ADRIEN ARPEL'S 3-WEEK CRASH MAKEOVER/ SHAPEOVER BEAUTY PROGRAM

ADRIEN ARPEL'S 3-WEEK CRASH MAKEOVER/ SHAPEOVER BEAUTY PROGRAM

ADRIEN ARPEL

with Ronnie Sue Ebenstein

Illustrations by Gail Schneider

PUBLISHED BY POCKET BOOKS NEW YORK

Material quoted from *The Perfect Exercise: The Hop, Skip and Jump Way to Health* by Curtis Mitchell, © 1976, is reprinted by permission of Simon & Schuster, a division of Gulf & Western Corporation

Color plates by Al Giese

POCKET BOOKS, a Simon & Schuster division of
GULF & WESTERN CORPORATION
1230 Avenue of the Americas, New York, N.Y. 10020

To Lauren—my beautiful child

Acknowledgments

I would like to thank Seligman and Latz, Inc., for making this all possible, with special thanks to John Kubie, my boss and friend; Iris Segal-Gallin, who gave me my start; Mike Blumenfeld of Bloomingdale's, who was willing to listen to a different drummer; Ronnie Sue Ebenstein, a wonderful writer who worked so beautifully with me; and all the doctors who gave so freely of their time and knowledge.

Contents

ix

PART III
Three-Week Makeover/Shapeover Program . . .

21 DAYS OF BEAUTY ACTIVITIES
THAT CAN TOTALLY CHANGE YOUR
APPEARANCE

PART

I

Growing Up
in the
Beauty Business

Why I Know
My Program Will
Work for You

Before you read this book, there are a few things I think you should know.

I am not a descendant of Hungarian "royalty" who ran across the war zone clutching nothing but grandmother's face cream formula (and a faded diploma from a long-defunct Budapest "university of skin care").

I am not an ex-Hollywood star who decided to dabble in cosmetics after the celluloid faded into cellulite.

I am not one of the world's ten great *natural* beauties.

I *am* the president of a multimillion-dollar try-before-you-buy face treatment and cosmetic business located in over 350 major department stores around the world. My business, which I began when I was seventeen years old with $400 in baby-sitting money, is still based on two simple premises: 1) Help the customer realize that good makeup can't cover bad skin, but bad skin *can* be improved through the right treatment. 2) Give the customer an opportunity to try the makeup she needs before she buys it—and, most important, teach her how to apply it effectively.

BEGINNINGS

I started in the beauty business accidentally: not with the intention of founding a dynasty, but out of the frustration I felt when I realized there was no one willing to take the time to teach an insecure beginner (or, for that matter, someone who had been trying for *years* to get that porcelain finish) how to become more attractive.

My own beauty education began the day after high school graduation. I had little money but lots of time, so I visited the cosmetic counters of all the large New York department stores. After badgering the salesgirls about how to put on cosmetics, and never getting the same answers twice, I decided to teach myself about makeup (which probably made the salespeople very happy—I was so young I didn't realize that after they smeared five different foundation shades on my wrist, they actually expected me to buy something!). And I found, after much trial and error, that I could make makeup work for me. When I realized I knew almost as much as the "experts," who were there because they could make themselves beautiful, but had no idea how to translate their skills for the woman who needed help, I opened my first shop in New Jersey, at age seventeen.

Since my tiny shop was barely visible to passersby, I decided to bring my "try before you buy" idea to the women themselves, and I convinced local beauty salons to open try-it-first counters in their establishments. I trained girls who were good at applying makeup, installed them in the salons, and we were in business (in these early days I developed my makeup line from the Yellow Pages—looking under toiletries, I found companies willing to produce a private label line for me).

Though I was amateur and immature, I was the only one offering this service, and the women in salons responded immediately.

Within several years our service-oriented operation and our now professional, nature-based cosmetics line caught the eye of a $180 million beauty conglomerate, Seligman & Latz, Inc., who took us under their wing and established us in the hundreds of department store salons where we're now located, and where we've grown to include facilities for skin cleansing and renewing facials—such an important part of a beauty regimen.

NOT PROMISES, BUT PRACTICES

If I confess that I don't fit the current mold of those writing beauty books (how many of these "experts" grew up in the beauty industry?) I must also tell you that this won't be like any of the celebrity-circuit self-improvement books you may have seen (the only one who *hasn't* written a beauty book yet is Snow White—I hear she's holding out for better terms!). My book *isn't* geared to some mythically beautiful woman born with a silver eyebrow pencil in her mouth. That means you *won't* be getting nonsense on the order of: " . . . my friend Countess Edwina, Europe's foremost beauty, says putting beluga caviar on your face and wrapping your body in formaldehyde is a terrific wrinkle-preventer . . ." Nor will I waste your time with such "revolutionary" advice as ". . . in the spring, pink is so becoming . . ." Or the trendy ". . . at my rejuvenation spa I'll inject you with youth-preserving sheep placenta. . . ."

You *will* be getting a first-rate practical guide for redesigning every part of you, based on the program tested by thousands of women who have signed up for my makeover clinics held in top department store beauty salons (Saks Fifth Avenue, Bloomingdale's, Neiman-Marcus, Burdine's, Robinson's, Harrod's of London, etc. etc.). Because I've literally spent the past ten years, eight hours a day, in these salons, I've got notebooks filled with the "how to" techniques perfected by the salon superstars, techniques that I'll explain step by step so you can make them work for you at home.

I will also tell you how to duplicate the most popular facials offered in the salons. They're popular because they work. And I'll honestly tell you which beauty routines should be left to the experts.

I want to take you home with me! Before I outline my program, let me tell you how I happened to write this book:

We still follow our total facials with a free makeup application, and no matter how sophisticated the woman, her response is always the same: "I wish I could take you home with me." Because most women don't have the painting skills of a Picasso, they need constant reinforcement to keep applying their makeup correctly as the styles (and their faces) change. (Ever notice a woman who paints a terrific 1940s mouth . . . still?)

These women wanted a manual that would explain in black, white, and color the marvelous things I was doing for their faces, something they could refer to when they were getting "rusty." This, then, is how my book began—as an aid for the woman who wanted to keep me by her makeup mirror. (I often feel like the Lone Ranger of cosmetics. I fly into town, make up a few hundred women, and leave with the following words ringing in my ear: "Who was that mascara-ed woman?" "I don't know, but I'd like to thank her!")

OK. The book *started* as a way to get my face care and makeup ideas into the hands of the many women who wanted them. But it grew into a total beauty book as I tried to answer the many questions women ask me about every aspect of "looking good." Now that you've taken me home with you, here's what you'll get:

The book is divided into two comprehensive parts: The first is the mini-encyclopedia of health and beauty, which provides in-depth answers to many of the behind-closed-doors questions you've never been able to bring yourself to ask, and avoids the boring, oft-repeated beauty fluff (you know: Walk in the spring rain for a dewy complexion—if only it were that easy!).

You will learn what to do *when* . . .

You're beginning to droop? Check out the "Sag Alert."

You've got to lose five pounds fast, and are thinking about amphetamines? Read "The Second Most Popular Indoor Sport."

You're afraid those acne scars are hopeless? Scan "The Good, the Bad, and the Ugly."

I've asked the experts the questions *you've* asked me, and I'm very proud of the information I've been able to gather.

I was determined to present new facts about the nitty gritties, because if I've learned one thing from my frequent promotional visits to department stores, it's this: Today, women no longer believe that beauty can be bought in a jar. (I don't believe it, and cosmetics are my business, so why should you?) Women want the whole picture, and they're not embarrassed to ask me questions about the nitty gritties, including:

- How to get rid of acne scars.
- How to lose weight without going crazy.
- How to make over your teeth with just a few dental visits.
- The lowdown on plastic surgery and "invisible" scars.
- How to remove unwanted hair . . . professionally.
- How to get rid of those spidery lines on legs.
- How to duplicate the super-nail treatments that cost $35 in salons.
- The good news *and* the bad news about skin and hair care, hair coloring, diet, exercise, and more.

The beautiful people may find pomegranate seeds the key to health, but the girls and women I've spoken with want sensible advice. That's what this book provides. Yes, I have watched the salon pros work their magic, but, equally important, I've also talked with top doctors in every conceivable beauty-related field. Many of these specialists are my friends, and they have gladly shared their personal knowledge with me.

I do admit I have had a healthy interest (my husband might say obsession) with my looks ever since I had my nose fixed at age fifteen. (I had it done early—my mother wasn't taking any chances!) As an adult, I've actually submitted my face and body to many of the medicine men's newest treatments, so I'll tell you what works . . . and what doesn't.

Like you (and like my customers), I want to look the best I can. Sure, Mother said, "if you're beautiful inside, you're beautiful outside." (That thought and a bag of Fritos has seen many a teenager through adolescence.) But let's be realistic. Most men aren't going to bother learning about your 24K heart unless it's wrapped in an attractive package. I'm going to help you make that package worth claiming in the comprehensive three-week activity-filled makeover/shapeover program. It's three weeks of cosmetic therapy (cheaper, more fun, and less time consuming than analysis) that will help you look like yourself, only much better. I *know this program will help you,* because I've seen what bits and pieces of it do for the women who take the makeover program in our salons . . . and if it didn't work, I would no longer be in business.

HERE'S THE SET-UP:

Each of the twenty-one days features one superduper beauty step-by-step treatment (based on professional salon secrets) you will learn to do yourself. Also included is a *daily check-out* (diet, exercise, and grooming pointers you must keep in mind each day). And, on certain days I've included a *beauty bonus,* extra activities you'll delight in trying when your three-week makeover is complete. (And the program will be liberally illustrated with photos and line drawings for easy learning).

The best way to explain that this is truly a learning guide to describe some of the activities for you now:

Day 1: Primal Scream Facial

Group therapy for your skin, a most successful salon deep-cleansing face treatment for all skin types. Included are directions for making special pore-flushing herbal formulas, a honey and almond scrub based on the one used in Arpel salons, the draw-it-out impurities masque and more.

Day 2: Nature and Nurture Hair Treatments

Expensive natural, organic hair treatments you can make inexpensively at home . . . something for every hair problem.

Day 3: Three for Your Nails

1) The makeover manicure, step by step to a *professional* manicure . . . 2) The nail wrap, shows how to mend broken nails, keep the nails you've got . . . 3) The art of applying acrylic nails like a pro (this last one alone costs $35-plus in top salons).

Day 4: Climate-Control Face Care

Routines to help your skin survive beautifully in any climate . . . facials for all around the country.

Plus: BEAUTY BONUS . . . tailored treatments designed to correct skin and hair faults.

Day 5: The Personalized Pedicure

Including a do-it-yourself foot pumice paste, fragrant foot bath and magnificent foot massage.

Plus: BEAUTY BONUS . . . Just for Your Feet: Five additional feet treats that keep the beautiful people on their toes.

Weekend One: The Sensuous Milk Farm

Day 6: Super Milk Farm Face Treat

A comprehensive facial featuring all kinds of dairy delights, including a variety of masques. Also included are Sweet Dreams Milk Baths, featuring you-know-what.

Day 7: The Egg-and-I Milk Farm Hair Treat

A quick and nutritious way to feed your hair. Also included is the Creme de la Creme Bath Oil . . . spas charge a fortune for good-for-your-body treatment baths like this.

Plus: BEAUTY BONUS . . . the "Super Six" milk farm face treats. More performance-oriented facials to try at your leisure.

Day 8: The Skin Ironing Face Treatment

A fabulous treatment based on three beauty ideas: the wax masque of ancient Egypt; the skin ironing of old Romania; the skin feeding favored by the rich/chic in ultramodern Swiss clinics.

Day 9: Highlight Your Hair—How to Henna

The most complete guide to flaw-free henna application this side of Cairo. All the how-tos, when not-tos, hints from the pros, the "hennicure" and more.

Day 10: Removing Unwanted Hair

The nittiest of the gritties. For the first time, you'll learn how to wax every area of your body, professionally and privately at home. It's the training we give to the girls in our salons. Bleaching, shaving, chemical depilatories and more are also covered.

Plus: THE BODY FACIALS, how to bring the goodness of facials to that vast uncharted area below your neck.

Day 11: The Senuous, Sensational Massage

Physical *and* psychological benefits are yours when you
try these three: 1) The Stimulating Scalp Massage; 2)
The Salon-Style Face Massage (based on a series of
movements the estheticians employ in my salons); 3)
The Do-It-Yourself Sensuous Body Massage.

Day 12: The Revival Hour

A brace of simple, fast routines to pick up your tired
hair, face, and body.

Weekend Two: The "Sea Cures" Spa

Day 13: The Deep-Cleansing Sea-Spa Skin Treatment

The facial that has the beauty press talking: makes use
of sea salt, sea kelp and glorious mud, based on the
steps performed in my salons.
Plus: BEAUTY BONUS . . . Sea Salt Body Treat, a
terrific bath.

Day 14: Sea-Spa Hair Treatment

Two based on sea kelp. *Plus* . . . the Mineral Mud Body
Treatment, based on famous mud baths of Europe.
  BEAUTY BONUS: Two for Your Face, two quick sea
cure facials.

Day 15: Organizing for a Perfect Makeup

Today you begin your glamorization process, a five-day
series of makeup lessons. Featuring tools and products,

how to confront the cosmetic saleswoman, how to buy the right cosmetics without making costly mistakes, makeup removal and cleansing rules, treatments for everyone, your basic makeup and more. A practical, factual guide for the woman with no time and less patience . . . and little natural skill in applying makeup.

Day 16: Contouring and Face Color

The essential gear, essential philosophy and easy-to-follow steps for this so important makeup procedure.

Plus: NIGHTWORK (how to do this step for night lights) AND MAKEUP LANGUAGE (what you reveal by the way you color your face).

Day 17: Eye Makeovers

Professional makeup artist tips and tricks for creating beautiful, expressive eyes. How to correct all eye shapes via makeup. How and when to use all the latest tools. Pages of tips clearly explained, so even the fumble-fingered can get results.

Plus: NIGHTWORK AND MAKEUP LANGUAGE (see Day 16).

Day 18: The Makeover Mouth

The mechanics of making up lips: Literally everything a woman should know about choosing and using today's products. How to correct lip shapes. Makeup Language.

Day 19: The Ten-Minute Everyday Makeup

The previous days' lessons are combined into an illustrated putting it together lesson.

Plus: NIGHTWORK AND MAKEUP LANGUAGE.

Weekend Three: Body and Soul Spa

Day 20: The European Cellulite Treatment Wrap

In Europe this treatment is one reason *thin* and *rich* are synonymous. Now, try this water weight-shedder inexpensively at home.

Day 21: Total Relaxation Routine

The fifteen minute yogi's way to put your mind and body in harmony.

Now that I've given you a preview of what to expect, I hope you can't wait to begin!

PART

II

The Comprehensive Mini-Encyclopedia of Beauty

CHAPTER

1

The Good, the Bad, and the Ugly

THE TRUTH ABOUT SKIN

You can hide your hair by twirling scarves around your head or encase a less-than-perfect body in a tent dress, but unless you singlehandedly try to resurrect the little-hat-with-veil, your complexion is there for everyone to see.

Only women who spend their lives hermetically sealed in Baggies can avoid skin problems; the rest of us are better equipped to deal with the rigors of childbirth than with the hard labor needed to banish pimples and prevent wrinkles.

That's why I've put together many of the skin-care questions women have asked me over the years and tried to make the answers as free of medical jargon as possible. If you've always wanted to be a dermatologist, the words *comedone, occlusion, senile lentigo* may have appeal—but I prefer *blackhead, blocked pore,* and *liver spots.* Much simpler!

17

First, let's get the basic biology out of the way. I don't want to bore you, but if you understand the workings of the skin, you'll also understand why my skin program will work for you. Here goes:

Skin can be divided into two main parts, the epidermis and the dermis. The *epidermis,* or topmost horny outer layer, is made of a substance called keratinized protein. This "K.P." protects your skin from the cold, cruel world, dryness and the army of airborne bacteria that can cause skin problems. The lower layers of the epidermis are the new cell manufacturing sites, where the real action takes place. As the new cells grow, they push upwards toward the surface. By the time they reach the top, they've completed their life cycle and are actually *dead* protein—no longer reproducing.

No magician can make these dead cells "born again," so you've got to remove them to make way for those eager young cells ready to come forth and sacrifice themselves for the sake of your ever-glowing epidermis. *We remove the dead surface layer by thorough cleansing.* Upon this simple thought cosmetics empires are built. Drop-dead-gorgeous models earn their $250,000 a year just to convince you to wash your face. And, if the message gets through, they're worth their tax shelters! (Of course, these beauties were born that way—in spite of the moonbeam sets with the Rolls-Royce in the background, the bottle of cream you buy can do only so much. The rest, alas, is genetics.)

Beneath the epidermis lies part two, the *dermis* or "true skin," and though you can't see it, you'd better know what it is—this is where trouble often begins. The dermis forms the support system of the skin. In it are found oil and sweat glands, hair follicles, blood vessels, and fat glands. The dermis is also the home of collagen (which you might call "support hose" for your face), a protein that gives your skin its elasticity, i.e., keeps it firm, well toned, youthful looking. Obviously, damage to the collagen is to be avoided, unless, of course, you're in a hurry to win a Grandma Moses look-alike contest.

This short "technical" explanation should help you understand what your dermatologist or facial expert is saying, without having to resort to *Gray's Anatomy* for help. Now, if you're still with me, let's get onto the questions women most frequently ask me.

● *I call my complexion "the good, the bad, and the ugly." Magazines call it combination skin. How do I handle it?*

Many women have combination skin at some point in their lives. It's characterized by a shiny-looking forehead, nose and chin (called the T-Zone, collectively) prone to occasional breakouts, and surrounded by normal-to-dry areas needing different attention. But, whatever kind of skin you have, whether Sahara-dry or Shah-ful of oil, the *three basic care steps* are the same.

1) Cleansing—to remove accumulated dirt, pollution, and dead surface skin cells

2) Toning—to stimulate and tighten the pores after the skin has been cleansed

3) Balancing—to return precious oils or moisture removed in the cleansing and toning processes, making the skin feel supple; to seal in the skin's natural moisture

If you have combination skin, you'll have to care for dry areas with one set of products, oily with another.

The care, treatment and cosmetics for all skin types are discussed in Part III, Day 15. You're not sure what kind of skin you're in? The following tests will tell you how to professionally determine your individual skin type.

KNOW THYSELF SKIN TYPE TEST 1

For this test you'll need looseleaf reinforcements (those little white circles that keep notebook paper from falling apart); a magnifying glass or lens; a peel-off masque (many companies make them); glass slide (or bottom of glass plate or drinking glass).

1) Put three reinforcements on your clean, dry face: one on outside of cheek, one on chin, one close to nose where large pores may be located. (Note: Keep well away from eye area.)

2) Cover reinforcements completely with a *very thin* layer of peel-off masque.

3) Leave in place for five minutes (or till dry), gently pull off glue and reinforcements in one piece.

4) Place reinforcements on glass side or plate, and examine with magnifying lens.

When you look through the magnifying lens, what you see is an impression of your skin's surface. (Don't faint—only a man equipped with a bionic eye will ever get so close a view!) This graphic picture of your skin's little irregularities and problem spots will help you see your skin with a cosmetologist's eye. What do all those little indentations mean? We perform this same test in our salons; compare your skin with the magnified view on pages 22–23, and discover your problem areas.

SKIN TYPE TEST 2: THE BLOTTER METHOD

All you need for this test is a thin brown paper bag (no, you won't have to put it over your head if you fail).

Before you go to bed, cut the bag into strips: one for your forehead, one to cover your nose and chin, a third to use on your cheeks. (Don't want to use paper bag? Buy a package of oil-blotting tissues from your druggist.)

First thing in the morning, before washing your face, reach for your papers. Rub one strip back and forth across your forehead. Is the paper getting *shiny?* Your forehead is somewhat oily. Is the paper *transparent?* Your oil glands are working overtime! Follow the same procedure for your nose/chin paper, and compare the results. If a few swipes of the paper across your cheeks also reveals shine, you're an all-over oily-skinned lady. If the cheek area shows up relatively clean, but you can wring out your forehead papers, you've got classic combination skin. If all three papers look clean, head for your moisturizer; you've got dry skin.

SKIN TYPE TEST 3: RATE YOUR FACE

Get out your magnifying mirror and really look at yourself. Don't dwell on your too-closely-set eyes (there's plenty of time for that later!) or terrific dimples. Instead, peer at your skin closely. Place the index fingers of each hand closely together on skin, gently pull them apart, slightly stretching skin. You're looking for enlarged pores. Make a knuckle with the second and third fingers of your hand, gently squeeze skin together. Thickness indicates an oily skin, thinness means dry. Continue your analysis.

- *Your face looks shiny, a bit greasy around the nose; your chin and forehead have a tendency to become shiny as the day wears on; your skin feels a bit coarse*

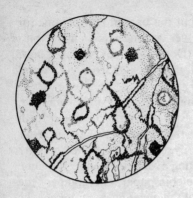

OILY SKIN

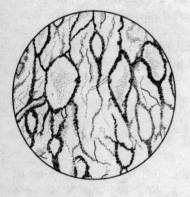

ROUGH SKIN

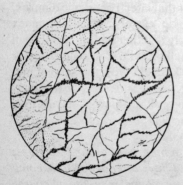

DRY SKIN

WRINKLED SKIN

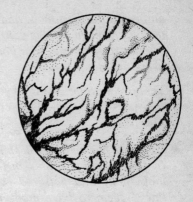

PERFECT SKIN

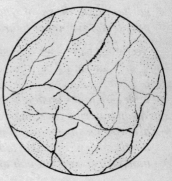

and rough to the touch; and blackheads appear all too often. When you flip your mirror back to reveal a normal-sized image, your pores still look like they're being magnified.

Yes, you've got *oily* skin. If you've just spent $50 on a super-rich, thick, all-night cream, give it to your mother.

● *Your face hurts when you smile, your skin feels tight. In cold weather your skin feels not only rough, it looks flaky and gets red easily. Your fine "laugh lines" seem to have made their appearance a bit earlier than those of your friends. And enlarged pores? You've never heard of them.*

You may have had oily skin as a teenager, but it's now *dry,* and must be treated accordingly.

● *Your skin looks basically clear and rarely breaks out. When you run your fingers over your face no lumps are waiting to surface, and skin feels neither greasy nor flaky-dry. Your skin looks good with a light film of moisturizer and a touch of blusher.*

Heredity has been good to you and the environment hasn't ruined you—you've got *normal skin* (a rarity), and have to work to keep it that way (if only the rest of us were so lucky!). You're probably around twenty-five; skins much older or much younger usually have some visible problems.

The Skin-Type Hangup

Why all this attention to skin typing? I've met mature women so unsure of their current skin condition that they're still hung-up on the treatment regimen they were using to combat teenage skin traumas. Many young women with once-oily skin continue to use drying soaps, followed by oh-so-drying alcohol based astringents. But as you start approaching your thirtyish birthday, the skin under your eyes develops a wrinkle or two, and those very *unfunny* laugh lines start appearing. So *stop* acting as if you had sixteen-year-old skin so oily you could fry an egg on your face.

The above skin tests should give you a better idea of the state of your skin, but the best way to face the truth about your complexion is to have a licensed cosmetologist or facial expert examine your skin. Your monthly professional facial can be as important to keeping you young-looking as your yearly physical can be in keeping your body in tune.

Once you know your skin type (it may change from season to season, hence the monthly or seasonal skin check), forget your inhibitions and visit your favorite cosmetics counter with your face devoid of moisturizer or makeup (you can't expect a cosmetics saleswoman to believe you have dry skin if you approach her counter with enough oil on your face to stop the energy crunch).

If you're thinking of investing in a series of facials, consider the following:

Before your first appointment, ask the cosmetician to show you the facial room, and have her explain the techniques she uses. Insist on *absolute* cleanliness. Ask for an explanation of any machines to be used on your face.

Look for a facial specifically designed for your complexion needs. Don't be afraid of new treatments—old-fashioned facials may work wonders for your psyche but do little to correct skin problems.

Beware the skin care expert who promises you

perfect skin. Good facials will help, but anyone who promises a Hollywood contract plus a flawless complexion is, shall we say, exaggerating.

Observe the way your first treatment is given. Your cosmetician should look at your skin under a magnifier and tell you what your problems are. If you're lying down, your eyes should be covered whenever creams or sprays are applied. Your facial should be given by a "quiet" person, in a quiet room, who isn't afraid to tell you what she's doing and why. If you're over thirty, your skin care expert will use alcohol drying agents *only* on blemishes.

Realize that the professional aesthetician is not a replacement for a dermatologist. If you have psoriasis, seborrhea, or allergies, see a doctor. If you have relatively minor problems, and you don't see an improvement after your third facial, you might also need to consult a dermatologist.

Never have a first facial the afternoon of a big affair, unless you know how it will affect your skin. Certain types of facials purposely redden the skin, giving it an "angry" look because deep-seated infections are being cleaned up and disinfected.

● *How do I give myself a facial?*

You'll be performing many face treatments for yourself during the three-week *Crash* program. The instructions for each are outlined on the day you'll be doing them, but here are some general pointers to keep in mind:

1) You will have most of the ingredients at home. Others are readily available in the supermarket, health food store, or pharmacy.

2) Since the formulas usually contain perishables

(fruits, milk, egg, etc.), they should be stored in the refrigerator—in *glass* jars that are *well labeled* (my daughter Lauren once mistook my "freshener" for a mint-colored soft drink!).

3) You can always take shortcuts by substituting one of your commercial products for a home-made recipe. For example, if you're delighted with your toning lotion, you don't have to make mine, though I think you'll enjoy experimenting.

4) If you'd like to add scent to a recipe, you should know that "fragrant oils" and "essential oils" are virtually the same: it's the essence of the scent, put in an oil medium, and that's what I had in mind. You'll also see the term "extract." European manufacturers started using the French term *extrait* to denote per-fume-strength scents; these are fine, too.

5) Always cover your hair when you're giving your-self a facial, or you might get greasy near the hairline. If you're steaming your face, a towel wrapped turban-style will help keep your hair from going limp.

6) A facial should be a sensuous experience. When you've applied your masque, lie down in a darkened room, put on some soft music, set a timer so you won't have to look at your watch, cover your eyes with water-dampened cotton pads . . . and enjoy!

● *Every 8-ounce bottle of everything from bubble bath to cleanser is extolling the virtues of* pH *and the* acid mantle; *is this something else I have to worry about, or is it just industry "hype"?*

If you're confused about the importance of the acid mantle, don't worry. So are the scientists. You needn't get a PhD in pH theory, but you should know what the fuss is all about. Basically, pH refers to the relative acidity or alkalinity of the skin's surface. It is believed that the skin has an *acid mantle*—a light, invisible covering made up of dissolved secretions (sweat, oil, etc.) that push their way to the skin's surface, protecting it from harmful bacteria. Because this mantle is acidic (measuring 4.5 to 5.5 on the pH scale), some skin experts and scientists believe you should avoid using anything highly alkaline that could alter the acidity of this protective layer. Thus, the theory goes, highly alkaline substances (like detergent-based soaps and shampoos) can destroy this acid mantle, leaving an exposed epidermis. And, while "exposing yourself" this way won't get you arrested, it will open your skin to all manner of problems.

Sounds straightforward. Why the confusion? Some dermatologists claim there really isn't anything to this whole pH business. But until we get a clear-cut answer, it's better to err on the side of acidity.

If your skin type demands frequent washing (if you have acne or over-active oil glands), you'll especially want to avoid harsh alkaline substances. How to test whether you're using an acid-destroyer? You don't have to open your own chemistry lab or invest in a Bunsen burner to become a qualified pH tester. Just buy Squibb Nitrazine papers from your druggist, dip the paper into the solution you're testing, and match it to the color chart provided. Yellow means you're using a nice, mild, acidic product—that's what you're aiming for. Instructions are included on the package.

You should know that major cosmetic companies are aware of the acid mantle theory, and are terribly anxious to create products that will help your skin. We've also got Big Brother, in the form of the Food and Drug Administration, peering over our shoulders . . . an added incentive to do the job right!

● *Instead of inheriting my mother's big brown eyes,
   I'm stuck with her large pores. How can I shrink
   them?*

A pore is an opening onto the skin's surface through
which oil escapes. Too much oil, and the pore stretches
to try and accommodate that flow. Once stretched or
enlarged there is *no* treatment that will permanently
shrink it to invisibility. What you can do, however, is
temporarily camouflage your pores by using a good
astringent. An astringent is really a fascinating product.
The "tingling" sensation it produces is an indication
that the astringent is doing its work, slightly irritating
the skin. This irritation causes the skin *surrounding* the
pore to swell, thus blocking the pore opening from
view. This pore-minimizing trick should last a few
hours, so apply the astringent right before going out, or
your pores may reappear by the stroke of midnight.

● *My skin is so colorless, I look like I'm ready to play
   the death scene from* Camille. *Why don't I look as
   healthy as I feel?*

The best treatment for pale skin is a trip in a "Time
Machine." You were just born in the wrong era.
Ancient beauties went to some lengths to achieve the
fragile, on-the-verge-of-fainting look you come by naturally. They applied a whitening powder made from lead
to their faces which, not surprisingly, made them feel as
wan as they looked. (They also swallowed lead; seems
they felt it was an ideal form of birth control—it was,
since the fertile women usually didn't live long enough
to reproduce!)

What gives skin its healthy glow is a good supply of
red blood flowing near the surface. Could be you're
slightly anemic; ask your doctor for a hemoglobin (red

blood cell count) test, or perhaps your blood doesn't zip around your body as fast as it should. Many women feel yoga postures such as the head/shoulder stand bring their blood into their face, giving them a bit more color. Perhaps you're staying up extra late with someone you like? Plain old exhaustion may be causing your problem.

If your wan look isn't due to a real medical dysfunction, consider epidermabrasion—a mild peeling of the surface with cleansing grains or any good scrub (honey and almond brew, which you'll learn to make in Part III, Day 1, for example), or judicious use of a mechanical exfoliator (exfoliation is the process by which the skin's dead surface cells are sloughed off) like 3M's Buf-Puf will get rid of dead cells and bring up a glow. Once your skin is scrupulously clean, the proper application of the right makeup can give you the healthy look you want.

● *Will a moisturizer (or anything) help my skin stay young-looking?*

Let me tell you what a moisturizer really does, then you can decide for yourself. First, a moisturizer isn't used to plop on lubrication (surprise!). But it does do something equally important: seal in the moisture that is already produced by your skin. And, that *natural* moisture is *water*—yes, it's the H_2O in your cells that keeps skin soft, not the oil. But we all know water can *evaporate* (central heating, dry weather, not enough liquid in your diet, overexposure does it), so you need a moisturizing agent to *lock in* the valuable water your skin manufactures, and to keep parched skin feeling soft and comfortable.

The right moisturizer can make your skin look and feel better as well as protect it from the elements. If you're not super-oily, consider it essential. If you are oily, look for a non-greasy moisturizer. You'll enjoy the protection it provides.

But a moisturizer is only the first step toward staving off the dry skin that makes you look older. You must also provide your skin with nourishment in the form of treatment creams. I'll discuss who needs what, and when, in Part III, Day 15, where I outline care and cosmetic needs for all skin types.

If younger looking skin is your goal, you must also look to your life style. Late nights, alcohol, sun worshiping, smoking (heavy smokers are always screwing up their lips as they puff; the above-the-lip skin develops fine wrinkles early anyway—why hasten the process?), and crash dieting do nothing to improve skin elasticity.

Let's not forget the heredity factor: If mother and dad started crinkling and wrinkling early, you may be in for a similar fate (in which case, you'll want to be especially diligent with your treatment creams and oils—a little bit of skin care can pay off big dividends).

● *My skin erupts more frequently than Old Faithful, and I have craters that rival the Grand Canyon. I know it's acne—but what causes it? How can I get rid of it?*

If I could give definitive answers to these questions, I'd probably be awarded the Nobel Prize for medicine. (I might even get the eighteen-year-old vote for President!) There are, alas, almost as many different acne experts as there are sex therapists. Luckily, much has been learned about both fields. Before I tell you about suspected causes, and the most effective means of controlling acne, here is some of the latest thinking in the "gray area" of acne knowledge:

- There is still no known cure for acne.
- Chocolate, pizza, and deep-fried foods may make you fat; they probably won't give you acne.
- Dirt won't help your skin; neither is it a number-one acne cause.
- Tension can make acne worse, but it won't convert good skin to bad overnight.
- Vitamin E applied to breakouts can do more harm than good.

Certain of these ideas are at odds with mom's teachings? You should still remember her on Mother's Day, but when it comes to acne, be aware of current thought.

SUSPECTED CAUSES. While the experts can't define the causes to the point of preventing acne, much *is* known about this skin disease. The greasy skin, blackheads, pimples, and cysts that we associate with acne are related to an overproduction of *sebum* (oil and fatty substances), which is usually caused by increased hormonal activity. (I hope all this talk about sebum won't make your eyes glaze over in boredom and your hand reach involuntarily for junk food; a little healthy scientific talk *is* necessary if you're to understand what sick skin is all about.)

That's why most acne appears during puberty, when the output of the hormonal glands increases—sometimes wildly. Dr. Michael Kalman, assistant professor of dermatology at Mt. Sinai School of Medicine in New York City, says it's androgen, the male hormone, that causes these disturbances of the sebaceous glands—and, alas, men aren't the only ones possessing mischief-making androgen. When the extra sebum can't make it through to the surface because the surface is already blocked by oil, skin trouble begins. By the way, you also have oil glands on the back, shoulders and chest that are affected by hormones; that's why these areas break out.

Why, then, doesn't every teenager fall heir to acne? We're not sure, though *heredity* is believed to play a part. Does your family gather round the fire to listen to grandma complain she could have been Miss America if she had all the acne medications available today? If there *is* a history of severe acne in your family, you have a better-than-average chance of continuing the break-out chain, karma after karma, generation after generation.

Though greasy foods do not greasy skin make (remember, excess oil is a by-product of hormonal activity), there is one dietary factor to consider: If you've been to a dermatologist he's probably told you to avoid shellfish. (Maybe God made them so ugly because they make our skin so ugly!) This anti-shrimp, etc., bias still holds . . . seems too much *iodide* (found in a variety of foods from shellfish to table salt) is bad for the acne-prone. So are bromides, found in many medicines.

If your acne condition has grown markedly worse, or you've suddenly gone from clear skin to such a disaster area you're thinking of calling in the Red Cross, look to your medicine cabinet—certain prescription or non-prescription drugs could be causing the problem. If this is true, your acne should disappear when you stop taking the medicine. (But don't drop the medicine without consulting the prescribing doctor. Contrary to what you may feel when you first look in the mirror, death is *not* preferable to acne.)

If you've changed cosmetic lines recently, your new purchases could be causing an allergic reaction. Do without for a few days; if your break-out attack subsides, you've saved yourself the cost of a visit to the dermatologist.

• *OK. I think I understand the link between over-active oil glands and acne. But I'm interested in a cure, not the cause. Any suggestions?*

Control—not cure—is a realistic goal. There are two parts to the management of skin problems: 1) at-home skin cleansing routines, 2) professional help. Take advantage of both. (You were hoping I'd suggest some unusual routine like wrapping your face in tin foil and praying to the sun god for relief? Sorry! Gimmicks may sell books, but only common sense will clear acne.)

UNBLOCK AND TACKLE. While this sounds like something a football coach might say, it's your key to better skin. You've got to *unblock* the surface so the excess oil can escape freely. The next explanation always amazes my clients: Everyone in the world thinks a blackhead is a pore filled with dirt. Not true! *Trapped oil* causes blackheads, which are really plugs of hardened oil that turn black or oxidize when exposed to air—it's a chemical reaction; the color has nothing to do with dirt. Oil excess also causes whiteheads (covered blackheads), pus-filled pimples, and other niceties we can do without.

To unclog the pores, do the following:

1) Apply hot towels to the face (or steam it à la Primal Scream Facial, your main activity for Day 1 of the program—see Part III) to loosen the plugs, making it easier for you to remove them gently . . . if they're ready.

2) Follow-up with an anti-acne soap. But don't plunk down extra money for these "acne" soaps unless they contain sulfur, salicylic acid, or resorcinal. These are all *peeling agents,* designed to remove the top layer of skin, including the clogged blackhead/whitehead openings that are keeping the oil trapped. If it's adult acne

you're fighting, you may not want to indulge in all this peeling and drying, since that may age your skin. You'll have to decide which you detest most, wrinkles or pimples.

3) Treat yourself to a blemish-fighting masque (you'll find many to choose from in Part III, the *Crash* Program).

If your problem persists, you'll want an expert to tackle your skin. Look for a competent, licensed cosmetician, if you think your skin will benefit from the deep cleaning she can provide. But to make sure you're doing all you can, also check in with a dermatologist. He or she can perform many treatments (and offer medications) that only an M.D. is qualified to do. Consider the following:

Acnesurgery

This is the fancy name dermatologists give to the process of clearing the infectious matter and debris out of your skin (sort of a professional picking!). The doctor or nurse will extract blackheads and whiteheads, drain pimples and cysts. What about scarring? Most dermatologists say leaving these blemishes unattended will leave behind scars, and treatment minimizes this possibility. But I must say at this point that I personally have found (from the women who visit my salons) that though it cures infection, acne-surgery may also leave some scars. If your case isn't severe, ask your doctor to begin your treatment by prescribing a drying lotion; the peeling induced by these agents may be all you need to clear your skin.

Should you pick it yourself? Another New York dermatologist my friends and I have badgered, Dr.

Hillard Pearlstein, associate professor of clinical dermatology at Mt. Sinai School of Medicine, says our fingernails are *lethal weapons,* and we should leave acnesurgery to the pros. But since many of us can't resist, I'll teach you the safe way to do it yourself in Part III, Day 1.

Antibiotics

Since acne is caused by an infection of the sebaceous glands, antibiotics may be prescribed to help clear the problem. When taken in low doses, antibiotics can be used safely for a long time. Tetracycline is still the most commonly prescribed; it works by inhibiting the oil glands which overproduce in the acne sufferer. But side effects are possible. Dr. Alvin Weseley, a gynecologist associated with University Hospital in New York City, says antibiotics can cause problems (one is monilia vaginitis—you get a white discharge and itching) because they kill good bacteria as well as bad. Yogurt helps balance the bacteria—make it part of your diet whenever you're taking antibiotics. Topical (in lotion form to put right on skin) antibiotics have fewer side effects, but they give less dramatic results.

The Freeze

This form of treatment involves cryotherapy or skin freezing. The application of such substances as liquid nitrogen or dry ice leads to skin peeling, which helps remove sebum and blackheads, and generally unblocks the surface of the skin so the various cellular debris can reach the top and be removed.

Trick or Treatment?

Will Vitamin E help cure acne? The medical profession says no. Since Vitamin E is marketed as an oil in capsule form, you wouldn't want to apply it to an oil-troubled skin. Besides, many people develop an allergic reaction to E, and some say it stimulates the production of androgen, so if you've got acne to begin with, don't fool with this vitamin. And Vitamin A? You can overdose on it. Too much Vitamin A, taken internally, can cause a variety of ills from hair loss to brain damage. Vitamin A acid, applied to the face, is another story. If you've got lots of blackheads, it may prove helpful.

● *The Pill may have done wonders for my "peace of mind," but it's done nothing for my skin. How come?*

As I mentioned earlier, skin eruptions are related to hormonal functioning, and androgens (male hormones) seem to be the trigger. These androgens can be produced either by the ovaries or adrenal glands. If your androgens originate in the ovaries, the Pill can help: when ovulation is suppressed, so is androgen production. But if your *adrenals* are producing too much androgen, the Pill won't help.

Even if the wheres and whats of androgen production have no particular bearing on your case, your Pill may contain the wrong estrogen/progesterone ratio to help clear your skin. If so, your gynecologist may be able to recommend an oral contraceptive that will control breakouts as well as pregnancy.

● *I no longer break out, but my face has some scars left over from the bad old pick and squeeze days. Can anything be done, or must I live with "the pits"?*

Ask your dermatologist or a plastic surgeon if you're a candidate for *dermabrasion,* an office procedure. Some pockmarks and scars may be helped by this method of skin planing. First the skin is anesthetized, then a small, rapidly rotating stainless steel wire brush is worked over the face to remove the top layers, planing it down to make it "level" with the indented scarred area. Following sanding, your face is bandaged and you're sent home. The next morning you remove the bandages and crust formation begins. When the crusting-and-oozing finally ends about ten days later, smoother skin should result. Be prepared for some pain and discomfort. And be aware that this treatment works best on skin that is terribly pockmarked (also, the better your doctor, the better the results); it's not worth the trouble if you only have a mild case.

A second course of action is *chemabrasion,* or chemical peeling. Here, powerful chemicals burn away the top level of the skin. Obviously, you'd better put your face in the hands of a highly skilled doctor. Too much chemical, or chemical poorly applied, can be dangerous. Again, expect some pain with this treatment—and don't plan your wedding day post haste: Your skin will be peeling away for several days and you don't want to look like the Bride of Frankenstein! If you had really severe scarring to begin with, you may see dramatic improvement.

Which is best? It depends on your specific problem, of course, but most of the doctors I spoke with preferred dermabrasion—they have more control over the sanding tool. Once a powerful chemical is applied to your skin, they (and you) are in the hands of God! Neither of these treatments should be performed by a cosmetologist, though some wrongly do this work. In our salons, the peelings are done using organic materials only—vegetables and salts.

The above treatments are designed to minimize the appearance of *indented* (below-the-skin) scars. For protruding, lumpy scars called *keloids,* your doctor may take another tack: injecting the keloid with steroids like cortisone (an anti-inflammatory agent) to shrink them.

I recently heard of a new (to me, at least) way to camouflage the visibility of *icepick* (long, deep, narrow) scars. Dr. Michael Kalman told me he uses a punch (something like a cookie cutter) to actually lift out the "hole" causing the scar. He throws out the "hole" and replaces it with filler skin taken from behind your ear. You actually have enough tissue behind the ear to do twenty to thirty skin grafts; the doctor might be able to do four or five scars in one sitting—in his office.

There's another way to fill out acne scars. Injecting *pure medical grade silicone* into the troublesome indentions. But the silicone must be medical grade, and the doctor must be skilled. A former favorite with topless dancers, silicone *breast* injections long have been banned. But liquid silicone is getting a good press when it comes to face work—depending on where, how, how much, and who does it. I'll discuss silicone further in the plastic surgery chapter.

You should know that though the medical profession finds silicone injections useful, its use is still limited and controversial.

Those of you who are plagued by dry skin and fine lines instead of acne shouldn't feel slighted: Face peels and silicone may also help you. Silicone injections can be used to "plump up" wrinkles (see Chapter Ten). A mild chemical face peel, properly performed by a skilled doctor, can get rid of finely hatched surface wrinkles (not deep furrows) including crow's feet for as long as five years. In fact, some women have super-mild chemical peels twice a year: Their friends wonder why they look so refreshed, rejuvenated . . . only their dermatologist knows for sure!

● *Since I found out the man in my life is married, my sex life has consisted of studying the* Joy of Sex *illustrations. Can this sexual starvation be causing my skin to break out?*

You don't have to be Masters and Johnson to know that good sex is one of the best youth-retaining, beautifying treatments—superior to coating your face with $50-an-ounce wrinkle cream or being derrière-injected with chicken embryos.

The theory: When sex, romance, love (whatever *you* want to call it) is working right, you're less tense, seem to have an inner glow that oozes through your pores. In fact, in the good old double-standard days, a boy with a bad case of acne would be advised that losing his virginity would mean a corresponding pimple loss. Young girls, however, were told to wash their faces more frequently. At least the new morality has done away with "double-standard" acne!

CHAPTER
2

Split Ends and Spilt Milk

THE TRUTH ABOUT HAIR

Who invariably makes a hairdresser grimace with pain? The customer waving a photo of Farrah Fawcett-Majors, saying *"This* is how I want my hair!" Now, unless the snapshot-bearer and Farrah are identical, she can't have Ms. Fawcett-Majors's "look" without possessing Farrah's thick hair and fabulous face.

I'm not saying you have to toss out your movie star photo collection (with the nostalgia boom, I consider my autographed picture of a *thin* Elizabeth Taylor a collector's item), but if you were *born* with scraggly, limp hair, you've got to forget the "impossible dream" and learn what you can *realistically* do to make the most of what nature gave you. In order to maintain and improve your hair, there are certain essential facts (and new therapies) you should understand. Here is what you must know to revitalize the hair you've got.

Hair is 97 percent protein. If you looked at an individual hair shaft under a high-powered microscope, you would see three layers. (I confess, I don't spend my Saturday nights doing this!) The outer layer, or *cuticle,* is made up of a hard protein called keratin, just like the outer (or horny) layer of the skin. And, like the skin, the cuticle protects against penetration of bacteria from without and holds moisture within. Inside the cuticle is the *cortex,* where the pigments that give your hair its color are produced. Scientists are still debating the function of the *medulla,* or innermost layer.

Hair grows out of the follicle in the scalp, where it's nourished by blood and oxygen. By the time your hair protrudes from the scalp, it's already *dead* protein. So when we treat the hair, we're doing all we can to make this dead substance look better. But the actual birth and maturation process takes place beneath the surface.

Each follicle produces just one hair strand. Blondes have the most follicles (about 140,000 on a healthy head); carrot tops have the least (90,000) because red hair is thicker, coarser, and it takes fewer thick hairs to produce adequate head coverage. Brunettes fall somewhere in the middle in this numbers game.

How do you determine the health of your own hair? Many salons now offer the services of a trichologist, a scientifically trained hair analyzer who gets to the root of your hair problem by performing a sophisticated series of strand tests using a variety of machines. I'm going to help you make similar hair determinations at home.

"TRICH" TEST ONE: STRETCH

Remove a strand of hair from the crown area and gently stretch it. Healthy hair should stretch about 20 percent of its length, and then snap back to normal.

"TRICH" TEST TWO: CURL

Researchers at Redken, Inc. (they supply many beauty salons with hair care products) suggest holding a hair strand between your thumb and forefinger of the left hand. With the thumbnail and index fingernail of the right hand, run the distance of the hair strand rapidly (pretend your hair is a ribbon and "curl" the strand with your fingernails substituting for scissor blades). Next, pull your suddenly-curly strand into a stretched position, hold for ten seconds and release. Your hair returned to its newly-curled pattern? You have good elasticity, which is a sign of healthy hair. If only half the strand returned to its curly shape, your hair is structurally weak. None of the hair bounced back? It's *very* weak . . . needs lots of care.

"TRICH" TEST THREE: CUTICLE CHECK

Take a strand of hair (this is the last one, you won't go bald), and run your fingers down its length from the (hopefully not split) end down to the root end. Does it feel scaly, rough? If so, the cuticle (outer layer of the hair shaft) is in bad shape.

Now, to answer your most frequently asked hair-related questions:

● *My hair seems to be thinning out. Can women go bald?*

Don't worry: You'll lose your present husband and your waistline long before your hair falls out!

A certain amount of hair loss is perfectly *normal*. About 85 percent of hair on a healthy head is said to be in the growing (or anagen) phase. The other 15 percent (said to be in the telogen phase) is probably what you see on your brush each day—this shedding, or old, hair is being loosened in the follicle to make way for a "new" hair to appear. The lifespan of the anagen hair is from two to six years. The telogen phase lasts only a few months—so the hairs that fall out are replaced rather quickly by long-lived new hair.

Most authorities feel that loss of up to 100 hairs a day is natural, so chances are you needn't worry. However, there are some factors that contribute to abnormal hair loss among women. Consider the following:

Age

Alas, as we grow older, the hair-producing mechanism, along with everything else, slows down, and it takes longer for new hairs to grow back; some may not grow back at all. But while this leads to thinning hair, few women suffer enough hair loss to look "bald."

True MPB, or male pattern baldness, is genetic in origin and afflicts very few women, though 65 percent of men will suffer from MPB at some time in their lives. This hereditary male baldness is linked with the workings of the male sex hormone, androgen. A dermatologist told me that women who suffer from *diffuse* pattern baldness (all-over thinning, rather than on the crown first, as happens in MPB) can blame androgen, too. This hormone is twice-bad: while it may contribute to thinning hair on our heads, it also makes us hairy where we'd rather not be; on breasts, arms, and belly.

I should mention one thing: If you're linked up with a man whose obsession is rubbing everything from orris root to eye of newt on his recalcitrant locks (and he's considering consulting the local exorcist), give him the bad news: There is no way to cure the balding process, although hair transplants can correct the damage.

Health

Serious illness, high fever, and surgery can often cause hair loss. The problem is usually reversible—when you're feeling better, your hair will grow back. Certain medicines (e.g., chemotherapy for cancer) can also cause this problem.

If you're a fad-diet addict, you may also notice hair loss. (Vegetarians rarely have luxe locks!) You need fats to produce glossy hair and proteins to ensure adequate hair growth. In fact, hair loss is one of the first signs of malnutrition (and remember, nobody ever made a pass at a *bald* size 8). A vitamin-poor diet (lacking B-complex, E, C, and trace elements) may also contribute to hair decline. Conversely, a do-it-yourself vitamin regimen overly rich in A and D can cause baldness, among other health problems.

You're sure your mother-in-law is spiking your martini with arsenic? Here's something even Sherlock Holmes didn't know: Minute traces of poison can show up in your hair before they turn up elsewhere in your body. Knowledgeable criminologists are actually using hair analysis in murder detection.

Pregnancy

A closet full of Pampers isn't the only result of pregnancy; hair fallout may occur, too. Be assured that baby-making hair loss, which often begins about three months after the birth, is usually temporary. As your shape returns, so will your hair. Do consider hiding any bald patches or thinning spots by coloring your scalp with a soft eyeshadow pencil in a hair-matching shade. A man with thinning hair can use this trick successfully, too.

Traction Alopecia

When I was a teenager, status was a ponytail that would make Seattle Slew envious. I still have memories of ponytails and blue gym bloomers swaying in the schoolyard. Thank God the style lost popularity before we became the first generation of *bald* teenagers. Dermatologists (they're hair care as well as skin specialists) agree: All that traction (pulling) of the hair in the rubber band, even if the band is coated, can cause hair loss. Ditto sleeping on brush rollers. Besides being highly uncomfortable and making you look like an exchange student from Mars, this practice is highly damaging to the hair. Stop the unnatural pulling, and your hair will, hopefully, return. Meantime, you don't have to be pregnant to dip into your makeup bag and pull out a baldness-concealing eyeshadow crayon.

Trauma

Any shock to the body or psyche can cause more than jangled nerves and broken bones; you may wind up with your hair in a pile at your feet.

Appearance of Baldness

You may just *think* you're going bald. Hair that has been damaged by overprocessing often breaks off near the scalp, giving you a very unangelic halo of broken ends.

• *Can anything be done about thinning hair?*

I put this question to Dr. Hillard Pearlstein, who has done a good deal of research on hair. His answer, surprisingly, is, "Yes." Of course, there is no miracle cure for male pattern baldness, but if your hair loss is being caused by seborrhea of the scalp (which looks like a severe case of dandruff), for example, there is a treatment. This seborrhea is a reversible inflammation of the hair follicle which causes hair to fall out. By injecting steroids into the scalp (ouch!), you stop the inflammation and the follicle can again produce hair. Alopecia areata, a rare scalp disease (cause unknown) that may result in circular bald spots all over the scalp, can also be injected with the steroid cortisone.

And remember, you don't have to be a male politician or a macho movie star to have a hair transplant. This office procedure (which should be performed *only* by a doctor) *can* have an almost 100 percent success rate. Transplants are being performed regularly on women as well as men. The idea: If healthy follicles are transplanted to a new (bald) area, they will behave (produce hair) as they did in the old site.

Hair loss caused by accidents, operations, and infections can be improved by transplants, too. The procedure: You're given a local anesthetic, and small plugs (5/32 of an inch) of scalp skin containing several follicles are lifted from your donor site and transplanted where needed. You'll leave the office with a bandage over your head which you can remove the following morning. A scab forms over the site. When it falls off, in about ten to twenty days, you're left with a pinkish circle from which the transplanted hair gradually falls out. Dr. Pearlstein says not to worry. New hair will appear in about twelve weeks, to the tune of about six to twelve hairs per graft. How many sessions you'll need (from ten to thirty plugs can be moved per visit) depends on how much hair you need. There is some discomfort with this procedure and it takes a while to see results. But for the woman who does suffer from hair loss, it's a possibility.

You *may* look strange during the growing-in process. I once had a date who was in the midst of his transplanting sessions—he looked like a farmer whose crop was sprouting—on his head! You can camouflage *your* new growth with a hat or scarf—it won't interfere with the development of your new hair.

- *My idols are Rapunzel and Lady Godiva. I treat my hair well, but it just won't grow long. How come?*

If your hair and scalp are healthy, check through the family album; heredity may be the cause. As I mentioned earlier, the average hair life cycle is from two to six years; the average hair can grow six inches a year. If your hair is the victim of a short, or shorter than usual, life span (which is genetically determined), you probably just can't grow hair longer than six to twelve inches. Have you considered making Audrey Hepburn or Joan of Arc your idol?

What you can do is coddle the growth you get, treat it gently, and you may prolong the inevitable early fall-out.

In case you're curious, eyelashes, brows and other body hair operate on a much different life cycle—so you'll never have lashes down to your knees.

- *Do pH and the acid mantle have any effect on hair care?*

Skin and hair have much in common. They're both

composed of dead keratinized protein by the time they reach the body's surface, and both are protected by an acid mantle. Healthy skin and hair have a pH reading of 4.5 to 5.5, which makes them mildly acidic. Current thinking has it that the hair and scalp products we use should fall into a similar range—acidic rather than alkaline to protect the delicate acid mantle that in turn guards the internal structures, and locks moisture within both the hair and skin.

Here's why acidic products are recommended:

The cuticle, or outermost layer of the hair, is not completely flat—rather, under a microscope it resembles the overlapping scales of a fish. When alkaline products are applied to hair, the scaly cells are raised, allowing potentially harmful substances to swim right into the hair shaft. Thus, alkaline substances impair the cuticle's protective function.

What do mildly *acidic* cleaners and treatments do? They make the cuticle contract (just as your mouth does when you eat something acid), which is advantageous because (a) the barrier quality is enhanced, locking in moisture and locking out harmful bacteria, and (b) the cuticle, which is transparent, becomes a smoother surface. When the outer layer is smooth, light is reflected off of it . . . and you have shiny hair.

Mildly acidic treatments also lock water into the hair shaft. Without this natural moisture your hair will feel dry and look dull. You can test the acidity or alkalinity of your hair care products with the same Nitrazine papers you used to test skin aids in Chapter One.

● *Can anything be done about split ends?*

There's no use crying over spilt milk or split ends— mop up the former, chop off the latter. Once you've gotten rid of your current splits, you'll want to prevent the problem from recurring.

First, are you deliberately causing tress-stress? True, there's no Society for the Prevention of Cruelty to Hair, but too much processing, heat (incorrect use of hair dryers and other appliances), and teasing can split the ends and cause these ends to continue splitting right up the hair shaft.

The best treatment (aside from refraining from further hair-wrecking practices) is to use mildly acidic hair care products containing protein.

Of course, no company claims that its products will actually rebuild the hair, but the right type of protein can help strengthen what hair you've got. But here's the Catch-22: It's practically impossible for the layperson (even if equipped with her trusty packet of pH papers) to be sure her protein products possess the correct molecular structure. Your hairdresser should know, so ask him/her to recommend a corrective treatment line to help solve your hair problem. How can you tell if you're doing right in this molecule madness game? If your hair looks better and your split ends aren't recurring, assume you're using a good thing.

If you're not totally thrilled with your hair, and really believe your treatment routine rather than a genetic act of God is responsible, you'll want to explore some of the new professional products and processes available. You needn't don a pith helmet to canvass an untried territory I've always found rewarding: *the beauty supply shop*. Here, you can often get professional-type gear, whether you're looking for a shampoo, blow dryer, or boar bristle hairbrush. Look in your local Yellow Pages under "beauty salon equipment and supplies"—if there *is* such a place within driving distance—and if they don't discourage retail browsers, pay a visit. You'll see all manner of products you didn't know existed, and the salespeople usually know what they're doing—after all, they have to answer the questions posed by the experts.

You can often get a better price at these professional emporiums than you would at your drugstore, especially if you buy larger sizes—so go with a friend and buy in bulk.

● *A black dress is very elegant; dandruff falling on the same is* inelegant. *How can I have one without the other?*

Assuming a *strapless* black dress won't solve your problem, let's look at the types of dandruff, their causes, and cures.

You know what dandruff is—an itching, flaking scalp. If your hair and scalp are neither oily nor dry, your flaking problem could be due to the fact you're not getting rid of the normal amount of shedding scales. Thorough brushing will remove any loose debris on the scalp, including flakes. Another excellent way to stimulate a sluggish scalp and remove loose particles is through massage (see Part III, Day 11, for how to). Do you use hair spray? Though spray won't cause dandruff, too much spray will build up, and when you brush your hair, the excess will flake off, resembling dandruff.

If none of the above pseudo-dandruffs resembles your condition, you've probably got the real thing. Unfortunately, doctors don't know all there is to know about dandruff—no philanthropist is willing to leave $2,000,000 to the study of this disease, but it is widely believed there are two types, each related to scalp condition:

Oily dandruff results when the sebaceous glands of the scalp produce too much sebum (I *know* you're bored with sebum by now, but we can't ignore it!), and the rate of turnover of the outer layers of the scalp becomes abnormally rapid. This oily sebum causes the keratinized scales of the scalp's surface to clump together. The buildup of dead, greasy cells "stuck" on your scalp starts flaking off as dandruff.

Dry dandruff is produced by a water-poor scalp. Lack of moisure gives the cells on the scalp's surface nothing to cling to, so they start flaking off.

If you have dandruff, try curing your itchy problem by using specially formulated shampoos containing sulfur, zinc, selenium pyrithione, tar, or salicylic acid. Buy a few shampoos containing these medications and juggle their use so your "druff" is subjected to a varied assault. If these provide no relief, see a dermatologist. She or he may be able to provide a stronger, specially formulated anti-dandruff shampoo. Or, your doctor may diagnose your problem as something entirely different. You could have seborrheic dermatitis or psoriasis.

● *My hair is so thin. How can I beef it up?*

Hair is the one part of the body where *fat* is better than thin. But eating pounds of butter and fatty meat thrice-daily won't fatten up skinny locks. The diameter of the hair shaft is genetically determined. You can, however, beef up the *appearance* of individual hairs by coating them with products that make hair look fuller. Cheat Mother Nature in the following ways: Use protein body-builders and conditioners with balsam that envelop the hair shaft, imparting a bit of (temporary) width. *Coloring* your hair with an aniline deriva-tive tint (see Chapter Six, about hair color) will slightly enlarge the hair shaft by making the cuticle stand away from the cortex. A permanent wave is another body booster.

Note: Make sure your thin hair isn't actually *thinning* hair due to a vitamin deficiency: the B-complex vitamins, along with vitamins E and C, are considered important for healthy hair.

Remember that thin hair has nothing to do with the number of hairs on your head. It refers to the width of *each* hair strand. Just because your hair is thin, and probably lacks the medulla or innermost layer, don't think it's unhealthy—you're just unlucky. (Coarse hair, the other extreme, means the hair shaft has all three layers, and is thicker than normal.)

● *My hair looks thinner in winter. Why is that?*

Because it probably *is* thinner. I mentioned that hair appears in cycles: a long growth period, a shorter rest period followed by fallout. It is also affected by the seasons and weather. During the fall and winter, more hairs enter the telogenic phase, i.e., falls out, so you actually do have a little less hair. And then, the arrector pili muscle, found underneath the follicle, contracts in the cold, making hair hang there, looking limp.

Static electricity is another winter-related problem (symptoms are dry, fly-away hair). To calm your hair, brush it back in one direction only—this way the cuticle will stay flat, and won't pick up as much electricity. Add a bit of moisture to the hair (any hair cream or water will do) to counteract environmental dryness. In central-heated winter, you must add your own moisture to reduce your hair's shock (and fly-away) value, whereas in August, the humidity in the air provides a moisture-barrier, reducing electricity.

Those hot summer days that make your feet swell do the same to hair (the knee bone really *is* connected to the thigh bone), so it looks fuller. If you live in a high humidity area, your hair will, of course, have more of a tendency to curl . . . it looks like more than crop failure can be blamed on the weather.

- *When I leave the beauty salon I look like a young Ginger Rogers. Two days later I'm a ringer for Fred Astaire. How can I keep my hair healthy-looking between appointments?*

No matter what type of hair you have, do the following: *Brush* thoroughly, especially before washing. This will detangle the hair, remove surface dirt, and move the oil deposited on the scalp along the length of the hair shaft. The 100-strokes-a-day rule was probably invented by the founders of the Spanish Inquisition; this overkill can hurt your hair—brush adequately, but not with a vengeance. A natural (animal hair) bristle brush is preferable, especially if the nylon-bristle variety you're using has stiletto edges that can tear the hair. To add volume to your hair by brushing, bend your head so all your hair is hanging toward your toes. Brush vigorously. When you flip your head upright again, your hair will look fuller. Some women make this a two-fisted process: they hold one hairbrush in each hand and alternate strokes.

Treat yourself to a do-it-yourself scalp massage once or twice a week; it will ease tension while stimulating the follicular blood flow. (Exception: If you're battling unusual hair loss, forget scalp massage until your problem is diagnosed.)

Keep your hair clean. Aren't you tired of shampoo makers who tell us to wash our hair every night, once a week, during a full moon? *You* know when it's time by looking, touching, smelling. Use a gentle shampoo, and you can wash as often as you wish (sometimes nightly is necessary, if you have extra-oily hair). Washing won't cause baldness unless you scrub so hard you tear your hair out. In that case, I recommend a Valium instead of a sudsing. Here, the newest thoughts on how to shampoo:

First, check the pH of whatever shampoo you're using with your Squibb Nitrazine papers. A pH of 4.5 to 5.5 is the magic acid range; 3.5 is even gentler. If yours doesn't fall near these magic numbers, add ½ tablespoon of citric acid crystals (also called sour salts—look for them in your supermarket's spice display) to 8 ounces of your shampoo. This should lower the pH of the product; the lower the pH, the fewer frizzies you'll have, the more sheen you can expect.

When you *do* shampoo, wet hair thoroughly, apply shampoo and massage lightly into hair (don't rub and scrub as if you're pummeling an old algebra teacher). Leave lather on hair for three minutes—don't touch. Massage again, adding only water. Rinse thoroughly, and you're finished.

If your shampoo is the proper pH, one sudsing is enough. And, though we're all conditioned to believe in the "squeaky clean" philosophy, your hair will actually hold its set better if you don't wash all the life out of it! You needn't rub wildly—unless you want to tangle, snarl, and break the hair. If your scalp is oily, all that vigorous motion further stimulates the sebaceous glands, something you want to avoid. Let your shampoo do the work, not your fingers.

How long you rinse depends on what kind of water you've got: "hard" water is heavy on calcium and magnesium; "soft" water lacks these minerals. When it comes to H_2O, less is more—soft water is preferable. If you've got hard water (call your local water department and ask), you've got to rinse longer to remove soap and accumulated debris.

Drying: Your dog obeys your wishes more readily than your hair? That's no reason to dry it as if you were performing a strand-by-strand exorcism. Blot gently with a towel. Never brush hair while it's damp or wet—you may accidentally tug some of it right out of your scalp. And, even if you don't pull it out, you may stretch it: water-logged hair loses elasticity. Always use a wide-tooth comb for detangling, not a brush.

Take it easy with rollers, rubber bands, curling irons, blow dryers, and other potentially hair-damaging products.

Coddle hair that is being treated with alkaline processes (e.g., coloring, straightening, permanenting—see Chapter Six for details).

Here are specifics for treating your kind of hair:

Oily Hair

Use a shampoo especially formulated for oily hair (it will say so on the bottle) and use it as often as necessary. True, you may feel that you spend half your life with your head under the faucet, but at least you don't have to walk around with a mayonnaise cap twice a week!

Since oily hair means an oily scalp, brush often to dislodge "grease" from the scalp. Conditioners coat the hair strand—avoid them; you've got a natural coating process. Anything additional will make your hair dull.

To effectively clean oily hair, a shampoo must contain a greater degree of detergent, and is, therefore, more alkaline. As you know, alkalinity swells and separates the outer scales of the hair shaft—an undesirable side effect. To contract or smooth the hair shaft after washing, follow with an acid rinse—the simple Good Behavior Hair Rinse (see Part III, Day 2) will do the trick, giving your hair the tight cuticle that means shine. (But don't confuse shine with grease—if you rub your hair and come away with enough oil to make hand cream unnecessary, head for your hair washing gear.) If you can't shampoo (though you should), blot some astringent on your hair: it's a good grease cutter.

Dry Hair

To treat this condition, first determine the cause of your dryness. If you've "overdone" your hair with too much bleaching, straightening, or permanenting, you can't expect your hair to ooze moisture. By now you can probably *guess* why: All of these hair changes require the application of lavish amounts of alkaline chemicals. That doesn't mean your hair must remain in its virgin (untouched by processing hands) state. It does mean you have to process with care and moderation, and give a little more attention to been-around-the-track hair. Even formerly oil-gushing hair can dry up after too much treatment.

The cure? At the risk of sounding like a 1970s Timothy Leary, I still must answer: acid, acid, and more acid! I *am* hooked on shampoos with a pH in the acidic range, and conditioners heavy on the protein. These will provide temporary aid to your ailing hair by bolstering the protein content and tightening the cuticle. But the only way your hair will return to normal is to let the damaged hair grow out, fall out—then treat the *new* growth with more kindness.

The good news about hair: Processing damage affects the hair from the scalp outward; the growing structures of the hair root (fortunately) can't be touched by human hands—so each new hair that reaches the surface is, once again, a virgin. Treat it with delicacy and care, and it will retain its virginal health.

You've never done anything to your hair but give it a wash and set and it's *still* dry? You're a victim of the oil-poor scalp syndrome. Hair contains natural moisture (water). But your scalp doesn't produce enough oil to coat the hair, so what moisture you do have is leaking out. (Put another way: You have a defective acid mantle!) You should see an improvement if you follow your acid-based shampoo with a conditioner that will stick to your hair (for instance Wella Balsam or Clairol condition). This will block the escape route of the moisture you are producing and give your hair a more voluptuous appearance. There *is* one benefit to dry hair: If you're trapped in an elevator for a week, your hair will probably still look clean when you emerge.

You might also consider a hot oil treatment. It feels good, and, though its effects are temporary, it will give your hair a lush, pampered look. Take olive oil (any vegetable oil will do) and heat till very warm (not boiling). With a wide-tooth comb, part the hair into sections. Using fingers, massage oil into the "part" lines your sectioning has created. Keep parting and sectioning till whole scalp is covered. Wrap your head in Saran Wrap and sit under a bonnet-type hair dryer (if you have one) for forty-five minutes. Or, put a thin towel over your head, and drape with your heating pad on a low setting for thirty minutes. No plans for the evening? Cover your Saran Wrap with a shower cap, skip the heating pad, and sleep this way, giving your head an *all-night* treatment.

Normal Hair

If you've managed to reach age twenty-one with thick, healthy, normal hair you must have either (a) a mother who drilled you in good grooming habits while the other kids were out playing doctor; (b) a marvelous set of genes; or (c) incredible savvy. *Your* program of hair care: Keep up the good work, and give advice to the less fortunate.

● *My analyst says it's because my mother wanted another Shirley Temple . . . anyway, I want curly hair and I'm stuck with the "straights." How do permanents work? Are they harmful?*

To answer the *how,* a bit of biochemistry is needed. (Stay awake, this won't take long!) Simply put, your hair is made of protein; the protein is linked together by four sets of chemical bonds. Three of these bonds can be broken and re-formed into a temporary curly pattern merely by wetting and setting your hair. The fourth, the disulfide bonds, are extremely strong and determined to resist curl: These are the bonds we attack with a permanent.

The cold waving lotion that does the job is composed of thioglycolic acid and ammonium hydroxide. It's strong, it's alkaline, it chemically breaks down the bonds, it's applied to your rolled-up hair and allowed to "set" for the required (by the hairdresser or manufacturer) time.

Step two, with hair still in "curlers," involves neutralizing, which accomplishes two things: it helps compensate for the alkalinity (neutralizers are acidic) and it allows the tough disulfide bonds, broken in step one, to *re-form* in the new curled position. It also induces hair "amnesia"—your hair forgets about its formerly straight bias, totally embracing the curly look until the perm grows out.

If you're still with me, here are some facts about permanents to remember:

How long you keep the lotions on is determined by the condition of your hair and the amount of curl you want. If you're doing it yourself, follow package instructions to the letter (too long a processing can give you terminal frizzies; too short, and your efforts will have been a waste of time. The only lingering effect will be a dreadful smell).

You should know that most home perm mistakes are due to customer misuse, *not* fault with the product. If you're all thumbs, have a friend do it . . . this is no time to test your manual dexterity. In fact, I recommend having a *professional* permanent if it fits into your budget. Beauty salons are filled with gone-wrong home permanent refugees. We can always tell these victims— they enter with hair wrapped in a babushka, wailing in tongues about frazzles, frizzles, and other hair-raising misadventures that caused them to cross over to the professionals.

If you're planning to both color and perm your virgin hair, do the permanent first, then wait ten days before tinting. I'm assuming you're talking about a one-process coloring job (no bleaching). If you're contemplating going from dark to blond, *and* permanenting your hair, you may be overdoing it. Too many chemicals are involved; there's too much chance for damage.

Conditioning is essential for permed hair since it has been subjected to an alkaline treatment. Any good conditioner designed for dry, weakened, or damaged hair will do—just make sure you use it regularly.

Should you get a permanent? If your hair is *not* overprocessed or damaged, but *is* lacking in bounce and curl, two characteristics you want, a permanent can make a remarkable difference. A perm can also bring thin, fly-away hair under control. And don't forget "spot" permanenting to add body, bounce, and wave to specific areas of your hair.

● *I don't dream about freight trains rocketing through tunnels, or being kidnapped by sex-crazed pirates. My secret fantasy is to have s-t-r-a-i-g-h-t hair. Is this possible if my hair has a curl?*

Y-e-s, b-u-t.

Hair straightening is the flip side of the permanenting coin—that is, it is a chemical procedure most often using either thioglycolates or (for the newer home curl relaxers) bisulfites. In straightening, the strong disulfide bonds are broken, and the hair is continuously combed for about twenty minutes in a straight position. (This is the equivalent of the "setting" in the curling process.) The neutralizer is then applied to reduce the effects of the alkaline solution and to "harden" the hair in its new straight bonding pattern. The result: straighter hair.

B-u-t, points to remember: First, there are no rollers used, so the straightening chemicals have a better chance of coming in contact with the scalp. Second, the chemicals for straightening remain on your hair longer than during the curling process—again, there's more time for damage to take place.

There are two good reasons why straightening should be done in the salon *only*. Even if you just want to "spot straighten" (for example, your bangs), leave it to the professionals. You've heard of entering hat-in-hand? Straighten improperly and you'll make your "grand" entrance hair-in-hand.

Follow your salon-straightening procedure with a mildly acidic shampoo and protein conditioner and don't attempt any other processes on straightened hair.

- *You've talked about care, conditioning, and hair processing. What about styling?*

Styling should be discussed last, because no matter how you choose to wear your hair, it won't look right unless it's well-conditioned.

Today, style starts (and often ends) with a haircut. The idea is to get as perfect a cut as possible, so you'll have to do a minimum of setting and fussing. Here, I must tell you one bad news basic: You can't give *yourself* a decent (let alone terrific) haircut. Your best friend's mother can't give you a good cut either. You must go to the best salon you can find, and put your hair in the scissors of a pro. Here are some tips that will help *you* guide the *experts,* so they can give you the look you want.

GETTING THE MOST OUT OF YOUR HAIRSTYLIST

Don't pick a stylist out of the Yellow Pages. Look for one who has given a friend a look you like (but if all your friends look as if they were cloned from the same picture, keep looking).

Read the women's page of your local paper—hairstylists as well as other beauty/fashion experts are often interviewed, and their creations are photographed for the press.

The first time your new stylist sees you, don't greet him clad in one of those shapeless salon wraps with your head dripping wet from shampoo. He should get a look at the way you look in "real life"; otherwise he can't tell whether you need a styling to go with a free-flowing gypsy personality or a more controlled junior executive look. The stylist isn't clairvoyant, either. You have to express any definite likes and dislikes you have, tell him problems you've had with different styles in the past and give him a good idea of the look you want. A picture may be helpful, but if the competent stylist says "It's not for you," respect his judgment.

The worst thing you can say to your hair cutter is, "Do with me what you will." Given such license, he will let his creativity (not to mention his scissors) fly, and you may not be pleased with the results. So don't go for a haircut until you've thought about what you want.

Tell him just how much effort you intend to devote to upkeep. If you've got yardstick-straight hair, and don't *ever* want to bother with electric rollers or a permanent, a curly look is not for you.

If minimum upkeep is your goal, go in the direction of hair growth. Respecting natural parts, cowlicks, curliness, fine-hairness, and other quirks, rather than trying to plaster them into an unnatural shape, will mean an infinitely easier care job for you.

Watch your haircutter work:

- Hair is usually best cut while wet.
- Make sure your stylist gives you a precision cut. Whether you're getting a layered look or an all-one-length blunt cut, the competent stylist will follow a system, sectioning hair before cutting, and keeping hair not being worked on anchored out of the way with clips. The cutter who snips a fistful of hair here, there, and everywhere needs a refresher course.

Discuss the price of each service suggested in advance, so your total bill won't exceed your total expectations.

While your hair is being cut, study the work of other salon specialists—the colorist, permanent-waver, manicurist. As part of your total makeover, you may want to use their services at a later date.

Make sure you and your stylist are speaking the same language. You both speak English? That's just the beginning! You both must define terms the same way. Your idea of a short cut, for example, may be one that comes out chin length; your stylist may think you want a look that just grazes your earlobes.

When you're trying to decide on a style, consider how your hair can be made to emphasize good points and detract attention from the less-than-perfect. On the night you're washing your hair, step out of the shower, leave a little lather on your head and try molding your hair into different shapes. (The lather makes hair pliable.) You'll notice the following effects.

- Hair piled on top of the head elongates a round face.
- A narrow jaw line will look wider with hair massed in curls at either side.
- A long, unending forehead falls into proportion when covered with bangs.
- Chubby cheeks will look less rotund if hair is brought forward on the face to camouflage them.
- The older woman will look younger when her face is surrounded by soft waves (harsh, angular cuts just aren't as flattering when you reach what the French politely call *"un certain âge"*).

When you do find a style that suits you, keep it up—that means a haircut when your style first starts struggling out of shape.

- *I can play the piano like Van Cliburn, and thread a needle blindfolded. But when it comes to using a blow dryer, my fingers grow numb. What's the secret?*

Plug-in hair power revolves around three separate appliances—the hand-held (or blow) dryer, the curling iron, and electric rollers—and I want to say a few words about each.

BLOW DRYERS: CHOOSING AND USING

Don't be overpowered. The dryer that delivers 1,000 watts of power or more, with temperatures above 160 degrees, is probably too hot for the amateur to handle.

Don't overburden yourself with attachments. Unless you have the hands and eyes of a pro, concentrate on learning to wield the dryer itself with proficiency. Hold the dryer in your hand before you buy. If it seems to weigh more than an M-16 rifle, you'll have trouble keeping it aloft during drying time.

If you use a gun-type dryer, you'll need a brush to help you smooth and style. Kenneth Pensiero of Enrico Caruso, my hairdresser for years, suggested I use a "vent brush"—it's least likely to stretch the hair, and air swirls through the brush to speed drying. Check one out at the beauty supply store. (I use a vent brush because it keeps my hair from getting wavy while I blow dry.)

If you have a near-terminal case of fumble-fingers, look for the comb-style dryer instead of a gun. You can literally "comb" this dryer-type through your hair, which means you can forgo the brush. (I'm looking for a dryer that comes with a third hand—that would really simplify matters!)

No matter how well manufactured the dryer, you can still have problems if you don't use it properly. Don't absentmindedly hold the dryer in one place too close to your hair—nobody is showing the "singed" look at the moment. You have to keep the dryer moving.

To use a hand-held dryer, you need practice and patience. Here are the rules for becoming an expert:

1) Hold dryer six inches from hair for safety's sake.

2) Develop a precision drying technique for best results: Divide hair into four sections, back, side one, side two, crown. Invest in a few long clips; clip sections not being dried out of the way. Always start with the back quarter; hair is thickest there. Work up in layers from the nape of the neck. Twirl a round brush underneath the hair, and dry the strand (don't take an enormous clump) at the roots first; gradually work your way to the ends.

Once the back quarter is 90 percent dry, do the sides. The top, or crown, comes last.

3) If you're curly-haired and you're aiming for a straight cycle, it will take you longer, because you must start with a wet head. Others should towel dry gently first.

4) Hair must be 90 percent dry before you start the final styling. A blow dryer with a two-speed motor is helpful, because once the drying is 90 percent complete, you can switch to the slower motor for styling; you'll have better control.

5) If you want more fullness for a casual style, try this old trick used by pro stylists at photography studios: Aim head to the ground and dry all hair going floorward. When hair is 90 percent dry, flip head back to an upright position and style. You'll be surprised by the added volume.

6) To make sure the ends stay curled under, the appliance people at Clairol suggest you put down your dryer and wrap the just dried hair around a round brush, hold in place until the hair cools completely.

7) For a smoother look, hold the section of the hair you're drying downward. For extra lift, angle the section you're drying upward.

Once you get the feel of blow drying, you will find it a convenient method for giving yourself a professional styling—if you've got the precision haircut as a base.

CURLING IRONS

If it's a wave and curl you want, you can't rely on your hand-held dryer; you need a curling iron to make tendrils, waves, etc. Here are a few suggestions:

- Have your hairdresser show you how, before you try it yourself.
- Your hair must be completely dry before you use the curling iron.
- Just as if you were using a clothes iron, you can get that overprocessed look by holding a hot iron in place too long (you'll get a ridge in the hair).
- If the wand is too hot and not used properly, your hair can break in seconds, and it will take months to regrow.
- When I'm in a humid climate, I run the curling iron the length of my hair to control the frizzies.
- I use a curling iron to straighten my bangs.
- You can only curl a small section of hair at a time, so if you're going to do a complete curly-headed look, you may want to opt for electric rollers (see next section).

- The wand itself can get very hot, so you have to make sure you don't touch it with your fingers— you're likely to get a blister. And *don't* let it rest on your scalp.
- When you make the curl, make sure the end is well tucked in, or you'll have a hanging wisp of straight hair instead of a flip or downward roll.
- Some women say it's awkward slipping the curl out from the wand—again, patience and practice. To make the job less sticky, look for a wand with a Teflon coating.

ELECTRIC ROLLERS

These versatile plug-ins can give you a whole-head set in fifteen minutes. When you're ready to buy, think about your hair condition and tell the salesperson you're looking for curlers good for thick hair, tinted hair, fine hair, whatever. The more information you give when looking for a hair appliance, the better the chance of getting a more tailored-for-you machine.

- The size/curl ratio is the same as for conventional rollers: the bigger the roller, the looser the curl.
- Start at the crown and work back down to the nape of the neck.
- Remember, the longer you leave the rollers in place, the tighter the curl. But electric rollers definitely won't give you as long lasting a set as the conventional kind, even if you leave the electrics in place for their maximum curling time.
- When you're ready for removal, start at the nape of the neck and work upward to eliminate tangling as you go. Remove carefully so you don't snarl your hair.

● After the rollers are out, don't reach for the hairbrush immediately. Let the curls cool completely first, and your plug-in set will last longer.

Bad News Basics Re: The Heat Wave

While all these appliances do wonders for your hair style, they do nothing for hair condition. Heat is your hair's enemy, so when you rely on plug-in power, make sure you condition your hair regularly (you'll learn many hair treatments in Part III). And don't engage in overkill. Your hair will be better preserved if you limit your appliance usage to twice a week rather than once a day.

● *I'm planning a ten-day cruise; what's the best style to see me from shore to shore?*

The most practical style is one you can care for yourself. Major cruise ships usually have only one beauty salon; there may be just three hairdressers to care for the needs of 750 desperate women passengers. (If you've been aboard ship before, you know there are two areas where long lines snake up toward the deck: 1) the dramamine dispensary; 2) the beauty salon.

The best solution: Bring a wig. I don't see wigs as a day-in/day-out styling aid, but there is still a place for one or two in a busy woman's wardrobe. And, if you started buying wigs in the mid-60s, you'll be glad to know they've improved a great deal since then. (When synthetic wigs were first introduced it seems that everyone found a relative in Hong Kong and made him into a wigmaker, and the results were often poor.)

WIG GUIDE: CHOOSING AND USING

I asked Edith Imre, internationally famous wig designer, for wig wearing advice.

Purchase your wig at a beauty salon or from a wig specialist who will trim and style it to do the most for your head. No matter how well designed the wig, it won't work for you unless it's professionally tailored.

When you try on your wig, look at it from the front, sides, top, and back. Check your appearance in a full-length mirror.

Understand that the set of synthetic wigs (real hair is expensive, hard to find, and totally unnecessary) will last about six months; when your wig starts looking frizzy, bring it back to the stylist for professional renewal.

Look for a cap made of criss-crossing strands of ribbon for comfort—it will let your head "breathe" and you will perspire less.

You put your wig on like a cap, but don't pull it down over your ears—this is the major cause of the wig-induced headache.

To care for your synthetic wigs:

- Brush with a wire brush before washing.
- Cold-water wash in the sink. Use wig shampoo or Johnson's Baby Shampoo—not a cleanser designed for sweaters or dishes.
- Rinse well in cold clear water and pat dry with a Turkish towel—don't submit your wig to a hair dryer.
- Never comb and brush a wet wig—you'll take out the set.

Wigs have been popular for some 4,000 years. You might find that one of the newer varieties will not only fit your head, it will fit your life style, too.

The Only Dirty Word
Spelled with Eight Letters

THE TRUTH ABOUT EXERCISE

I know there are women out there who jump into leotards and start exercising at the first buzz of the alarm, but I confess I'm not one of them. (My favorite morning activity? Bending my elbow to get a cup of coffee in the vicinity of my mouth; even that is an effort.)

But I've tried! I've swung from the rafters of the most fashionable gyms in Manhattan, swung my tennis racquet in my best imitation-Chris Evert style, and strung myself to so much machinery I've been mistaken for a walking coronary care unit. I gave up all of these attempts because they were (a) uncomfortable, (b) time-consuming, and (c) boring. But I couldn't give up the guilt feelings not exercising can produce.

For health as well as cosmetic reasons, we all must make over our attitudes toward exercising. Because I knew I wouldn't do it unless I found a result-producing, non-time-consuming routine, it took me a while to come up with the Arpel Exercise Regime. But I've finally succeeded—I'll give you the instructions we've passed on to the thousands of women who attend our three-week makeover programs—busy women like yourself, who can never find the time or energy to kick that leg, toss that ball. Before I begin, let's go over the *whys* of exercise.

TO YOUR HEALTH. The President's Council on Fitness and Sports (charged with the difficult task of moving sedentary citizens off their ever-spreading bottoms) claims that almost half of all Americans never engage in regular physical activity. And the longer you put off moving your tending-to-corpulent body, the more damage you're doing to yourself.

USE IT OR LOSE IT. Your heart is a muscle, and when it isn't exercised, the slightest stress will cause a strain. Lack of exercise also causes your bones to deteriorate, your kidneys to malfunction, your whole body to degenerate—and your husband to seek out firmer flesh. I'm not trying to scare you, *but* women who exercise regularly can expect to live seven years longer (and be better-looking) than those whose only spare time activity is doing needlepoint. Even if you're a perfect size 8, you need exercise: thin doesn't necessarily mean in good shape.

Here's what the right exercises will do:

- Strengthen your heart and increase circulation.
- Make your bones more flexible.
- Make flesh firm rather than droopy.
- Delay the aging process.
- Promote weight loss by softening your fat, literally helping it melt away easier.
- Calm your nerves.
- Help you make it through the day without fatigue.
- Get you through the night (because of improved digestion, increased ability to sleep, better sexual performance).

- Extra bonus: You'll be thinking clearer, have more
  confidence, look more awake, more together.

Of course, the problem is finding the right exercise
program and sticking with it. Ten desultory leg lifts a
night is not going to turn you into a Nadia Comenichi.

What is your *real* attitude toward exercising? Take
the following True/False test that will tell you how
exercise-resistant you are (I failed it myself) and then
I'll outline the simple routines that work for me.

My last brisk, long walk was a three-
block trot to the candy store for ciga-
rettes.   T___ F___
My idea of a strenuous vacation?
Turning my body to tan evenly on a
Caribbean beach.   T___ F___
You don't have to be a three-year-old
to enjoy a fifteen-minute nap.   T___ F___
When I pinch the flesh on my stom-
ach, I grab more than ½ inch of fat. T___ F___
I'd rather miss the bus than run for it. T___ F___
Women who ski, play tennis, jog must
be descended from my eighth grade
phys. ed. instructor—they're no rela-
tion to me.   T___ F___

If, deep down in your gluteus maximus muscles, you
agree with the obvious anti-exercise bias of this tongue-
in-cheek quiz, join the crowd. You're one of the sedentary types, and though you may not see it or feel it, your
body is slowly decaying—the vital organs aren't doing
what they were meant to do, so they're atrophying. In
short, you've got the body-blahs, and now you're going
to get rid of them.

GET TO WORK. THE ARPEL EXERCISE ROUTINE

Most women, whether fat or thin, have two things in common: *Fatigue* and *lack of an engineering degree*. (To follow some complex exercise routines you have to school yourself in body mechanics. When an instructor shouts "turn your big toe ½ inch to the left while rotating on your ankle," I'm in trouble. That's why I believe in simplicity.)

Fatigue is such a common female complaint that doctors buy an extra condominium with the fees paid by women searching for an "*energy*-deficiency-anemia" cure.

To follow my program, you needn't join an exclusive gym. You can forget about gadgets that promise to work even if you don't expend energy. You can do these exercises alone, in a family prayer group, indoors or out, or with the family dog as your only witness.

You *will* need to do some heavy breathing. For exercise to work, you've got to work, too.

Just what are these "radical" get-fit exercises I'm proposing? *Jumping rope* and *jogging*. You may have heard them before—what you haven't heard is a way to do them that will make the most sense for you. After all, the point with exercise is not just to do it once, but to keep it up. And unless the routines are as simple as brushing your teeth, you, like me, will revert to your wicked sit-still ways after your first enthusiastic efforts.

The $1.98 Way to a New Body

Out of the hands of babes . . . comes a truly terrific way to get your daily exercise. Jumping rope met my requirements because you don't need exotic, expensive gear (I already have closets full of equipment I never use). Your paraphernalia must include: loose comfortable clothing, socks and sneakers, an old bra . . . that's all! Buy your rope at a sporting goods store or from your local hardware man. Mine cost $1.98. Just explain what you want it for, so you get a suitable weight. The ends of the rope should just reach your armpits when you're standing on the rope's middle.

WHERE YOU'LL JUMP. Here's the beauty of J.R.: do it almost anywhere. In your high-ceilinged den, 'neath the old oak tree, in your office before or after work (it's easier to tote a rope than a tennis racquet). Just try to avoid jumping on concrete—it's hard on the feet.

WHY YOU'LL JUMP. Rope skipping works wonders for your heart, gets more oxygen into your blood, improves the whole cardiovascular system. It can help firm your muscles, and because your lower half is in constant motion, you should see (not immediately, of course—this is no gimmicky cure-all) fat reduction on those areas most women find hardest to reduce: bulging thighs and hips. You'll also find yourself climbing stairs without that chest-pounding feeling.

WARNING AND WARMING-UP. Sure, jumping rope is child's play. But have you watched a child play lately? They move like whirlwinds, never let up for a minute— for kids, jumping is just part of a chain of events that is constant motion. If *your* idea of play recently has been bridge or backgammon, you have to ease into rope skipping, as you do into any exercise. *Another warning:* Don't start this or *any* exercise program until you've had a thorough medical checkup. Could be you've got health problems that mean you shouldn't jump or jog.

Assuming the doctor says "go," how do you go about it? Any exercise program, whether jumping, doing headstands, or diving off the cliffs at Acapulco, should consist of three parts: The *warm-up,* the *main routine,* and the *cool-down.* To warm up, devise your own ten-minute period of calisthenics or stretching exercises—leg raises, knee bends, arm swings, until you feel some of the stiffness leaving your body. (You can use some of the spot exercises you'll learn later on in this chapter.) To cool down, just walk around a little, stretch a little, after you're finished.

Now, to the matter at hand: jumping. *Five minutes a day, five days a week* is your ultimate goal. Start by jumping with a two-foot bounce (both feet land together). When you've mastered this simple step, jump by lifting one foot at a time, as if you were jogging with a rope (the step boxers use in training). You don't have to jump very high—just enough to clear the rope. You'll start with just a few jumps each day (25 for Day 1), and gradually increase. Don't be surprised at your lack of stamina—your heart is probably not used to any activity. If your heart does start pounding wildly, or you're just plain breathless, feel faint or uncomfortable, stop and rest before continuing. (You want to live to enjoy your new fitness!)

In fact, jumping theorists say you get the best benefits by jumping/resting/jumping. I now skip 200 times without stopping, rest for a minute, skip again and repeat. But it took me a while to get there.

I know this all sounds ridiculously easy (it won't seem like kid stuff when you try it), but it works. In his informative book, *The Perfect Exercise, The Hop, Skip and Jump Way to Health* (Simon and Schuster, 1976), Curtis Mitchell provides all the scientific evidence that proves why jumping is good for you. One of the experts

Mitchell quotes—yes, there are jump rope experts, too—says 500 skips non-stop in five minutes is top goal for everyone.

You want to know *how* out of shape you are? First, you've got to learn to take your pulse. Rest your arm, palm relaxed, on your lap. With your opposite hand, cradle your wrist with the two middle fingers about an inch below the thumb; feel around till you find your pulse. Count your pulse for 15 seconds, multiply by 4 and you've got your pulse rate per minute: 72 to 80 is considered normal. The following two tests from Mitchell's book will easily tell you how desperately you need to exercise.

TEST FOR RECOVERY FROM EFFORT
1. Take your pulse, sitting.
2. Climb a flight of stairs.
3. Take your pulse again.

If your heart is fit, your pulse after climbing the stairs will be around 88 to 90 beats per minute. If you're out of shape, it can zoom to 160. Anything over 90 needs improvement.

JOG-IN-PLACE TEST
1. Run in place briskly for one minute.
2. Stop, sit, and take your pulse for 15 seconds.

Multiply by 4 to get your pulse rate per minute.

BEATS PER MINUTE	YOUR RATING
84 TO 96	VERY GOOD
102 TO 114	ABOVE AVERAGE
120 TO 132	AVERAGE
138 TO 149	BELOW AVERAGE
150 TO 161	POOR
162 AND UP	VERY POOR

Now you know why you need to exercise, and a simple exercise routine. Just build up your jumping *gradually*. This is an activity even the lethargic can learn to love. The only drawback? If you're an apartment dweller, you may incur the wrath of your downstairs neighbor!

Jogging

Jumping rope is an ideal solitary pastime, perfect for those who feel exercise should be performed only in the privacy of one's bedroom, between consenting adults. Jogging can go either way: do it alone, or if you're the social type, take to well-trafficked trails with friends. There are some 8,000,000 adult joggers out there—and what they're getting is more than a little fresh air. They're building up endurance, and (important for women) they're *not* building Mr. Universe muscles. Another plus: Jogging does not mean racing. There's no one clocking you and you don't even burn more calories by accelerating, so why rush? When seven medical experts rated fourteen sports according to the health benefits they produced, jogging came in first, bicycling was second, tennis ninth, bowling last. (Jumping rope wasn't included in this survey printed in *Medical Times*.)

BEFORE YOU START. You *must* get a checkup; jogging can be dangerous for certain individuals (especially if you've had heart, lung, or joint-disease problems). Also, you'll have to do limbering up (a good warm-up routine) exercises to get your body in shape so soreness and strain don't result first time around the track.

Jogging does take a little bit of investment: Buy proper shoes (Adidas, Pumas) in your local sporting goods store—this is essential. I've found that purchasing a sweatsuit is an added inducement—I feel guilty wearing it if I don't get moving. (This from the President's Council on Fitness and Sports: Never wear a *rubberized* suit. It won't encourage weight loss, and more important, it won't allow you to sweat properly, which means your body temperature could rise to unhealthy heights.)

Once you're geared up (if you wear a bra, make sure it's loose enough so you don't feel it), you can jog anywhere, indoors or out. In good weather, a dirt or grassy path is perfect (concrete is harder on your feet, but if that's what you're surrounded by, you've got no choice). If you feel the world isn't ready to see your sweatsuit-clad body, or you can't stand the heat/cold, jog in your basement or house until you're in more presentable shape. The only problem with housebound jogging? Boredom.

HERE'S HOW TO JOG: Stand up straight and don't look at your feet. Keep your arms bent at the elbow and let them swing naturally. Try to land on the heel of your foot, and push off from the ball of your foot. Remember, you're not running a race, so keep your steps short— don't reach out with your legs. If you become tired or develop any kind of discomfort while jogging, stop.

Jogging is a terrific way to gain physical fitness. The hardest part about practicing this discipline is getting up the courage to begin.

Experts say you should jog three times a week, for thirty to forty minutes each session. I usually jog twice weekly but I consider jogging a *back-up* to my skip-rope routine. You may get so high on jogging you'll only use your rope in bad weather. (Veterans say the lighter-than-air feeling that comes with your "second wind" is superior to any drug-or-drink induced euphoria. Some claim it's better than sex . . . I wouldn't go that far.) The point is, one or both of these exercises can get your body back to feeling *human* again.

The National Jogging Association (1910 K Street N.W., Suite 202, Washington, D.C. 20006) suggests the following program for beginners. (The N.J.A. is an excellent source for any jogging-related questions you may have.)

WEEKS 1-6

Warm up with walking and stretching movements.
Jog 55 yards, walk 55 yards (four times).
Jog 110 yards, walk 110 yards (four times).
Jog 55 yards, walk 55 yards (four times).
    Pace: 110 yards in about 45 seconds.

If you become a regular jogger, you can forget about fatigue. Your doctor will have to finance his condominium elsewhere.

As you get in shape, you'll also want to devote a minimum amount of time to a maximum-results spot-reducing program. I'll ease you in to exercises for body-bulge areas at the end of this chapter. I hope you do agree with me that you must exercise to stay healthy. Now, answers to a few commonly asked questions relating to exercise, body shape, and diet.

● *If I want to lose weight (which will translate into inches), won't dieting alone do it? I've cut down my calorie intake.*

Congratulations. You're *half-way* there. But unless you add exercise to your program, don't expect a real weight loss. Here's why: To control your weight you have to balance food intake with energy outflow—and it takes less food intake (calories) to maintain the body than we think. So, what are you going to do with those excess calories? Unless you burn them off with exercise, your body will store them as fat.

When the eating habits of obese people were compared with their normal-weighted counterparts, researchers found that in many cases the fatties weren't eating all that much more, *but* they were moving *much less* than thin people.

- *When I engage in strenuous activity, I get so hungry I'm ready to chew up my gym sneakers.*

If you're overweight, your post-exercise hunger is probably psychological. You see, during and after your work-out, your body can "consume" the energy you've already stored as fat—it doesn't need any extra food.

- *I get enough exercise turning the wheel of my calorie counter. To make any extra effort, I need some heavy inspiration.*

Dial-A-Prayer may not offer solace, but clasp your hands heavenward and chant this: I can be twenty-five pounds thinner next year at this time if I do just two things: (1) Keep my food intake constant (and reasonable). (2) Add thirty minutes of exercise to my daily schedule.

- *I buy sweaters in the boys' department; I have to order my skirts from an itinerant Bedouin tent-maker. Will exercise help re-align my body?*

Here I must tell you a bad news basic: If your mother, aunts and great-aunts are all wide of thigh and bountiful of hip, you're probably the victim of a hereditary figure problem.

The most rigorous exercise routine just isn't going to turn you into a body beautiful. But you should work to tone up what you've got. Did you know that muscle takes up much less space than flab? So you'll look smaller if you're in shape. Get out your jump rope, do the best you can, and learn to camouflage with the right clothes.

- *What about exercising to* increase *parts of the body, specifically the breasts?*

Exercise *can* develop and tone *muscles*. But here's another bad news basic: Your breasts, alas, have no muscle tissue; they're made from fatty tissue, so exercise won't increase them or make them firm. You can exercise to strengthen the pectoral muscles which support the breasts. Try this: Stand up straight, swing arms behind you, and clasp wrists together. Bend your neck back, hold for ten seconds, release slowly and repeat ten times. (This may help, but it won't turn you into a *Playboy* centerfold.)

If your small breasts bother you, read the section on augmentation mammaplasty in the plastic surgery section (Chapter Ten). You'll also learn about operations to lift drooping breasts, but if you're not ready for such radical procedures, wear an under-wire bra to counteract the effects of *gravity,* which causes our breasts to fall floorward as we age (the larger the breast, the longer the drop, so once past the age of thirty, those flatchested girls we taunted in high school have their revenge—small breasts look perky longer). Overweight, pregnancy, and hereditary factors can also be blamed for premature breast sagging.

● *I already lost weight; now my skin seems to be hanging around with no place to go. Will exercise help firm me up?*

As I said before, exercise only helps tone *muscles*. For a further discussion of sagging skin, see the diet and plastic surgery chapters.

● *A new gym with a set of exercise machines resembling medieval torture mechanisms has offered me a complimentary session. What do these machines do?*

Most experts feel that machines that propose to do the work *for* you . . . do nothing. All that fancy gear that wriggles your rear and pummels your thighs while the rest of you stands around yawning is to be avoided. Some of these machines have even been "credited" with causing heart attacks.

Take advantage of the complimentary gym offer, but join the exercise classes that will firm you up and burn up calories. The machines will help if you let them gather dust!

THE BODY BULGE ATTACK

Though I'm not a great fan of routinized exercise (mainly because I'm too lazy to do it), if very specific areas of your body need whittling, you're going to have to expand your exercise effort to include movements to firm these target areas.

What exercises do I recommend? The following are adapted from our makeover/shapeover classes headed by Patty Snyder in Robinson's, Beverly Hills. The women who do these regularly report excellent results.

Because you're jumping and/or jogging, you will see an *all-over* body improvement, so you (we hope) won't have to do *all* of the following. But do be merciless in your personal body assessment; if you need it, include the carefully tailored exercises for your problem area(s) in your three-week *Crash* program. You'll be surprised at the results the Body Bulge Attack will provide.

STOMACH

Cross Your Heart

Lie on your back, legs straight, hands clasped behind head. Bend left leg touching knee to right elbow, and return leg to straight position. Bend right leg touching knee to left elbow, and return to straight position. Alternate legs 20 times each. Remember . . . keep a brisk, steady pace and breathe!

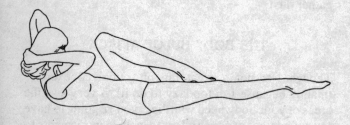

Semi Sit-ups

Lie on back with hands clasped behind head and elbows on the floor. Lift both legs up over chest with slightly bent knees. Raise upper half of body to meet knees, pulling elbows forward. Return to starting position by rolling back down, with elbows back in place on floor. Repeat exercise 20 times.

HIPS

Roll 'Em Over

Lie on back, arms extended, palms up. Bring knees up to chest. Keeping knees together, roll legs to right until hip touches floor, then bring them back over the chest and roll to left. Continue rolling from left to right,

keeping shoulders down and knees high, close to elbows on each roll. Repeat 20 times.

THIGH-TRIMMER

The Swing

Lie on your right side, legs together and straight, with both feet flexed. Lift left leg upward about 18 inches with outer thigh toward ceiling and knee and toe pointing forward. Lower leg to starting position. Repeat 20 times. Turn on your left side and repeat lifts with right leg 20 times. Remember . . . keep a steady pace and breathe deeply and often. Gradually build to a count of 50 per leg.

ARMS

Arm Twist

Stand up straight with feet together, buttocks tucked under, rib cage lifted, stomach tight and arms straight out at shoulder level with fingers extended. Turn arms over forward until palms are facing ceiling, then turn arms over backward (180 degrees) until palms are facing ceiling again. Repeat forward and backward twist 50 times, keeping arms out and at shoulder height. Repeat series with fists clenched 30 times.

DERRIÈRE

The Tight End

Stand with feet together and knees slightly bent, stomach in, rib cage lifted and arms relaxed by sides. Contract buttocks muscles, hold tightly for 1 second and release. Complete 9 contractions and hold the 10th for 15 seconds. Repeat series 4 times. Remember . . . pull and hold as tightly as you can each time. Make your efforts count!

4

America's Second Most Popular Indoor Sport

THE TRUTH ABOUT DIETING

I was born 400 years too late! If I had lived in the seventeenth century, my body would have been the toast of Europe. Rubens would have admired my always-dieting-to-stay-thin body almost as much as he worshipped the flesh of those darlings of the day (whose slightly more than ample behinds were sought after by kings and counts) he immortalized on canvas. Because in the good old days a bare-bones woman was not considered the height of fashion. (Have you ever seen pictures of a *skinny* courtesan?)

Styles of beauty do change, unfortunately. More recently, flat-chested women cringed at pictures of Jayne Mansfield in the 1950s, the rest of us started quaking when Twiggy became the sex symbol of the sixties. Who would have thought that bony knees could turn on a generation of otherwise normal men?

But thin is still in, and whether you're ten pounds over the mark or sixty, you know it's time to go on a diet. Next to sex, Americans spends more time discussing, practicing, and feeling guilty about dieting. We've also been exposed to more diets than the Kama Sutra has positions: the stuff-yourself-with-sweet-cream diet, the can't-fail-fasting program, the drinking-man's, thinking-man's, and drink-the-contents-of-your-office-water-cooler diets. So, how come at least one in five of us in grossly overweight, and most of the rest of us could stand to lose five or ten pounds?

The problem lies with education. We have to understand not only what we put in our mouths, but the when and why of eating patterns. We have to *think* before we eat. I don't know of one friend who looks wonderful and is past thirty who eats whatever she wants. The goal of weight loss should be to keep off what we work so hard to take off.

Obviously, *staying* thin is the problem. So I decided to find a diet that would do the work for us. I interviewed many weight control experts and came to one bad news basic conclusion: There is no easy way to do it.

What I *have* discovered is a way to take off and keep off those few extra pounds that plague most of us. After I tell you my program (which doesn't require starving!), I'll try to explain some of the more popular approaches to weight control, so you can review other diets available.

THE ARPEL SACRED COW DIET

This is a diet you must follow *faithfully*. In fact, I'm going to "convert" your eating habits, turn you into a disciple of the dieting rituals practiced in Bombay, New Delhi, and Calcutta. I am insisting that you start believing *the cow is sacred*. That's right . . . no beef at all during your makeover. In India, where the cows are never touched by true believers, eating beef is a sin. So will it be for you.

Forget Beef and Lose Weight

Ask any thin model if she eats meat. I assure you the answer will be "never" or "rarely."

Aged beef (and its cousins, lamb and pork—avoid them, too) may well be a good source of protein, but it contains too much fat to make its consumption worthwhile. And, don't think you're getting rid of the fat by trimming around the edges. Even if the aged beef looks lean to you, there is invisible fat hidden in the muscle fibers. But don't take my word for it. The lean beef myth is illustrated by Dr. Robert Levine, a New York weight control specialist.

CALORIE CONTENT OF BEEF (7 OUNCES)

	Protein	Fat	Total
Porterhouse steak	216	268	484
Rib roast	190	380	570
Ground chuck	218	308	526

You don't have to be a math major to realize that the fat content in each of the above portions actually is higher than the protein. Nor am I suggesting you must eat gauze (some yogis do . . . helps clean out the system) for the rest of your days. The trick is to substitute foods that contain less fat while providing more protein:

CALORIE CONTENT OF BEEF SUBSTITUTES (7 OUNCES)

	Protein	Fat	Total
Roast chicken	312	54	366
Baked bluefish	260	58	318
Veal cutlet	226	78	304

You don't need the help of a pocket calculator to figure out that by making these substitutions, you're cutting your calorie intake by 25 percent, and you're also eating well. Of course you know that you should bake or broil your chicken or fish, not fry it. (Cook chicken with the skin on to preserve the natural juices, but don't *eat* the skin—it's fattening.)

There are two other commandments thou shalt not break:

Boycott Salt

Quite simply, the sodium in salt retains water in your body. You might as well lose this excess water bloat along with the fat you'll be dropping.

Boycott Booze

I'm not telling you to go on the wagon permanently, but if you want to lose some weight during this three-week period you've set aside to make yourself over, forget drinking. You've all seen the bad news calorie content of many favorite cocktails listed on any calorie counter.

After the three weeks are over, why not confine your drinking to white wine, one of the least fattening, most enjoyable of drinks? A Manhattan contains 145 calories, a whiskey sour 140, but 2 ounces dry white wine adds just 45 calories to your intake total. Drinking to excess also *ages* you—another good reason to stop saying "just one more."

To review—the Sacred Cow Diet is based on a fanatic devotion to cutting the following five from your diet for three weeks: *beef, pork, lamb, salt, and booze.* When the three weeks are up, indulge yourself in the above no-nos rarely and sparely (if at all), and you'll keep off the weight you've lost. Here are the specifics of the Sacred Cow Diet. I worked these guidelines out with Dr. Levine—he's young, healthy, attractive, and practices what he preaches. (Some of the diet doctors I've visited are a bit on the chunky side, which hardly inspires confidence!)

When to Eat

In order to gain control of runaway eating habits, you must school yourself to eat three meals a day: breakfast, lunch, and dinner. Snacks at any time are out— Monday's well-behaved carrot turns into Tuesday's crackers and cheese and Wednesday's chocolate brownie.

Eat Smart

Cagey dieters are aware of the following:

When your mouth is watering for a baked potato, get the mood without the substance by eating just the shell. If you must have a bagel or roll, toss out the insides.

Beware of cheese. It's deceptively fattening and calorie-full (there can be 100 calories in a paper-thin slice of processed American cheese). Europeans understand that cheese belongs in the treat category; that's why they serve it for dessert. You should avoid cheese altogether during your three-week makeover, except for skim milk cottage or pot cheese.

Beware of "diet" foods. What makes most of the supermarket-shelf diet foods slimming is their size, not their contents—micro portions of anything have fewer calories than macro. So, just because the label says dietetic, you can't eat triple portions and still be sticking to a weight-control regimen.

Consider a new craze, frozen yogurt—it takes a long time to eat, so you get the impression you're consuming something filling (a little positive self-delusion never hurt a dieter). But don't think you can eat this and then eat dessert. An 8 ounce container of a vanilla-flavored frozen yogurt contains 180 calories and with fruit it's 210. For the dieter, yogurt is a meal substitute, not an appetizer or dessert.

Understand that health food is not always slimming. Granola, for example, may give you more bounce to the ounce, but it also provides lots of calories per ounce: at least 130. There are 115 calories in one ounce of wheat germ—this adds up if you eat wheat germ as your breakfast cereal. Eat Bran Buds instead—it only has 70 calories. Special K, also allowed on this diet, contains 110 calories per ounce.

If you think you're eating dietetic as well as healthy by having a big salad, don't think you're automatically feeding thin. I don't want to bore you with charts but you should know you must monitor your salad dressing with care: one tablespoon of Italian dressing can add 85 calories to your salad. French, Russian, and cheese dressings contain even more. Before you know it, you can have a 500-calorie salad—not quite what the diet doctor ordered!

What to Eat

This sensible diet is really a high-protein, low-carbohydrate, low-fat diet. Chicken, veal, and fish are in; mature beef is out. So is adding salt to your food. One more important "in": vegetables and citrus fruits, which are so essential for good nutrition. Since this is the Sacred Cow Diet, I've divided your "can" and "cannot" foods into two categories, the Abstinence (or "out") and Indulgence (or "in") food lists. Keep in mind the following, culled from advice Dr. Levine gives his patients:

Abstinence

The following are not allowed for the duration of your three-week makeover:

- Fruits and fruit juices with the exception of half a grapefruit or orange (or the same equivalent in juice) for breakfast ONLY, and a small wedge of melon, for dinner dessert ONLY.
- Chinese food
- Carbonated diet sodas
- Buttermilk
- All sweetened drinks
- Bread and butter (except for two slices of protein bread, very lightly spread with butter or oleo, permitted daily)
- Hot cakes, sweet rolls, waffles, pancakes, hard rolls, soft rolls, bagels, crackers
- All cakes, cookies, pies, pastries
- Puddings (this includes "dietetic" puddings), rich desserts
- Cereals (except Special K or Bran Buds, which can be taken three times a week for breakfast only)

- Spaghetti, macaroni, noodles
- Fats
- Avocado
- Potato, hominy, rice, corn, peas, grits
- Salad dressings (you may use lemon juice or white vinegar only)
- Chicken roll or turkey roll
- Butter sauce, cocktail sauce
- Dried fruits
- Fatty or fried meats, breaded meats, delicatessen meats, smoked meats
- Smoked fish, fish canned in oil, herring, gefilte fish, sardines (you may have water-packed tuna or water-packed salmon)
- Cheese (other than skim milk cottage cheese, or skim milk pot cheese)
- Coffee-Mate or dairy substitute
- Creamed or thickened soups or soups containing non-allowed vegetables
- Dried peas or beans
- Alcohol, wine, beer
- Catsup, relish, cranberry sauce, sauerkraut, cole slaw, horseradish, chili sauce, mayonnaise
- Ice cream or ices
- Sauces, gravies, creams (sweet or sour), oils (corn, cottonseed, safflower, etc.)
- Pickles (sweet or sour), olives, nuts
- Flavorings or extracts

Indulgence

In case you're worried that you have nothing left to eat, the following is your allowed foods list:

- Veal, eggs, fowl, and seafood—nothing fried, all visible fat trimmed off, and without sauces or gravies. (You may have "fried" in a Teflon pan, or in pans sprayed with Pam.)

- All vegetables with the exception of peas, corn, rice, winter squash, potatoes, and beans (string beans are allowed).
- Tea, coffee, or skimmed milk—but no sugar
- Plain (unflavored, unfruited) yogurt, once daily
- Dietetic gelatin dessert
- Any condiments not listed on the "Not Allowed" list.
- Sugar-free gum
- Bran Buds or Special K cereal three times a week, for breakfast ONLY
- An orange or half a grapefruit (or the equivalent in juice) for breakfast ONLY
- A small wedge of melon (watermelon excluded) for dinner dessert ONLY
- Cottage cheese (skim or low calorie)
- Pot cheese (skim or low calorie)
- Water-packed tuna or salmon
- White vinegar only
- Vegetable juices
- Two slices protein bread daily (lightly spread with butter or oleo).
- Small amounts of lemon juice allowed on salads or in cooking.

As I mentioned earlier (and as you can see from the above lists), this is no gimmick diet. You can't eat all you want of everything you want and still lose weight. But if you are willing to make some sacrifices, you can lose ten pounds in three weeks by following the Sacred Cow, and you won't starve or make yourself sick in the process.

Maintenance

If you want to keep the weight off, you will always have to eat within reason. But instead of excluding the abstinence list completely, add a forbidden food to one of your daily three meals in moderate (never gargantuan . . . who are you trying to kid!) portions.

To maintain your ideal weight the most important thing is not what you eat, but when you eat—three meals a day, breakfast, lunch, and dinner, no snacks. Never vary from this pattern.

Do you have a weight problem? Most doctors tag you obese if you're 20 percent above the poundage considered average for your height. But *you* can tell if you're overweight by performing a simple two-step test: 1)Take off all your clothes. 2)Look in a full-length mirror. Unless you're myopic, you'll know how much weight to lose. I asked Dr. Robert Levine if there were any categories of overweight people who *shouldn't* diet. His answer? "Yes . . . those who don't want to be thin."

My diet will help you keep off excess pounds. But to really get yourself down to where you want to be, you should know the latest diet-related thinking. Here, as promised, answers to questions you'd probably like to ask.

● *A friend of mine is taking diet pills. They seem to be working. What exactly are they?*

Trying to get a doctor to reveal what pills he prescribes is almost as hard as trying to find a best seller without sex. Most medical men are uncommunicative on this subject, but I have found out the following:

The Crutch of Crutches: Amphetamines

The diet doctors who dispense amphetamines (also known as "speed" and "uppers") may not be around much longer, as the government continues to look into amphetamine abuse. The idea behind amphetamines is that the pills will keep you running in such high gear you won't feel depressed about dieting, and yes, they do suppress your appetite. But take them for too long a period, and you may become addicted. And when you stop the pill your appetite will return because you haven't learned how to control your food urge while pill-popping. Even the hippies who turned on to drugs in the sixties were aware of the dangers associated with amphetamines. Their slogan? "Speed kills."

Every diet-conscious woman knows that amphetamines will help you lose weight when you first start taking them. But upper-stuffers also report anxiety, sleepless nights, excessive talking, edgy nerves, even bad breath. I myself tried amphetamines to lose five pounds (before I went cold turkey on the Sacred Cow), but my experience was not good. I decided thin and *paranoid* was not a winning combination.

If your diet man is free with these pills, but stingy on long-term dieting plans, you'd better look elsewhere.

Thyroid Pills

Some diet doctors claim an underactive thyroid gland is a prime fat causer. The pills prescribed to counteract this problem hype up your thyroid, and raise your metabolism so you will burn more calories. But few cases of overweight are truly thyroid-related. What happens, then? The pills do most of the work, your thyroid gets lazy and doesn't work on its own. Result:

Your thyroid gland could atrophy (the old use-it-or-lose-it principle) from lack of hard work.

Diuretics

These help you get rid of water weight, not fat. If used for a long time, your kidneys will grow dependent on them, and won't be able to function without their aid. Diuretics are often prescribed at the beginning of a diet—the doctors hope the quick weight loss that occurs when you "drop your water" will encourage you to stay on the regimen they provide. Diuretics may be double bad news: They drain water from your skin cells, too—prolonged use makes the skin look wrinkled.

Diet pills have many negatives and very few positives, but if you still decide to take pills to supplement your weight program, ask the doctor just what's in them, what they're doing to and for your body. If the doctor won't tell, ask your druggist or call the pharmaceutical company—it's your body, and you have a right to know exactly what effect everything you put in it will have on your health.

- *There are so many diet programs available, I could probably lose weight if I just read one of these books at every mealtime. How do I know which program will work for me?*

Diet and nutrition experts are still trying to answer this one. But as one doctor told me, when so many possible cures are put forward for a disease (and obesity *is* a disease), the medical profession is really admitting it's stymied. Here are some of the more popular diets that have gained public attention, and worked for some of the people, some of the time.

The Calorie Count

This is the conservative, time-honored approach. Each food is given a calorie count. If 3,500 calories equal a pound, you have to reduce your intake by that much to lose one pound of body weight. Extra calories that you don't burn off by physical activity are stored in the body as fat. So, the theory goes, eat less, gain less. Or burn up more calories than you take in, and your body will use the energy in its *stored* fat reserves, shrinking them, and you at the same time.

The good news: Even though you're cutting caloric intake, you can still eat a well-balanced diet composed of foods from the four basic groups you studied in junior high home economics class: 1) milk group; 2) meat group; 3) vegetable-fruit group; 4)bread-cereal group.

The bad news: If you're a 2,500–calorie–a–day person who is cutting down to 1,200, expect to go through withdrawal. Symptoms: Severe hunger pangs.

Dr. Atkins' Low-Carbohydrate Diet

The opposite of the calorie count. This diet proclaims you can lose weight *sans* hunger pangs. Dr. Atkins allows his patients to eat such "no-nos" as bacon, butter, heavy cream, roast duck, pastrami, and other high calorie foods. What you must count is carbohydrates, not calories. Dr. Atkins begins by demanding carbohydrate cold-turkey of his patients, then they continue on a very low-carbohydrate diet. Atkins says we don't need carbohydrates at all, the "carbs" actually "prevent you from burning up your own fat and stimulate your body to make more fat."

The good news: Dr. Atkins says his disciples are never hungry because they can eat a variety of rich foods banned on calorie-counting regimens.

The bad news: The medical profession as a whole does not share Dr. Atkins' enthusiasm for his diet—some of its members feel it could have detrimental side effects.

There's another problem: bad breath. Acetone is formed when the fat breaks down, and the body is in a state of ketosis (throwing off ketones, which Atkins describes as "little carbon fragments"). To minimize the bad breath, drink plenty of fluids . . . lots of water. (Note: Other diets cause bad breath, too.)

I should also mention that I tried the Atkins diet to lose my stubbornly clinging five pounds, but it didn't work for me, possibly because I'm not a sweet eater to begin with; but I'm sure this diet would help Sesame Street's Cookie Monster.

Fasting

The no-carb, no-cal, no-nothin' diet. Fasting has been popular for thousands of years. The idea: Eat zilch and you'll purge your system of impurities while dropping the pounds. In his book *The Ultimate Diet,* Allan Cott, M.D., says fasting will also make you feel euphoric and lower your blood and cholesterol levels.

The good news: Some fasters say you don't feel hungry because you're not regularly exposed to the stimulation of food that even small morsels provide.

The bad news: It may be the wrong kind of weight loss. Recent research shows that prolonged fasting causes the body to "eat up" lean tissues and important muscles before the fat is gone. There have been cases of fasting-related deaths. If you want to fast, consider cutting out food for thirty-six hours tops . . . but first ask your doctor if you can cut it. The side effects (including headaches, dizziness, weakness) may cause you to break your fast even sooner. *Prolonged* fasting demands constant medical supervision; it can be highly dangerous and does nothing for your hair and skin, which need nourishment to maintain their glowing good looks. Obviously, if you're fasting, you won't jump rope or jog—a brisk walk is about as strenuous as you should get.

Dr. Stillman's Quick Weight Loss Diet

Stillman said you can burn up to 275 extra calories a day if you eat what's on his list . . . which is *protein only* (beef, lamb, chicken, veal, eggs, fish, etc). No carbohydrates or fats are included. You also must drink eight 10-ounce glasses of water a day because all the protein burns up much more of your body fat than a balanced diet would. "This leaves in its wake the waste products or ashes of burned fat . . . which must be washed out of your system. . . ."

The good news: You'll certainly get lots of high-energy body-building proteins.

The bad news: He said you can eat all the beef and lamb you wish . . . but what about cholesterol? Besides, his list is very restricted and you may get bored before you reach your ideal weight. Because 80 ounces of water daily are required, you must be possessed of a) an unquenchable thirst; b) the constant availability of a bathroom. This is not the diet to follow when driving cross-country.

The Vegetarian Diet

While I'm a vegetable lover, I don't believe in such a limited approach to dining. Vegetarians don't get the complete amino-acid protein needed for good cell reproduction and growth. They rarely get the protein punch packed in vitamin B-12. (Note: Liver is probably the best source of this vitamin. If you haven't touched the stuff since you were old enough to say no, look for dessicated liver tablets in the health food stores.) Besides being (in my opinion) unhealthy, I think chicken, fish, and veal are much more interesting and can be prepared in a variety of ways.

The Protein Sparing Fast

Another form of fasting. All the dieter consumes for nourishment is a daily dose of predigested liquid protein. It supplies the necessary amino acids. When the dieter is consuming this protein (the *only* sustenance allowed for the duration), it is claimed, very little lean body mass must be broken down for energy, so it's really the fat you're losing. (Weight lifters and wrestlers have been using liquid protein for years as an energy supplement; what's new is the concept that it can be used for total sustenance.)

The good news: It is said that you won't be hungry, dizzy, weak, afflicted with low blood pressure (some side effects of no-nothin' fasting), and you *will* lose weight. (I know someone who has done well on this regimen.)

The bad news: Though a variety of predigested liquid proteins are now on drugstore shelves, you have to know what you're doing when you take them—you need the proper vitamin and mineral supplements and *you need a doctor's supervision.* And, there's the question of how you'll eat when you end the protein-sparing fast. If you return to your former eating habits, your weight will return, too. It may tax your kidneys;

the blood urea and uric acid must be monitored. So put yourself in the hands of a doctor before you begin.

Before I leave the subject of weight loss, I want to say something *in favor of* flesh. A few pounds hanging from your bones are essential, serve to plump up facial wrinkles and keep your breasts from looking like empty envelopes (especially as you pass forty). If your daily diet consists of starvation rations month in, month out, the price you'll pay for unnatural skinniness will be nervousness, irritability, and an all-around ogrelike personality. If ever the cliché *moderation in all things* was applicable, it's in the realm of dieting.

5

Mad Dogs and Englishmen

THE TRUTH ABOUT SUN

Do you know what would make me supremely happy? A hot, sunny day . . . and a long expanse of empty white beach. I would take this mythical empty beach as a sign that women have got the "sun damage" message, and are happily sipping piña coladas at the bar till the high noon rays cool off.

Why do I sound like an enemy of Caribbean resort owners? The following answers will explain my shade-loving bias.

● *I've finally managed to squeeze myself into a size 8 bikini. Now I'm told that the sun may be hazardous to my health. Is this true?*

Noel Coward said it best: "Mad dogs and Englishmen go out in the noonday sun." If you don't fall into either of these two categories, avoid sun overexposure as you would the swine flu. *Sun will age you faster than your fortieth birthday.* My definition of too much sun? *Any* time spent sun-bathing . . . especially without protection, and that means a hat, effective sun-block, umbrella, the works.

Here's why: Prolonged overexposure to sun means those powerful ultraviolets are not only browning or burning your epidermis (depending on how lucky or careful you are); they're also reaching right down to your dermis, the secondary layer that contains collagen and elastic fibers. If you remember from our "Truth About Skin" discussion in Chapter One, collagen provides the skin with elasticity. When the elasticity goes, the skin loses its "snap" or "tone" . . . and it's goodbye to your youthful appearance. Guess what's a prime collagen-destroyer? That's right . . . the good old sun.

Vanity isn't the only reason you'll have it made in the shade. The scientific jury has been out, deliberated and returned with a verdict: Sun is guilty of being a prime cause of skin cancer. According to the AMA *Book of Skin and Hair Care* (ed. by Linda Schoen, J. B. Lippincott & Co., 1976), about 90 percent of skin cancer is found on areas of the body exposed to sunshine, particularly the face. People in the southern states (where there is more sunshine and more sunshine worship) report more cases of skin cancer than their northern neighbors. And blacks, who are less susceptible to sunburn, rarely develop the disease. The AMA further warns that one severe sunburn can result in skin cancer developing years after the initial over-exposure.

Now that I've given you the bad news about skin cancer, here's some less-scary information: Skin cancer is rarely fatal; it won't infect other organs; a variety

of treatments are available. If you're looking at a lump
or discoloration on your skin and reaching for the
telephone in panic, remember that the overwhelming
majority of skin irregularities are *not* cancerous. Still,
leave it to a doctor to check out anything that makes
you suspicious. No sense worrying for nothing.

● *Can't anything good be said about the sun?*

If you suffer from severe acne, exposure to the sun
can help by causing the top layer of your skin to peel.
This peeling process will help unclog the pores, allowing the oil and other matter to flow to the surface to be
removed. Just remember, however, that your peeling
efforts could be damaging the collagen fibers that will
keep your skin young-looking after the acne has sub-
sided. (Obviously, my admiration for sun worshipping
is not quite on a par with my affection for chicken pox.)

● *What causes a sunburn?*

I was hoping you'd ask. Maybe if I explain why you
burn, you won't allow yourself to fry again. When your
skin is subjected to an overdose of ultraviolets, proteins
sensitive to these uv (ultraviolet) rays are injured. At
the same time, the blood vessels begin to dilate. The
combined result is a red, swollen look that will make
you look like you should be served with drawn butter.
To avoid a burn, take the sun in small doses. This gives
the pigment-producing cells time to produce more
melanin, the protein that tans you. Tanning is actually a
build-up of cells designed to protect the body against
further uv penetration. Caution: The faster the build-
up, the faster new cells reach the skin's surface and die.
The result: peeling.

We know that burning is the skin's way of crying too much, too soon. You also probably know by now that if you're fair-skinned and fair-haired, you'll have to take the sun even slower than oily-skinned, olive-complexioned women.

You should also know that your skin seems to have a memory longer than an elephant's. When your burn has disappeared into a painful memory, your skin will remind you of the assault with freckles, wrinkles, and the leathery look.

Assuming you *still* want to tan (I admit, it makes everyone look terrific), here's the safest way to get golden, short of applying cosmetic bronzer.

The Agony or the Ecstasy. Carefully read the labels on tanning products before you buy. A sunblock will keep out the maximum number of unltraviolets, giving you the minimal chance of burning. Sunscreens allow some of the uv rays to penetrate, making gradual tanning possible. You're looking for one containing PABA (paraaminobenzoic acid), a truly effective sunscreen. Whether you choose an oil, lotion, or cream, don't be stingy with the application. Slather your whole body in your PABA-product from *day one* in the sun. Include the forgettables like back of neck and soles of feet. There's nothing uglier than swollen, sunburned feet painfully stuffed into little gold evening sandals after a day's overdose of sun. (And nothing ruins a romantic Caribbean jaunt *à deux* faster than one partner crying in sunburned agony at the touch of her mate.)

You know from experience if certain areas tend to burn faster than others. Sensitive lips and noses may benefit from an additional coat of zinc oxide, that old-fashioned thick white cream beloved by lifeguards.

Night of the Iguana. Time yourself diligently, allowing no more than fifteen minutes a day for your first few exposures. If you don't, watch yourself get that leathery lizard look; you may be declared an endangered species. If you're going to a resort nearer the equator than your own backyard, realize the sun there is more intense. Try to get a base tan before you leave for vacation.

The Spy Who Loved Me. Equip yourself with the right accessories. Buy a little extra protection like good sunglasses and a hat to protect your hair (sun can damage dry, colored, straightened, permed—even normal—hair). Better to be mistaken for a mystery woman than the barbecued main dish at the evening luau.

Don't Unveil at Vail. Remember, you can get a worse burn skiing (snow is a great reflector of sunlight) than you can sunbathing; protect yourself accordingly.

Story of No. The sun warns you when you're getting a burn—when you start hurting, put down that sexy book and head for the shower. But the uv's may still be doing their damage on a *hazy* day, so don't plan on putting a dent in *War and Peace* just because you can't see the sun . . . it's up there under the clouds, you know.

A girl's best friend may be her sunscreen. Reapply after every swim. Even if you never go near the water, reapply your tanning gear every two hours (more if you're engaged in a sweat-producing activity like tennis).

Sit in the cinema between 11 A.M. and 2 P.M.; this is when the sun's rays are strongest; this is also when the theater is most deserted. Catch up on your sleep if you've already seen the current epic.

● *What are the best kind of sunglasses?*

I asked Alfred Poll, a New York optician who is the
eye fashion consultant for *Women's Wear Daily,* what
he would recommend. First you should know that the
ultraviolet and infrared rays that can sunburn your skin
can also cause eye damage. To reduce the risk of
sunstruck eyes, you want a good, absorptive lens in a
dark brown, gray, or green (forget pastels if protection
is your goal). The lenses can be plastic or glass, as long
as the material is deemed impact-resistant by the Food
and Drug Administration.

As Alfred Poll points out, it's hard for the layman to
judge the quality of lenses by trying them on indoors,
but there's a sixth-sense test that can't be beat: Put on
the sunglasses of your choice and walk outside on a
bright day—if you still squint, you need darker, more
absorptive lenses.

Photochromic lenses (those that darken when you're
exposed to sunlight) are favored by many people. But if
you want *instant* sun protection, the transition period
from light-to-dark may take too long . . . and the
photochromic lenses just never get *that* dark.

For information on choosing frames to fit and flatter
your face, see Part III, Day 17, where I discuss eye
makeovers.

● *After my last sunbath, I developed an itchy burn and
   brown spots on various parts of my body. What
   causes this?*

You may be photosensitive. Certain substances,
when they come in contact with your skin and the sun,
produce an allergic reaction. Oil of bergamot, for

example, is a potential sensitizer found in many perfumes. If you scent yourself before going to the beach, a burn followed by brown *spots* may show up where you dabbed on fragrance. Your deodorant soap may also contain photosensitizing ingredients; shower with a gentle nondeodorant variety prior to a sun-soak. If you *are* the "sun-sensitive" type, not only will your skin feel like it's on fire, you may resemble a trusty Dalmatian if you expose your body to sensitizing ingredients before heading for the beach.

Certain medications may be photosensitizing. If you're suddenly burning unusually often or severely, ask the doctor about the prescriptions you're taking. Some oral contraceptive users develop brown splotches on the face; the sun may aggravate this condition. If you're a *pregnant* sunworshipper, you may get this same splotchy look—called chloasma, or the "mask of pregnancy"; it *can* develop without sun exposure, but why increase the chance of this happening?

If you're an older woman, you probably call your brown areas "liver spots" (they have nothing to do with the liver). Again, sun exposure will increase the chance of developing this hyperpigmentation, too. These discolorations can often be removed. But if you've read about miracle cures while thumbing through the backs of magazines, go back to reading the main story, and call the only official spot remover, your dermatologist. She or he will use one of three methods: (1) cryosurgery—a freezing process; (2) electrosurgery—which employs a needle propelled by electricity (also called electrodesiccation) or (3) chemosurgery—a chemical peel making use of acids.

● *What's the best sunburn cure?*

Now that you've read the previous pages, you won't let yourself get burned again, right? In the meantime, do the following:

Soak in a tub filled with cool water and colloidal oatmeal (available at your pharmacy) for about fifteen minutes. This may ease the burning sensation while treating your skin to at least a little moisture (sun dehydrates the skin as well as burns it). But don't loll in the tub *indefinitely—too much* water will also dehydrate your skin, giving it a wrinkled prune appearance. Follow with a slather of après-bath emollient cream that will help lock in the water your skin has just received in the *short* tub session.

CHAPTER
6

Color Yourself Super

THE TRUTH ABOUT HAIR COLOR

Remember Clark Kent, the mild-mannered comic book reporter decidedly lacking in "oomph"? All he had to do to change his image was slip off his glasses, don his blue and red gladrags . . . and *voilà*! Superman, super hero. Even if blue and red aren't your colors, and you seem to look the same in a sweatsuit or a Halston, you can transform your appearance by changing drab *hair color* into super locks.

The only villain in the super color story is proceeding before you know the facts. First, here are a few thoughts to set your head at ease.

A new and improved hair color is one of the best psyche boosters I know . . . cheaper than a designer-initialed handbag, less time-consuming than analysis, less *angst*-inducing than plastic surgery.

The most popular coloring agents are also the safest, so unless you plan on drinking your dye with dinner, chances of developing a bad reaction are rare.

Such a variety of colors, formulations, and procedures are available that you're a minority of one if you claim you can't find a product to suit your taste.

But there are some limitations as to how drastic a change you should make. Here are the procedures, the products, and the pros and cons.

For convenience's sake, the easiest way to categorize hair coloring is by its *longevity,* the length of time it will stay in your hair. There are, then, three main types:

1) Temporary

These are the color equivalents of a one night stand, lasting only till your next shampoo. Why do they rinse out so quickly? Temporary coloring molecules are too large to pass through the protective outer cuticle of the hair into the cortex, where pigment changes take place. So they really just coat the hair's surface.

The good news: Because "temps" *don't* penetrate, they won't alter the hair structure. Also, temporary color rinses are acidic in nature (which means, as you know, not as harmful as alkaline tints). But this same structurally helpful acid also closes the cuticle, another reason (along with big molecules) that color doesn't seep into the hair shaft.

Temporary coloring is available in rinse or shampoo formula. But whatever the formula, don't expect a dramatic change with these products. Use them to highlight your own hair color or provide subtle shade uplifts. You're a brunette looking to go blond? Keep looking . . . this isn't for you. You're a coward about coloring your hair? Temporary shades will provide a perfect introduction to the color spectrum. You'll be surprised at the lift a little color can give your hair, presuming you've chosen your shade wisely. And if your reaction is more glum than glee . . . well, it all comes out in the wash. (Note: In the trade, the terms dye, tint, and coloring agent are used interchangeably. A toner is really a blond-shade tint.)

Temporary hair colorings usually use acid dyes approved for food, drug, and cosmetic use by the FDA, so there's no patch test warning required for these products. But if *your* chosen "temp" package does advise you to patch test—by all means, do.

The bad news: Since "temps" wash out easily, don't use one the night before you go to the pool—it might *run*. Ditto if you're caught hatless in a rainstorm.

2) Semi-Permanent

Expect these coloring agents to last through four to six shampoos. Here's how they work: Because these products are just slightly alkaline, they cause the cuticle to swell, allowing some molecules (which are smaller than those of temporary acid colorings) to slip through the cuticle into the cortex.

When you rinse out the slightly alkaline formula, the cuticle contracts again, trapping the molecules that made it to the cortex inside, allowing a degree of color-fastness to remain. Of course, with each washing, the cuticle (like the sun) once more rises, allowing additional color to again escape from the cortex. That's why these products are *semi*-permanent.

In case you're interested (and you should be!), semi-permanent formulas contain no peroxide and don't change the hair structure. They *do* provide more substantial results than the temporaries, especially if your hair is more "blah" than brunette. Use them to highlight, make gray more beautifully gray, or cover gray hairs while leaving your non-grays their own natural color. There's a bonus for the lazy: they fade gradually, all over; no root retouching is needed; and tedious parting and sectioning isn't necessary.

3) Permanent

Hair treated in this manner will remain tinted until you cut it off or alter it with dye-stripping chemicals. There are three kinds of permanent dyes.

A) VEGETABLE DYES. Yes, Virginia, camomile, indigo, and henna (among others) were popular in the good old days. Egyptian henna is again favored by those who want dramatic highlights and color, and don't want to apply anything "artificial." Henna, made from plant roots and stems, *is* the safest thing you can use—it's non-toxic even if you accidentally swallow it. But, assuming you can tell henna from hamburger, the fact that it isn't poisonous is only part of the story: henna paste is messy to use; it will mess up any projected permanent wave (it penetrates the cortex in such a way as to alter the bonds you must change for permanent curling); it can be unpredictable, if used incorrectly. Does that mean I'm *against* henna? Of course not! I'm just against using it improperly. Henna fans are legion once again, and those who apply it *right* know the dramatic difference it can make in the hair's condition as well as color. On Day 9 you'll learn the expert how-tos, so you can choose a gloriously radiant henna color that will turn you into a fan—not a victim!

B) METALLIC DYES. These work by depositing a thin metallic coating on the hair. But, as you know by now, when the cuticle is coated, light can't be reflected off of it . . . and your hair will be flat and dull. When you've got metallic salts in your hair, you absolutely must not use a peroxide tint (your hair may disintegrate); nor should you attempt a permanent wave or straightening till the metallic-dyed hair grows out.

Bad news basics: If your metallic dye contains silver, your hair may turn green. Lead may turn to purple; copper to red.

Today, these formulations are chiefly preferred by dye-shy men because metallics, when combed through the hair, cover gray gradually, day by day (in fact, they used to be known as progressive dyes). But, assuming you've gotten over the "does she or doesn't she" hang-up, there are better ways to cover gray or change your color, chiefly:

C) ANILINE DERIVATIVE TINTS. This is the stay-in product beloved by beauty salons and major manufacturers. This is what I use.

These dye kits come equipped with two bottles: a tint base and a developer, hydrogen peroxide. (If the word peroxide conjures up visions of brassy 1930s gun molls, you've been seeing too many old films. Today, these dyes can give lovely, subtle results.) Here's how these minor miracles work: The components are mixed together right before application, and the *tiny* colorless molecules of the tint base have no trouble working their way right through the cuticle into the cortex where they mix with the peroxide which is deposited in your hair shaft by a chemical reaction known as oxidation. When color molecules are thus trapped within the cortex, you've got stay-put hair color.

You can give aniline-dyed hair a permanent wave (not right away, please), because the chemicals don't interfere with the waving bonds the way hennas do. But, sweet anilines definitely weaken the structure of the hair, so hair thus treated should be tended with care.

Also, you must do a patch test before you use an aniline dye to determine whether or not you're allergic.

Though you are interested in doing *yourself* over, a permanent dye job that is poorly done can make you look like a Central Casting natural for a grade Z horror production. I would recommend you see a professional colorist for any permanent processing.

Before I go on to questions and answers, I want to give you some advice, based on my years of salon-watching experience: If you're new in the hair coloring market, confine your first experiments to temporary rinses or semi-permanent hair colorings that wash out in four to six shampoos. These formulas will give your hair the highlights that can make it look new. But I do feel that drastic changes (for instance, from dark brown to ash blond, a double-process job) should be left to the professionals. It takes great skill to do a dramatic shade change correctly.

Now, re-read the last few pages. Molecules, oxidation, chemical bonding— it *is* rather difficult to digest— but you only have one head of hair, and understanding how hair color works can point you toward the products and processes that will give the best results.

• *I have dark brown hair, brown eyes, and a desire to learn first-hand if it's true "blondes have more fun." What do you think?*

Ever since the advertising geniuses of Clairol dreamed up that slogan (and for eons before), dark-haired women have longed for sun-colored hair. We known Egyptians used henna, indigo, and sage. Roman women looked with awe at the blonde Teutons hauled back by a triumphant Caesar; Roman royalty used saffron and a form of arsenic (a twenty-first birthday must have been a rare event) to blond themselves à la Teutons.

Should *you* switch? Consider the following *bad news basic:* Nature (or heredity) is far from capricious when it comes to allotting hair color. The same genes that code your eyes also take into account skin color and texture before gracing you with dark hair. If you're olive-complexioned, tend to have an oily or combination skin, and have truly dark eyes, you might look strangely unnatural as a blonde. If you're a blonde, with the accompanying super-fair skin, you may look more witchy than bewitching as a brunette. If your skin is ruddy or pink, stay away from auburn or red shades.

Before you take a drastic color plunge, bring a friend you trust to the wig department and get his/her reaction to a wide color selection (just don't tell the saleslady I sent you). If you do decide to color, remember, you can't make a big shade change unless you go (straight to a professional, I hope) for a permanent double-process tinting.

Consider some alternatives: Jazzing up your hair with rich, red highlights . . . seeing how you'd look with a lighter version of what you've got . . . trying one of the streaking processes that can give you the look of light, without fright.

Because shade selection is such an important part of successful hair coloring, I want to give you a few more specific points:

1) Don't expect your color to match exactly the shade of the model's on the package. In most cases, her hair was bleached completely white before the formula was applied (I hope she was well paid!), so unless you have the coloring of an albino, the look may vary slightly on your own head.

2) Before you decide what your natural color is, try to stand in true north light. Cosmetic companies test their lipsticks and blushers in northern light, artists choose studios with the same exposure—so go to a north-facing window with your mirror. Looking at your hair under fluorescents is no way to make a decision.

3) Follow your clean, well-lighted space with clean, dry hair. Wet or oily locks look darker than they really are.

4) If your hair is gray, and you're considering returning to your "natural" eighteen-year-old color, this may be a case when a little artifice will give the best results. You see, as you age (*that* should be a four-letter word) and your hair whitens, your skin also gets a shade or two lighter. That's why you should consider a hair color shade one or two steps lighter than the true color you grew up with. Too-dark hair looks garish against a fair, less-than-young face.

I persuaded Clairol's technical experts to part with some of the color selection tips they teach professional colorists. Here's what I learned.

To match hair color, check a strand from the back of the head near the scalp (where it's darkest) *and* a strand from the front hairline, which is usually the lightest. Decide which depth of color you prefer, remembering that most people see you from the front, where your hair is lighter.

So you can speak the colorist's language, understand that a *shade* is only a subtle degree of difference between colors. As you know, there are various shades of light brown hair, blond, and so on. *Tonal value* describes the tone of the color: drab, red, or gold.

If you're trying to decide between a lighter or darker color, select the lighter shade first. You can always go darker next time, but it's more difficult to make colored hair lighter.

If your hair has been permed, straightened, overexposed to the sun, or abused by your hair dryer or electric rollers, it is more porous and color-absorbent than healthy, closed cuticle hair. Check the color of your still-healthy hair near the scalp, and use a formula at least one shade lighter (assuming you're aiming to lighten your own color). Note: If you've permed or straightened, you'd be a step ahead by following this advice—three giant steps ahead if you let any color work be done by the pros.

- *What is double-process blonding? Toning? Streaking?*

It's not enough to know the kinds of dyes available. You must also know what and how they do what they do. So, settle back with a carrot and a glass of skimmed milk (you didn't think I'd say brownies and a cigarette!), put up your feet, and read the following explanatory guide to permanent hair coloring procedures.

Single Application Tint

A one-step process that both lightens and colors. Peroxide is mixed with the tint base and applied using a procedure the professionals call "sectioning and parting": Hair is divided into four sections, tint applied first to hair strands ½ inch from scalp to within 1 inch of ends. (Scalp border and ends are done last because they absorb color faster.) This is a tricky procedure, and unless you have eyes in back of your head or incredibly nimble fingers, you shouldn't attempt to do it yourself. Leave it to the experts. If that's not possible, corral a non-hostile friend to do the application.

You can make rather dramatic color changes with

this process: from several shades deeper or lighter than your original color. Here are some tint tips:

1) To cover gray without disturbing your dark hair, choose a shade most closely matching your original.

2) To brighten hair that's partially gray, go one shade lighter than your own color. (If you have lots of gray hairs in front, fewer in back, you may need to use a different formula on each area of your head to get a balanced look—see a professional.)

3) To go from dark to blonder (not from black to blond . . . though from medium brown to golden blond *is* possible in one step) when your hair has natural red highlights which you'd prefer not to show up, a *drabber* (another chemical) must be applied. This is mixed with the tint—never used alone.

Two-Step Tint

More commonly called double-process blonding (or the "ouch process"—some women say it hurts). It's the only way to go from truly dark hair to the light or silvery blonde. *Step one:* Your hair must be bleached. A solution of hydrogen peroxide and ammonia water literally strips your hair of its natural color (how else are they going to "blond" you?). The bleaching action also makes the hair more *porous,* so it can absorb the *toner.* *Step two:* A toner, the name given to the delicate blond-toned dye, is applied to bleached-out hair. Toners are available in a range of shades from ash blond to platinum.

Two-step blonding should not be undertaken (pardon the pun) lightly. These chemical procedures can weaken the hair and dry it out. When hair becomes brittle, it can break off close to the roots. This is why some women who *do* double-process their hair complain they're going "bald."In reality, hair is just tearing near the scalp, but the *appearance* of hair loss in over-processed hair is a disturbing illusion.

So unless you know what you're doing, or don't mind looking like you've just stuck your finger in a light socket, leave it to the experts. The professionals know how to handle hair, will perform strand tests to see how the color is taking, can mix different colors to give your hair a beautiful customized look.

Note: If you're doing it yourself, don't take a short cut and skip the strand test. It's really a color preview. Wouldn't you rather catch a mistake on a few hair strands than have to correct your whole head?

Mind your As and Ps: If you do go ahead with a two-step process, there are two treatment points to remember. (1) A cuticle-closing *acid*-based shampoo specially formulated for colored hair will help offset the harsh treatment caused by alkaline-derivative dyes. Lather once—you don't want to overmanipulate processed hair. (2) Follow with *protein* conditioners to both coat and coddle the hair shaft. (3) Also, wear a hat or scarf in the sun; overexposure can damage hair and distort the color.

Out, damned roots! You complain your hair doesn't grow fast enough? Color it (especially double-process) and suddenly you'll wish your hair growth would slow down. Those telltale roots seem to sprout faster than gray hairs. They can be camouflaged temporarily with hair color sticks or crayons—find them where you buy your coloring kits. Another trick: soft hair-matching eyeshadow pencils. Permanent retouching involves the same procedure as your original coloring. But care must be taken to make sure the bleach and dye applied to the new growth don't *overlap* previously tinted hair. The result can be breakage at the "overlap" site.

You may think the vasectomy was a great discovery, but how about some applause for the colorists who first came up with frosting, streaking, and hair painting? These are the hair-saving processes that allow dark-haired girls to flirt with blonding.

Frosting

Strands of hair chosen from various sections of the head are lightened; the more strands, the more blonding.

Streaking

Larger sections of hair are subjected to lightening; produces the effect of wide bands of color.

Sunburst

Hair framing the face is lightened.
These effects can be accomplished one of two ways:

Cap Method

Selected strands of hair are drawn through holes in plastic cap with crochet needle. (The women undergoing this always look uncomfortable, but it works.)

Foil Wrap

Selected strands are wrapped in aluminum foil, then bleached. If necessary, a toner is applied over the bleached strands to soften the blond color. Many pros now use the foil method. The colorists who are foil fans say it's easier to control; besides it doesn't hurt like pulling strands through a cap sometimes does.

These processes are time-consuming because individual hairs are being treated. Though double-process tint jobs (your hair is first bleached, then a blond toner is applied to the lightened strands), they are much less damaging to the hair. First, because most of your hair is left in its virgin state. Second, the chemicals never touch your scalp. Third, retouching is needed much less often (two or three times a year), because the blond hairs blend in with your dark color as they "grow out."

Hair Painting

A relatively new process, it's really a surface frost. Using a small paint brush, the colorist (or you) merely paints bleach on areas where lightening is desired. This works best on light brown or dark blond hair; if you "paint" dark brown hair, you'll end up with garish-looking red streaks.

You want to try these frosting processes yourself? Kits are available. But if you couldn't even master painting by numbers, and your art teacher groaned at your clown collage, spring for a salon treatment. Again, the colorist can do it better—blending toners to give you a personalized look you just can't get from a kit.

All the procedures I've outlined so far in my quick guide to chemical permanent coloring (henna is another story—see Part III, Day 9) have one thing in common: I don't consider them do-it-yourself matters.

However, if you feel you're not a *"klutz,"* and want to improve your hair color without necessarily turning from Snow White to Cinderella, you *can* try a one-step shampoo formula that gives permanent results (read the package). You just shampoo, keep on hair for twenty minutes. You don't need to section hair to retouch—you redo the whole head. But these definitely contain a developer (peroxide); semi-permanent shampoo-ins do not. Don't confuse the two.

- *The only things I'm allergic to are blueberries and my boss's wife. Do I still need a "patch test"?*

Let's put it this way: Eat strawberries. Change jobs. And learn about *contact dermatitis,* which is a reaction to the chemicals in aniline hair dyes. The results can be swelling, itchy, uncomfortable red eruptions around the face, eyes—anywhere. And, though it's true this reaction is rare, sensitivity to the dyes can develop anytime. You can have used your favorite tint a dozen times; the unlucky thirteenth could cause C.D. symptoms.

That's why each aniline hair kit sold contains a warning, and the FDA isn't kidding. Patch test first, avoid problems later. If you're coloring at home: Mix a capful of peroxide with a capful of tint in the exact shade you'll be using (different colorings contain different percentages of chemicals). Wash your test site (behind the ear or in the crook of the elbow). Dry, apply solution with a Q-tip to an inch square area—then, hands off.

If, after twenty-four hours, your skin is unchanged, color away. If you notice redness, burning, any unusual eruptions, you've become sensitized. Throw out the rest of your kit and be thankful you didn't color your whole head.

Sensitization doesn't mean you have to abandon hair color completely. Try a shade similar to the one you like, but from a different manufacturer. It could be you're not allergic to the chemical combination in the second company's formula. Again, patch test before proceeding. A patch test and a strand test are necessary for safety and success.

● *I never should have colored my hair. How can I get back to my natural color quickly?*

It depends what products you've used to color your hair in the first place.

One or two shampoos will remove all traces of temporary dyes. Semi-permanent tints will fade after several shampoos. Since you didn't alter your hair's structure when you applied "semis," why use a color remover now? Your tint will grow out soon enough . . . or get a haircut if you're in a big hurry. You don't want a haircut? Clairol's Metalex lifts temporary and semi-permanent colors, but it may take more than one application.

To remove permanent aniline dyes, see a professional skilled in color corrections.

● *Is it safe to give dyed hair a permanent?*

Yes, but have the permanent ten days *before* a coloring session and choose a permanent wave designed to be used in conjunction with a tint. But I wouldn't attempt both processes without speaking to a professional—you don't want a do-it-yourself disaster.

● *You said earlier that tinting can actually be good for the hair. How?*

Aside from improving the appearance (increased sparkle, shine, and a more exciting color) a "tint job" that doesn't involve pre-bleaching (the most damaging kind) can actually make skinny hair look fatter. First, the alkalinity causes the cuticle to swell, slightly expanding the thickness of each individual hair shaft. Second, the coating of hair with coloring imparts another bit of fullness. This extra body can bring increased manageability to fly-away or unruly hair. I have my hair tinted professionally; I wouldn't do without it.

- *Where can I get information about how to highlight auburn hair?*

No matter what your natural hair color or the process you're considering to improve it, you can get personalized information from the Clairol Hot Line—just call the toll-free number 800–223–5800 in every state but New York from 9:00 A.M.-5:00 P.M. (If you live in New York State, dial 212–644–2990.) Some 100,000 dye-shy consumers make use of this question and answer service each year. You're welcome to join the crowd.

The following is a list of just a few of the many commercial hair coloring preparations on the market—it may prove helpful if you're considering tinting your hair for the first time:

Temporary

- Fanci-Full Rinse (Roux)
- Nestlé Protein Colorinse (Nestlé-Le Mur)

Semi-Permanent

- Color 'N' Tone (Nestlé-Le Mur)
- Happiness (Clairol)

- Loving Care Color Lotion (Clairol)
- Loving Care Color Foam (Clairol)
- Silk & Silver (Clairol)

Permanent One-Step Shampoo-in Color

- Nice 'N' Easy (Clairol)
- Miss Clairol Natural Wear Shampoo Formula
- Fanci-Tone (Roux)

Double Process Blonding

- Born Blonde (Clairol)
- Natural Blonde (Clairol)

Special Effects

- Quiet Touch Hair Painting (Clairol)—for dark blonde/light brown hair)
- Gentle Lights Finger Painting (Clairol—for brunettes)
- Frost 'N' Tip (Clairol)

One more hint: Before you buy, read the directions thoroughly to make sure the kit you're purchasing is designed to create the results you're after.

CHAPTER

7

*They Think
I'm a Free-Lance
Dishwasher*

THE TRUTH ABOUT HANDS AND NAILS

You may have predicted the demise of the French Twist
and the rise of the 1960s mini. But if your intuition tells
you that short, ragged nails will one day be featured on
the cover of *Vogue*, I tell you now, you are not psychic.
For thousands of years, long, elegant nails have been a
status symbol.

Nail infatuation (obsession?) has been traced back to
the ancient Chinese (Cleopatra wasn't the only beauty
innovator, you know). The Mandarins (male as well as
female) considered long nails to be a sign of wealth: The
possessor of two-inch talons couldn't very well do
manual labor (she could barely lift a chopstick), so nail
length effectively distinguished the working class from
the idle rich.

Today, you don't have to own a slice of Manhattan
Island to prove your nail-length credentials, but you do

have to be realistic: You can have "nails of the year" or be named "homemaker of the year," not both. But you can have well-groomed hands and well-tended nails no matter what your occupation or preoccupation.

Your nonexistent nails make it obvious there's not a trace of Mandarin blood in your veins? You could sit on your hands and pretend you're practicing a yoga posture (this may work if there are no gurus around and you don't have to hail a taxi) or say you're a free-lance dishwasher. Instead, read the following and learn how to turn your nails from $#%& to terrific.

First, the *whats* and *whys* of nail formation. Nails are made of *keratin,* and if you don't know what that is by now, go to the back of the class. (Hint: It's the same protein that plays a prominent part in hair and skin composition.) Your nails are actually dead protein (sound familiar?); their function is to protect the fingertips from damage.

All nails are divided into three parts: the *nail plate* (the part you're going to pamper and polish); the *nail bed* (the flesh on which your nail plate rests); the *nail fold* (skin surrounding your nail). Since the nail itself is, alas, dead, good nail growth is really a product of healthy skin around and *underneath* your nail.

Like your hair, the state of your nails reflects the way you feel. Poor nutrition, nerves, even serious health problems can be revealed by the condition of your nail plate. So if your doctor grabs your hand and stares intently at your fingers, he's not making a pass (sorry to destroy this fantasy); he *is* making a diagnosis.

● *Can anything be done to speed up nail growth?*

Assuming you're in good health already, you should know that nails happen to grow very slowly (about ⅛ inch per month); you can't rush the procedure. If it's summer, nails (like hair) will grow a bit faster than in the winter. If you're younger, your nails, like everything else about you, will grow more rapidly. Middle-aged or beyond? The general cell-reproduction slowdown that you curse when you study your hair in the mirror affects your nail bed (where nail production occurs), too.

While you may not have a green thumb, you probably do have an imperceptibly shorter thumbnail—the thumbnail grows the slowest of all fingernails. Your middle finger's nail grows fastest.

You hammered your finger instead ot the thumbtack? If the trauma led to nail loss, be super-patient: It takes a good six months to grow a completely new nail.

Though nails are the tortoise of the body when it comes to growth, you can't wear little white gloves (they've been out for thirty years!) till your hands become respectable. Your high school reunion is Saturday night and you want to convince old friends you married a titled count who insists you never lift a finger? Acrylic nails applied to a suitable lady-of-leisure length may be your solution.

The best of the genre are actually a form of dental acrylic mixed and brushed over your regular nail to whatever glamorous length you or your manicurist desire. You *can* do it yourself—there are acrylic nail kits for home use available—but it's not easy to do a professional job (that's why salons get $35.00 plus per complete set, $3.50 per nail. $3.00 per fill-in). Unless you're an ex-baton twirler or disciple of Houdini (in other words, you've got nimble fingers plus a touch of artistry), it will take some practice before you get it right. On Day 3 of the *Crash* Program I teach you how to do it professionally step by step. Here is the background information you should have:

The good news basics: Acrylics make it possible for women who just can't grow nails to have the elegant, well-groomed look long nails provide. (Nailbiters, you can finally pretend you're free of whatever neurotic impulse your psychiatrist claims is responsible for your self-nibbling.)

If you have plump fingers, the addition of these realistic fakes has a slimming, elongating effect.

If you have nine long, strong nails but number ten is embedded in the papier mâché confection you've been making in crafts class, an acrylic can even up your manicure. Your nail is cracked? The mixture will mend the crack and protect it till it heals.

The bad news basics: Acrylics make the nail under it softer than usual.

You may be more prone to fungal infections, which, though rare, can cause your own nail to lift up from its nail bed (if this is the case, see your dermatologist at once).

Water can get trapped between your real and your fake nails. The water turns green and stains the nail. Though this phenomenon occurs on top of your own nail (rather than underneath, as with a fungus), you still must remove the acrylic till the problem clears.

If you're allergic to the chemicals in sculptured nails, there may be itching and redness down around your cuticle; the skin under your nail might look bruised. Building the nail well away from the cuticle may counteract this problem.

If your sculptured nail starts lifting away from the real nail, don't try to mend it—remove it at once. This could be a sign that your real nail underneath those acrylic layers is infected. (Another warning: It *hurts* when the nail lifts up!)

It takes time to remove an acrylic nail: You have to

soak your fingers in polish remover, then carefully chip and clip away at the fake nail till it comes off. Start by trimming the free edge of the acrylic to the length of your own nail.

If you decide to forgo acrylics, give yourself a total nail wrap (explained in Part III, Day 3) to protect your own soft nails until they grow strong again.

You're active in the kitchen? The garden? At the typewriter? Long nails, whether real or fake, will be difficult to keep.

When you have these nails, pulling up a panty girdle becomes a traumatic experience!

● *What about eating gelatin to strengthen my own nails?*

What about baying at the moon? Both have the same effect on nails: zero. The gelatin myth is one of the longest-standing beauty misconceptions, and it's easy to see how it began: "Gelatin is protein. Nails are protein. Therefore, one protein helps another." Right? Wrong! Scientific studies have proved that gelatin, whether consumed or sloshed on nails, has no beneficial effect.

However, you should continue to eat a protein-rich diet; a protein deficiency will contribute to poor nails, skin, and hair—not to mention poor health.

While we're on the nail-nourishment myths, forget calcium tablets. For some reason, people often think nails are made of calcium. Though they do feel "hard," nails aren't composed of the same stuff as teeth and bones. However, if you've been biting your nails because of *insomnia,* calcium can be an *indirect* help. This mineral is one of nature's tranquilizers—it will lull you to sleep. If a good night's rest leads to less nail biting, well, calcium tablets just may contribute to nail growth.

● *I've been elected the unofficial hard-bitten hangnail queen of Houston. Suggestions?*

Assuming your title hasn't led to a Hollywood contract, cut (don't bite) off the excess skin and curb those closet-cannibal instincts that lead to hangnail munching by coating your nail and surrounding tissue with an anti-thumbsucking medication (ask your druggist). Perhaps your skin is overly dry, which can lead to cracking. If so, hand cream may help.

Here I should mention an important way in which nails differ from skin and hair: Hands and H_2O are a dangerous mixture. If your hands are constantly submerged in water, and you're not meticulous about drying them, raw skin and hangnails will develop.

Too much water leads to a variety of nail problems, especially if the water is combined with detergents.

● *How can I keep my nails from breaking, splitting, and dying an early death?*

The first step? Keep 'em dry. Water (especially when that water is combined with harsh alkaline detergents and other common household chemicals) weakens the nail, makes it prone to splitting, chipping.

Even if you're one of those totally liberated ladies who has turned her kitchen sink into a planter, you have to put your hands in water at one time or another. When it's your turn to make contact with suds and water, reach for rubber gloves. Those interlined with cotton work well. Don't go near the water without these nail-savers.

Besides keeping 'em dry, keep 'em out of trouble: Dial the phone with a pencil, not your nail . . . learn to pick things up with your fingertips, not your nail . . . keep nails smoothly filed, so there won't be any jagged edges to catch on sweaters, corners, or your married lover.

● *What nail length is considered most attractive?*

Rules-of-thumb governing nail length are few: If the nail edge doesn't extend beyond your fingertip, the nails are too short. Nails so long they should be registered as lethal weapons need a trim. You also have to match your nails to your lifestyle. It's hard to type 70 wpm with talons that would make Fu Manchu weep with envy. But, if you're a guitarist, longer may be better. It was rumored that billionaire eccentric Howard Hughes had fingernails so long they curled under. Of course *he* seldom left his room . . . even the Mandarins would have felt Hughes went too far!

● *What about nail hardeners?*

Some people swear by nail hardeners. Others swear *at* them. A key ingredient of these preparations is formaldehyde—it's used to preserve frogs in biology labs, and to preserve us, too, in embalming fluid. (Some of my friends look so well preserved I could swear they sleep submerged in the stuff . . . could be why they act so strangely when there's a full moon.) Formaldehyde is an irritant. If you're one of the allergic, you may have nail loss rather than nail gloss! Or your nails may start peeling.

● *My doctor says nail polish, not mascara, is causing my irritated eyes. How could I be so off-target?*

Here is my consulting opinion: If you wear nail polish (especially pearlized), and you spend half the day with finger-in-eye (try to be conscious of how often you rub your eyes and reapply eye makeup—it adds up for all of us), you're more likely to have a polish allergy than a reaction to mascara. Of all the cosmetics women use, nail polish is the number one allergen. If you're one of the unfortunate polish-sensitive, dermatitis (a rash) will develop where you touch yourself. If you develop a nail polish allergy, of course you must face the world bare-nailed.

Incidentally, some women are allergic to acetone, the key ingredient in nail-polish remover. Even if you're not allergic, acetone is drying, so it's not a good idea to remove your nail polish daily. Instead patch up the chips and save the polish remover for your once-weekly manicure. You might also add a few drops of lemon, olive, or castor oil to your remover—it helps counteract the drying effect.

● *Fred, not known for his generosity,* claims *the ring he gave me is 14K gold, but I've developed a rash under it. Is Fred lying?*

Let me give you a few "ring rash" facts. It is true that pure gold, as well as sterling silver, won't produce allergic reactions. The problem usually occurs with the nickel-containing alloys that are used.

But before trading Fred in for a newer model, realize that your ring rash may be nothing more than a variation of that nemesis of the water-logged, "housewives' hands." Here's what happens:

You wash your hands with soap or your clothes with laundry detergent. You don't remove your ring first. Some of the soap/detergent gets plugged up beneath your ring, causing the skin to break out. If this is your behavior pattern, your rash will occur even if your ring is platinum.

If your ring or other jewelry turns your skin green, coat the inside of the jewelry with clear nail polish—it's a neat way of protecting your skin.

● *My nails are discolored. Why are they, and what should I do?*

If your problem isn't disease-related, it's self-inflicted.

BLACKISH NAIL. While sweeping out of the car in an attempt to make a grand entrance, you slammed the car door on your hand, giving yourself a good whack (and your audience a good laugh). Wait for a new nail to grow out, and remember that pride goeth before a busted nail.

REDDISH NAIL. Have you been applying two or three coats of dark polish without applying base coat first? Your nail doesn't appreciate these shortcuts. The base not only gives your colored polish something to adhere to, it protects the nail plate from absorbing the color. Wait for discolored portion of nail to grow out.

YELLOWED NAIL. Could be one more side effect of smoking. Polish your nails to hide the yellow tone; try to remove nicotine stains from your hands by bleaching with lemon juice—rub half a lemon over afflicted area.

LITTLE WHITE FLECKS ON NAILS. As a child I was told that each spot represented one boyfriend . . . if only I were that popular! The real cause is far less romantic: the spots are usually just a minor fluke of the nail-growing process, nothing to start biting your nails about.

● *Can anything good be said about nail polish?*

I hope I didn't give the impression that allergic reactions to nail polish are a common occurrence. While polish *does* cause more reactions than other cosmetics, few women (numerically speaking) are actually affected. If you're one of the millions who can wear polish, then, like me, you're probably addicted. But there's no reason to worry.

Polish not only makes your nails and hands look glamorous, it adds a finishing touch to your grooming. It *also* protects the surface of the nail from external assaults and as such helps you grow your nails longer. I wear it every day without fear. (I feel more naked without polish than I do *sans* bra.) If your conscience needs clearing about your polish habit, why not let your nails breathe once in a while? Leave off the nail enamel for a few days between manicures and buff to give your nails some shine.

● *Can an already-broken nail be repaired?*

Start a Nail Bank. It's sentimental to save a lock of your hair, but eminently sensible to save a nail that has broken off. Here's how to manage a transplant:

Put a dab of Crazy Glue (or 5-Second Nail Glue—the same thing) or Duco cement on broken edge, and glue nail into place. Hold until it dries. But a word of warning: If you use a "crazy" type of glue, beware: They dry instantly, and if the glue lands any place besides your target area, you could wind up twisted in a

Toulouse-Lautrec position! You *lost* your broken nail? Buy Eve N Tips, a plastic tip kit, from the beauty supply store, and you'll always be ready when a heart-breaking, nail-breaking incident occurs.

If your nail is split, but still hanging on, cut a tiny piece of mending tissue (or coffee filter paper), saturate in mending liquid, and place over split. Brush end underneath nail edge. (This is part of the nail wrapping procedure you'll learn on Day 3.) Note: Whenever you're working with nail-mending tissues, moisten your finger in polish remover. A moist fingertip glides over the tissue easier, will help you press and mold it into place. Patches should always dry completely before applying polish.

TRICKY TREATMENTS/ODDS AND ENDS

Here are some ideas I've gathered from top manicurists:

To remove polish from nails you've messed up, don't hold remover-saturated cotton with correctly polished fingertips . . . *they'll* get smeared. Instead, insert cotton between the index and middle finger where they *join* (down by the webbing). Apply remover and you'll easily clean off the ruined nail without disturbing the rest of your manicure.

You don't want to wear polish? Apply white iodine to nails. It makes them strong.

If your hands and nails are discolored, use this old-fashioned remedy: Cut a lemon in half. Rub the pulp over hands, elbows (and knees) to bleach. Use the rind on skin around nails to cleanse and bleach. Rub vigorously over nicotine stains. Rinse with straight white wine vinegar.

Hot Hand Treatment

This one's easy: Heat olive oil in a Pyrex dish. Soak fingers a few minutes to soften cuticles and strengthen nails. Save oil for step two:

Handy Terrarium Treatment/Massage

Do this when you've got absolutely nothing left to do in the evening.

Take honey and almond scrub mix (you'll learn how to make this on Day 1, Primal Scream Facial), massage into hands and arms for 10 minutes.

Wrap hands tightly in hot hand towel, leave 10 minutes more.

Remove towels, rinse, dry and apply hot olive oil (left over from the simple hand treatment). Massage into hands, wrap hands in paper towelling or inexpensive cotton gloves.

Put plastic bag over each towel-wrapped/gloved hand, seal shut with rubber band around wrist. This will create a terrarium effect, locking in moisture.

Keep in place for 10 minutes. If someone asks you for a match—laugh, but don't move. (When you're wearing a facial masque, move—but don't laugh!)

CHAPTER

8

Small Package, Big Problems

THE TRUTH ABOUT FEET

Unless you have a foot fetish or are a student of ancient Chinese foot binding, the only time you think about your feet is when they hurt. And, if you're like the great majority, your feet do have painful problems now and then.

It's estimated that 70 to 80 percent of American women have foot faults. Along with your husbands, lovers, and children, we spend well over $200,000,000 annually on over-the-counter foot remedies. The American Podiatry Association reports that some 27 million patient visits are made to podiatrists annually.

Let me give you a few foot facts, then I'll answer the questions that may help you quit hobbling once and for all.

Your feet are incredibly complex: One-fourth (26 per foot) of all the bones in the human body are packed into the feet. The way you walk—your gait and posture—are determined by the state of your feet. It's rather

143

difficult to glide swanlike across a room when you're flat-footed or have fallen arches or painful calluses.

While "aching feet" are looked upon with about as much sympathy as a hangnail, you should know that foot trouble can signal heart, kidney, and liver diseases, arteriosclerosis, and other circulatory problems.

Let's discuss the less catastrophic (but still irritating) foot sores that plague many of us.

● *I haven't seen the inside of a locker room since I was in college. Now I have athlete's foot. How can I get rid of it?*

What is America's most common skin disease? If you answered *acne,* you're wrong. The number-one skin nuisance is none other than athlete's foot. And we spend over $8.5 million annually on remedies. If you also think athlete's foot is contagious (you can pick it up in a public shower), you're wrong again. Here is the truth about athlete's foot:

"A.F." is caused by one of several yeast-like fungi that can infect the feet. These fungi are present on just about everyone, but they need the perfect environment (warm, moist, and dark—like the inside of a tight shoe or old sneaker) to grow. They also may erupt after an illness, or when you're generally run down.

The symptoms can be cracking, blisters, scaling, and redness. One fungus attacks the nails, too. It usually infects the skin between the toes, then the bottom of the foot, the nails last.

If you think you've got athlete's foot, you need professional help. (You wouldn't expect to fill your own tooth; don't consider yourself a qualified foot care specialist, either.)

After the doctor determines what kind of fungus

you've got, he'll treat it with anti-fungicides. There's even a pill (by prescription only) that can "cure" certain kinds of athlete's foot.

To prevent this skin disease, dry your feet (between toes, too) after every shower. Wear 100 percent cotton socks. Remove your sneakers immediately after sports, and wear open-to-air leather sandals, weather permitting.

● *Why are high heels so bad for the feet?*

Besides causing postural problems, women can also get shortened hamstring muscles. When your feet are at the odd angle caused by high heels, your hamstring (the muscle behind your calf) doesn't need to stretch as far as if your heel had to touch the ground, so it atrophies (the use-it-or-lose-it principle again).

Women with shortened hamstrings walk around on tippy-toes, even when barefoot, because it hurts too much to lower their feet. I asked Dr. Benjamin Kauth, a New York podiatrist, what can be done about this. He recommends the following exercise you can do daily.

1) Stand three feet away from a wall, lean in and place your hands against the wall, stretching them as high above your head as possible. Hold arms straight. Push into the wall, hold for a count of 15. Repeat 10 times. If you don't feel much pull in the back of your legs, stand farther away from wall.

2) Try the towel-pull exercise I suggest in the Magnificent Massage, Part III, Day 5. Hold for a count of 15.

I'd also like to mention some other exercises Dr. Kauth recommends for specific foot areas:

To strengthen the forepart of your foot, turn the pages of a phone book, one at a time, with your toes.

For your arches, first come up on your toes, hold, throw the weight to the outside of your foot, come down slowly. Second, walk around on the balls of your feet.

- *My corns are making me cranky, and I can't even predict when it's going to rain!*

Corns are painful little growths that usually occur on the fifth or outer toe—the little piggy that gets squashed by tight shoes. The blood cells in the area dilate, the skin cells build up faster than the body can throw them off. When the cells become hard and impacted, you've got a corn. When these cells encircle the nerve, you've got an even more painful nerve corn. The doctor will shave down these corns for you. I always thought I had congenital foot trouble, but when I started having my corns and calluses shaved by a podiatrist, I found I was able to stay on my feet for hours without pain.

Even some people who swear they wear "sensible" shoes all the time may develop corns. These unfortunates probably are suffering from an inherited imbalance of the foot. The solution: orthotics, or mechanical devices that change the position of the foot to redistribute the weight. (The "thotics" are those plastic soles, made to measure, that you slip into your shoe.)

A callus is similar to a corn, but more amorphous, and it's usually located on the bottom of the foot. It's caused by the foot pressing down onto the shoe from an odd angle (for example, you foot is slanted due to high heels) or a natural imbalance. You can also get a callus on the heel. If it's not too serious, use your pumice stone to plane it. But don't abrade it completely: it's actually protecting the soft skin beneath it from further trauma.

You have to treat the cause of the callus (whether it's

just the wrong shoe style or a foot imbalance) to assure it won't come back.

While I'm talking about these foot-related nasties, let me say a few words about bunions and plantar warts.

What causes bunions? Ask Mother and Granddad to take off their shoes—do they have any? Bunions are usually hereditary. Hurting shoes can make them worse, of course, but even natives who go barefoot their whole lives can develop these "turnip toes"—so much for blaming everything on footwear! Bunion surgery can probably cure you.

If your mother has bunions and you want to try to avoid them, do this exercise religiously: Grab your foot with one hand. With the other hand, take your big toe, pull it away from your foot, rotate it gently. Dr. Kauth said this really helps. Do it in the bathtub; you're sitting down already.

Warts are caused by a virus. Which means don't touch them, mess with them, or they can spread. Plantar's warts have nothing to do with peanuts. Rather, they occur on the plantar (bottom) surface, or sole, of the foot. They can be treated with medications or surgical procedures (an electric needle or other methods).

● *How can I get my feet ready for tennis?*

The various exercises mentioned throughout this chapter should help your feet become good sports. But you have to be careful *while* you're playing. You've heard of tennis elbow—well, there's tennis toe, too. When you keep jamming your toes up into your sneaker, you're exposing them to constant mini-trauma. A bloot clot can form under the nail, said nail will turn black and you can lose it.

I'm not suggesting you throw the game, but you *can* wear an extra pair of socks, use a cushioned insole if your sneakers are too big, remove sneakers right after you win, and powder feet liberally.

Tennis fanatics are also prone to a ruptured plantaris (a painful status symbol, like the skier's broken leg), which is a frankfurter-shaped muscle in the back of the leg. It used to help our forebears climb trees. Now it's vestigial (useless). But when tennis players come down hard suddenly, and feel like someone has kicked them in the back of the leg, they learn (painfully) of its existence.

Joggers also must beware the sports-related injury. Improper shoes can lead to many problems, from fractured metatarsals to blisters. By the way, a blister can be more than painful. If it becomes badly infected, a blister can lead to blood poisoning, foot amputation, even death. Now, you needn't run to the doctor in terror every time you scrape your heels on a new pair of slingbacks, but a *serious* blister should receive treatment.

Remember the plastic molds people with foot imbalance need? Well, there are also special "orthotics for jocks." If you think your poor showing on the court or the course is due to a foot problem, these may help.

You are knock-kneed or pigeon-toed? Orthotic devices are probably all that can be used to encourage normal gait. Exercises help during childhood, but they won't do much once your bones are formed.

● *What causes swollen ankles?*

Look down at your feet this very minute. Are your legs crossed? Is one foot hooked behind the chair? If so, you're cutting off your circulation. Train yourself to sit with both feet on the floor, straight in front of you. This will reduce your tendency toward swollen ankles. Support hose also help, by giving the blood a "leg-up" on its journey back to the heart.

FINAL FOOT THOUGHTS

Beware the "bedroom fracture." People always *say* they broke their little toe while stumbling in the dark from the bedroom to the bathroom (I always fantasize that they've been chased around the bedroom by an impatient lover). Whatever the cause, nocturnal toe fractures are common. Have yours attended to, or you'll have a chronically swollen tiny toe.

You bought your shoes in an air-conditioned store? Double check to make sure they'll be *large* enough in a more natural clime. When you get home, put an old sock over your shoe (so you won't dirty the sole) and wander around the house for an hour. Your feet hurt? Exchange them. Remember, your feet will break down before your shoes are broken in.

Go barefoot whenever you can. Walking barefoot in the sand or any soft, yielding surface is terrific exercise.

While the following may seem almost as drastic as dancing on hot coals, it's a great exercise: Fill low-heeled shoes with dried peas or beans and start walking. Stop when you feel the (painful) need for first aid!

Sneakers aren't bad for your feet if they fit properly and you don't wear them twenty-four hours a day.

There's no substitute for real leather: it lets your feet breathe while providing adequate protection. Speaking of shoes, don't buy in the morning. Your feet swell during the day, and that perfect fit at 10 A.M. may put frown lines on your face by 5 P.M.

Vary your heel height during the day, but don't try to make up for your 5'2" height with 5-inch heels. High heels cause you to lurch forward, can throw your back out of commission along with your feet, and cause calluses to form on the balls of the feet. Stiletto and outrageous platform heels? Consign them to a costume museum.

Boots are basic, but if you're afflicted with varicose veins or other circulatory problems (even just tired legs), buy the zip-up variety. Then, when no one's looking, unzip: at your desk, in the movies, under the dinner table. Eight hours of wearing calf-hugging boots can cause sluggish circulation.

Cross your heart, not your legs. Raise your legs whenever possible—this eases the blood's climb back to the heart and relaxes your whole body. Sleep with your feet elevated—roll up an old blanket (or a couple of last year's phone books) and tuck it under your mattress.

When you're wearing sandals (Roman soldiers conquered the world in them), color up exposed feet with pearlized powder—it gives a sheen. Short stubby toes? Use clear polish only.

For nimble feet (or to exercise boot-cramped toes) try picking up a pencil with your toes.

CHAPTER
9

Behind Closed Doors

THE TRUTH ABOUT SOME INTIMATE BEAUTY RITUALS

There are certain beauty activities you'd just rather not perform *à deux,* certain beauty flaws you'd like taken care of in private, certain health questions you'd like answered without having to ask.

This chapter, then, is devoted to solving those uniquely feminine problems.

Let's start with a problem that heads many women's "most wanted" list—removal of excess hair. Thick hair is a girl's best friend, except when it's poking through her pantyhose or darkening her upper lip. Of course, you've probably been shaving since you were four-teen—even though mother warned such early use of the razor would transform your peach fuzz into monkey fur! (Shaving is the American girl's *rite de passage.* Margaret Mead should have studied hair removal pat-terns of the American teen-ager rather than coming of age in Samoa. Actually, the whole problem dates back to the American Indian, who considered excess hair a defect, and removed it with two clamshells held like tweezers!)

But today there's more to de-fuzzing than clamshells, and I'd like to answer your questions about both professional and do-it-yourself processes.

First, a few words about excess hair.

Hirsutism, the medical term for superfluous hair, is not a health threat. Excess body and facial hair (defined as more than you'd like) may just run in your family, making it another in the long list of hereditary characteristics. It is also race-linked: Latin and Semitic women are just plain hairier than Swedes or Orientals. Are you somehow abnormal if plagued with excess hair? Not at all! Facial hair increases around puberty and makes another great leap forward at menopause. But, if you're suddenly sprouting lots of hair when the family album shows you're descended from a line of seemingly follicle-less individuals, see your doctor. Your particular problem may be caused by a hormonal imbalance. More than likely, it's just a cosmetic problem, and can be dealt with *sans* the medicos.

- *What are the permanent methods of hair removal? Are they safe?*

There are just two hair removal techniques considered permanent, both salon-performed: electrolysis and Depilatron. Let me describe how each method works, so you'll know what to expect when you're in the chair. I'll also give you the good and bad news basics for each.

Here's what the two processes have in common. They both make use of shortwave radio frequencies (set aside for medical purposes) to attack the papilla, the source of blood (nourishment) for growing hair. The electric current provides heat which damages the papilla, hopefully making further hair growth in the follicle impossible.

But, the means of heating (destroying) the papilla sets electrolysis and Depilatron apart. In electrolysis, the heat is conducted down to the follicle through the pore opening via an electric filament, or needle. This procedure will loosen the hair, which is then picked up with a tweezer.

Here are the electrolysis bad news basics:

- It can hurt, because you feel the heat of the needle on your skin. (The upper lip and inner thigh are the most sensitive areas.)
- It can leave needle marks and redness, which should go away shortly after treatment, but if not performed *properly,* permanent small scars may result. So make sure you go to a well-known salon for this service, not to your local corner unisex boutique.
- If the hair is curly, the operator may miss the papilla on her first attempt. If she goes in too shallowly or too deeply, the hair might not be removed. Again, the skill of your electrologist is a factor in the success of your treatment.

The good news basic: It works. Electrolysis has been time-tested. When properly performed, hair should go away forever.

With the Depilatron method, an electronic tweezer replaces the needle, and the tweezer never touches your skin: The energy from the tweezer flows along the hair shaft and zeros in directly on the papilla. This means that even papillae attached to curly or oddly-growing follicles can be destroyed, and your skin won't redden or be scarred, because all the action is done with the current touching the hair, not the skin itself. And, one of the best news basics: no hot metal touching the skin means no pain. It doesn't hurt!

One bad news basic connected with Depilatron: Because the energy is partially dissipated (there's no needle to go right to the papilla) this process may take a little longer than conventional electrolysis. Also, because Depilatron is relatively new, it doesn't have the time-proven track record of electrolysis.

Time, Money, Patience

If you are considering permanent hair removal, you'll need an investment of each. First, you can't zip in and have all your hair removed (even from such a seemingly tiny area as the upper lip) in a few sessions. There are about 1,000 hair roots per square inch, and though all the hairs aren't poking through the surface at the same time, enough may be visible to make the process time-consuming.

And, since time means money to a salon operator as it does to everyone else, expect to pay. It may take a few hundred dollars to clear your mustache and sideburns, hopefully forever. But for the woman cursed with an abundance of hair, removal may be as much a cosmetic and psyche booster as plastic surgery is to her sister, and it's actually cheaper.

Why patience? In the words of the Depilatron people, you must remember that "permanent is not synonymous with immediate" . . . for either process. If the papilla isn't completely destroyed, hair may regrow, though it will be lighter and thinner in texture. Successive treatments will eventually prohibit this regrowth.

Also, because each hair may be at a different stage of the growth process, those new hairs you may be calling "regrowth" might not have been visible to the electrologist at the time of your last treatment. (It takes a good eight weeks for hair to grow from the papilla to the skin's surface.) But, if well done, each session should see 80 percent of the hairs treated disappear forever.

Because permanent hair removal is expensive, it's usually reserved for excess facial hair. If you've got the money and the time, hair can also be banished from your arms, underarms, legs, and body, too. Visit the best salon in your area for a consultation about the method of your choice.

● *Each summer I spend more time shaving my legs than I do at the beach. I thought I'd try waxing rather than permanent hair removal. How effective is it?*

Very—it can inhibit hair regrowth for weeks. That's why I've outlined the how-tos for waxing (and discuss other hair removal techniques) on Day 10 of your *Crash* program.

● *I have a mole I'd like to get rid of. What's the procedure?*

First, a few "definitions." A mole looks like a brown spot *raised* from the skin's surface; a beauty mark is a *flat* area of pigmented color.

Before your dermatologist removes a mole, he first will test it to make sure it isn't cancerous. There are several methods of removal, one of the most common being to inject you with novocaine so you won't feel any pain, and then to shave the mole flush with a scalpel. (Doctors I spoke with preferred this technique to the incision-and-stitch method, which leaves a linear scar.)

When the mole is shaved, it will be level, but you may have some brownish color (resembling a light beauty mark or freckle) left in its place.

If there's a hair in the mole, shaving won't get rid of the hair follicle—for this you need electrolysis, which should be performed *before* the mole is removed, but *after* the doctor has checked out the nature of the mole.

You have a flat beauty mark, but you don't like the dark pigment? Leave it alone. The pigment can be deep within the skin, and any attempt to remove it could leave a scar worse than the discoloration itself. Better to use a special makeup like Covermark, available at your drugstore.

● *My perspiration problem is embarrassing. Have any new "cures" been discovered?*

Unfortunately, there has been no great national outcry for a sweat control commission! You should realize that some perspiration is necessary—it helps regulate the body's internal temperature, so 100 percent blockage of sweat glands would be an absolute no-no.

Make sure you're using an underarm product marked *antiperspirant;* if yours is labeled deodorant, the manufacturer formulated it to deal with odor, not perspiration—so you may have to look elsewhere. Try a cream or roll-on antiperspirant; they offer greater protection than sprays. Because not all antiperspirants have the same percentage of sweat-controlling ingredients, it pays to try and compare several brands.

If your problem is really severe, one doctor told me there is an operation that can remove two thirds of your sweat glands, but you will have a scar under your arm, discomfort following the procedure, and a slow healing time. There are also pills given to chronic perspirers (the same pills used for ulcers in some cases, because the acid glands in the stomach are part of the same system as the sweat glands), but the results aren't guaranteed.

If you have an excessive perspiration problem, there is one fashion accessory that never goes out of style—dress shields.

If body odor rather than perspiration is your problem, frequent bathing, shaving under your arms, and an underarm product clearly marked *deodorant* (rather than antiperspirant) are necessary.

● *How often should I douche to get rid of a vaginal discharge?*

It depends what kind of discharge you're talking about. The normal vagina is warm, moist, and not meant to be sterile (it contains helpful bacteria). If you aren't having any particular health (infection) problem, douching just isn't necessary—your daily bath or shower will take care of inoffensive secretions. One Manhattan gynecologist I spoke with, Dr. Alvin Weseley, said the majority of women don't douche as part of their regular hygiene regimen.

If you do want to douche, the old one-tablespoon-of-vinegar-to-one-quart-of-water is still a good formula. (Why vinegar? The vagina has an acidic pH, too!) Betadine (available from your pharmacist) is an effective douche if you feel uncomfortable because of a vaginal infection (use as directed).

But, remember, douching won't cure a vaginal infection. Infection must be diagnosed and treated (by medication) by your doctor. If you have an odorous discharge, itching, burning, or irritation, let the gynecologist have a look; he/she can prescribe a cure.

If you're considering using a vaginal deodorant because you like the scent, you probably shouldn't bother. Doctors hear many complaints (redness, burning, irritation) from women who have used these sprays; in fact, one doctor I spoke with feels vaginal deodorants are on their way out.

● *I'm beginning to think the gap in my social life is due to the growing gap between my two front teeth; can I close up the space without taking out a bank loan?*

If you're dissatisfied with your smile, you should be aware of the newer, little-discussed tooth restoring techniques that come under the heading *cosmetic dentistry*. Some recent scientific wizardry has provided innovative dentists with new tools that enable them to correct annoying cosmetic flaws in just a few (sometimes even one!) visits.

The new technology is based on the development of composite resins that can be molded, shaped (like acrylic super nails), and affixed to your teeth in such a way as to camouflage defects.

A resin-savvy dentist can fill your gap with the putty-like material in just one visit, and it's a painless procedure. You don't need to have caps made—definitely good news, because caps (or crowns) require more than a few dental visits, and they're expensive. Besides, a dental thought has it that capping a perfectly *healthy* tooth may not be such a good idea: you have to file away the enamel of the tooth to cap it. Why deliberately injure a good tooth?

I asked a New York dentist skilled in cosmetic tooth work, Dr. Jack Kern (he has many famous show biz patients), to tell me some applications of the new technology (after all, why should the gap-toothed have all the fun!):

Discoloration. Your teeth can turn color for a variety of reasons. White streaks are caused by hypoplasia (lack of calcium). Children who take long-term high doses of tetracycline or other antibiotics during their teeth-forming years can wind up with unattractively mottled teeth. (Note: While fluoride in water is an excellent decay preventive, consult your DDS before giving your children fluoride vitamins—they may discolor teeth.) Smoking has an effect, too.

The newest way to greatly improve these problems is known popularly as "tooth painting"—a thin layer of the resin is brushed onto your teeth. This is where the dentist must be an artist as well as a craftsman: You may want whiter-than-white teeth, but if you're older or have a pale complexion, the dentist will give you the shade of ivory or eggshell that will be most enhancing to your mouth. Again, this procedure will probably take just one visit.

Malpositioned/malformed teeth. Let's say you have a peg-shaped tooth or one of your teeth comes to a vampiric point. Perhaps your teeth are twisted, and don't quite face front and center the way you'd like. Or, you may have a missing or chipped tooth due to an accident. The new resins can often take care of these problems without capping or bridgework. Again, a vast improvement in your smile is possible with minimum trauma.

If one tooth is sticking out, the doctor can file a bit off of one edge of this snaggle tooth, and use a resin to build up the other edge. By this addition and subtraction method, the tooth can often be brought in line with the rest of your mouth.

Your gum is pulling away from your teeth due to

gingival erosion? The dark area at the gum line (actually the root of the tooth) can be painted, so your teeth will once more be all of a color.

The only drawback: Since the acrylic-tooth technology is relatively new, doctors don't know how long the resins will last before starting to discolor. Dentists don't claim the newer resins will last indefinitely but if necessary the material can be removed and replaced without damaging the teeth. Dr. Kern showed me cases where the resins have been in place four years, and the teeth still look good to me.

Before you begin to chant a prayer of thanks to the tooth fairy, understand that these measures fix *cosmetic* flaws. There are certain times when you *must* cap your teeth. Your dentist can't use resins on your back teeth, for example. The rear teeth are under tremendous stress—they chew and grind your food. Because of their workmanlike function, they need the strength a cap provides. Also, the porcelain-jacket crown or cap can match your own tooth color better than resins. A word about crowns: If you do get your front teeth capped, don't ask for huge white toothpaste-commercial teeth. As Dr. Kern points out, a mouthful of Chiclets shouldn't be your aesthetic goal! (Tooth shape and color should be natural looking with slight irregularities.)

Besides cosmetic dentistry, you may want to consider adult orthodontia. That's right, braces. Certain tooth problems can be corrected only by the orthodontist—and more and more adults are making later-in-life adjustments rather than waiting to be reincarnated as Farrah Fawcett-Majors. There are removable braces, so you needn't attend special social functions looking as if you were wired for sound.

If your problem is tiny teeth surrounded by mammoth gums, the dentist can actually trim healthy gums to give you a more even, attractive gum line and teeth more normal-looking in size.

Though great strides are being made in dentistry, it's up to you to plan a maintenance program that will encourage tooth health. Consider the following:

1) Your twice-yearly dental checkup is as vital as your every-six-month Pap smear.

2) Brush your teeth and your gums twice a day with a soft-bristled toothbrush. Hard bristles can do damage, natural bristles are unnecessary. Move the toothbrush horizontally, not vertically, while you brush.

Avoid abrasive toothpaste. In fact, one dentist I spoke with says toothpaste isn't necessary. It makes your mouth smell good, but you could just as easily brush with plain soap and water (if you could stand the taste), as long as you remove all the between-teeth particles.

Work unwaxed dental floss between your teeth. Don't let your Water-Pik gather dust.

Massage your gums with the rubber-tip end of your toothbrush. Healthy gums contribute greatly to tooth longevity; more teeth are lost due to gum disease than to decay. If your gums are bleeding, see the dentist.

3) Check to see if you've brushed properly by using a disclosing solution or tablets every day. The harmless vegetable dye clings to decay-causing plaque, giving a graphic picture of areas that need re-brushing. You can buy disclosing kits from your druggist.

If you haven't visited the dentist since pliers and strong whiskey were the chief dental aids, make an appointment. Could be your smile (not to mention your tooth health) can be made over in less than the 21 days it will take to complete the makeover/shapeover program.

- *Lately I've been mesmerized (and depressed) by little
  spidery red lines appearing on my nose and cheeks.
  What's happening?*

Sounds like tiny broken blood vessels (doctors call
them telangiectases), and they can be the result of a
variety of causes, including diet. If you're a fiery foods
addict, curb your intake of chili and curry; a spicy diet
can cause or aggravate the condition. So can excessive
drinking—W. C. Fields didn't get a big red nose from
sipping camomile tea. Overlong exposure to extreme
heat or cold may be the root of your particular problem.
Or perhaps you've just been overzealous in "picking"
your face, and have injured the skin and blood vessels
lying below it.

Here are some possible solutions. First, you must
figure out what you're doing to cause the broken blood
vessels (hopefully it's not hereditary; the fair-skinned
are more prone to this curse), and stop doing it. Second,
see a dermatologist.

The doctor has two ways of dealing with this problem. The first, electrodessication, involves "sparking"
the blood vessels with a high frequency electric current.
The idea is to burn them off. *Bad news basics:* There's a
slight risk of scarring, and the technique doesn't always
work. (Because the doctor is so worried about producing a scar, he may not go in deep enough with his needle
to destroy the capillary.) After dessication, scabs will
form; when they fall off (after a few days) the area
treated will be red from the trauma. This redness will
last a few weeks.

A newer technique is cryosurgery, freezing the broken blood vessels with liquid nitrogen or dry ice.
Because these substances are sprayed on the face,
there will be no scar. The capillary may still be there,

but it gets sclerotic (dries up), which is what the doctor wants. Again, your skin will be red for a few weeks following treatment, and there's no 100 percent guarantee for either technique—but many patients are pleased with the results.

In case you're worried about the physical (as opposed to cosmetic) side effects resulting when blood vessels (no matter how tiny) are destroyed, you needn't be: as Dr. Robert Berger, a Manhattan dermatologist, explains, these are superfluous vessels, and there are plenty more to do the work.

- *My legs look like they've been etched with red and blue marking pens. I know they're not varicose veins (too small)—but what are they, and how can I get rid of them?*

These little sunburst-shaped capillaries are known as vascular spiders. Some doctors dessicate them, but this procedure may not work as well as you'd like because thigh skin (where "spiders" are most common) doesn't heal as well as the face.

Dr. Berger says he often prefers to inject the areas with a sclerosing (drying, hardening) solution which clots the (superfluous) blood vessels in question, so they will be absorbed back into the skin. But, the patient must be patient: When the fluid is injected, the clot turns a purple or brown, and takes a number of months (three to nine) to fade. The procedure can be done in the office, but, as with many things medical, there is no guarantee you'll get 100 percent of the results you want. Because I stand on my feet all day, I get broken blood vessels behind my knees—and every few years I get another shot here and there as new "spiders" appear. Just remember, this treatment doesn't work for deep varicose veins—that's a more serious problem.

● *What causes varicose veins? How can I get rid of them?*

According to Dr. Albert M. Schwartz, chief of the vascular department at Beth Israel Medical Center in New York City, the problem really began when our earliest ancestors—Cro-Magnon and his cousins—began walking upright, giving our (rear) legs a heavy burden to carry. (Members of the animal kingdom who still march about on all fours don't develop varicose veins.)

If you suffer from varicose veins, a more immediate cause could be a familial tendency toward this condition. (Hint: Did your mother or great-aunt try to corner the market on elastic stockings?) Jobs that involve long periods of standing, pregnancy, or tumors in the pelvis that press upon the veins can also cause or aggravate a congenital disposition towards VV. Age is not a prime factor—teen-agers can get them, if this vascular defect runs strongly in a family. VV are not for women only—men are afflicted, too.

Unfortunately, once you have a varicosity, it won't just go away—it gets larger as time goes on, even if you forswear crossing your legs. (Dr. Schwartz says the leg-crossing taboo is a myth—the prohibition is really just for older people with an arterial problem, so you can cross away without fear of causing VV.)

If your varicose veins are painful, this could be a sign of superficial phlebitis, and you should see a doctor. Your vascular surgeon will decide whether you have true varicose veins (don't confuse a varicosity with tiny vascular spiders) that should be removed (whether for cosmetic or health reasons), and he may recommend a vein stripping operation. You'll spend two days in the hospital, and when you come home you won't be bedbound. Once the unattractive varicosity is removed, it will be gone forever. All you'll have in its place are the scars from surgery; the scars are usually visible, but for most women, these scars are 100 percent preferable to the veins.

Will the varicose veins return? The ones you've had removed can't possibly reappear; they've been left behind in the operating room. If you do have a tendency toward varicosity, a new vein may "pop out." But a large recurrence in the future is the exception rather than the rule.

10

Is My Nose in Place?

THE TRUTH ABOUT PLASTIC SURGERY

As I went on my information gathering forays among the plastic surgeons I had to control myself to keep from bursting into this tune I learned as a child:

> Are my ears on straight?
> Is my nose in place?
> Have I got a cute expression on my face?
> Are my blue eyes bright?
> Do I look all right . . .
> to be taken home Christmas day?*

The song tells the poignant tale of a doll who has been repaired and is wondering if she's finally a pretty enough gift for a little girl's Christmas.

Though the song is sweet and naive, many of us never lose that insecure feeling expressed by these winsome lyrics. Most women go through life asking themselves

*Words and music by Mel Leven; permission granted by Blackhawk Music.

variations of the same questions. And, when the mirror answers in the negative, some of us opt for plastic surgery.

PANACEA OR PROBLEM-MASKER?

I think plastic surgery can do wonderful things for the woman (or man) who has a physical flaw that is making her/him self-conscious about her/his appearance. Current thinking has it that if you feel good, you look good. Well, I believe the opposite is true, too: If you don't look good to yourself, you're not going to feel good, either. Besides, having cosmetic surgery is certainly nothing to be ashamed of. There's no stigma attached to capping your teeth or streaking your hair. Cosmetic plastic surgery is undertaken for the same reason—*an improved appearance.*

At least that's the only reason it *should* be performed. The woman who seeks a nose job when she already has the profile of a fashion model, or breast augmentation when she's amply endowed, is trying to make up for some unknown insecurity that can't be cured by a scalpel, and the reputable plastic surgeon will gently turn away these unsuitable candidates for surgery.

If you and the surgeon *do* decide that your physical appearance will indeed be enhanced by cosmetic surgery, you should enter the hospital with *realistic* expectations. A well-done face lift, for example, can take years off the appearance of a forty-five-year-old woman. But if this same woman expects to leave the hospital a double for her twenty-year-old daughter, she will invariably be disappointed.

Should you or shouldn't you submit to the scalpel?

Here are the facts you need to help you make your own very personal decision.

The Myth of Invisible Scars

Before I answer questions about specific procedures, there is one *bad news basic* every cosmetic surgery candidate should know: *There is no such thing as an "invisible" scar.* It's the nature of human skin to scar after any cut is made; it's part of the healing process. We're not like earthworms that just separate and regenerate. What the doctor strives for is to make the scars inconspicuous—by placing them in skin folds, making "hairline"-wide rather than freeway-wide incisions. And, for many procedures, the scars will seem to disappear. (Some operations, like the typical nose job, leave no scars externally, because the work is all done from within.)

You should also know that some women have an innate tendency to heal better than others. Look over your body for other cuts, stitches, or incisions you've had. Did they seem to disappear within several months? If so, there's a good chance (though no guarantee) that your healing processes will work satisfactorily. Also, women with thick, oily skin may not heal as well as the finer-skinned surgical candidate, and there isn't much the doctor can do about this.

If your past scars remained thick and lumpy, you may not be pleased with the results of cosmetic surgery, because you have a tendency to form keloids—raised, large, irregular scars. There is no foolproof method for determining the keloid-prone in advance, unfortunately. Caucasians can keloid, though black skins produce keloids more frequently.

There *is* some good news about scars, however: The

face usually heals better than the rest of the body, and since facial scars are the ones we worry about most, it's comforting to know they also heal the best.

Dr. Paul Striker, a Manhattan plastic surgeon who is technical editor of the *International Microfilm Journal of Aesthetic Plastic Surgery,* told me that the same scars may appear different to women of different cultures. In Brazil, where the renowned Dr. Ivo Pitanguy popularized body-sculpting surgery (I'll explain in detail later in this chapter), body scars may be a *status* symbol. Some women feel they have arrived if they can afford this kind of operation, and the highly visible scars that result don't cause them to give away their string bikinis. An American woman seeing the same scars may find them a worse deformity than the original problem she wanted corrected. Everything is relative, but you have to be willing to trade the (sometimes) dramatic improvement in body contour for the scarring that will inevitably result.

There are three factors that will determine how you'll scar:

1) The surgeon's skill—his tissue handling and sewing expertise.

2) Your inherent tendency to heal well, or to keloid.

3) Environmental factors—post-operative infections, bumping into walls, too-soon sun exposure, etc.

SAG ALERT

Since many of the most popular plastic surgery procedures deal with staving off the effects of aging, I want to give you a guide to what you can expect to droop—then I'll answer specific questions.

How do you know when those first tiny signs of

deterioration you thought were your imagination are visible to others? If you agree with the statements below, the days when you had to show your driver's license to be served a drink are long gone.

- Recent photos of William Holden and Dana Andrews bring tears to your eyes.
- Your teenage son's friends are beginning to look physically attractive to you.
- Your body is exactly the same as when you were eighteen. You haven't gained a pound . . . but everything is two inches lower.

Before you reach for the hemlock, study the following illustrated Sag Alert. You may have been the only girl on the block who still wore undershirts at age sixteen, but at least when it comes to aging you're not alone. And you can, to a large degree, control today how you'll look in the not-so-distant future.

HAIR

You've seen pictures of spry octogenarians (Geritol's word for old folks) who still have lush, full heads of raven-colored hair. These women are rare creatures who chew tobacco and always seem to inhabit tiny Balkan kingdoms annexed by the U.S.S.R.! The rest of us will gradually find our hair thinning due to the general slowdown of age (new hairs just don't replace the dead the way they used to). Treat your hair gently now, condition it often, eat a protein-rich diet. If you're turning gray, by all means tint . . . it adds life and body to hair and perks up your face. But don't go too dark—black hair and wrinkles just don't mix. Obvious platinums are aging, too—the blonde bombshell look works

ADRIEN ARPEL'S 3-WEEK CRASH MAKEOVER/ SHAPEOVER BEAUTY PROGRAM

THE UNRETOUCHED before-and-after photographs on the following pages show how any woman can alter her appearance by learning how to apply makeup and adopting a new hair style. The professional tips you'll learn throughout Week Three's makeup lessons will show you how to adapt these techniques to your personal needs.

Jane

To give a twenty-five-year-old "child-woman" a more sophisticated look: Lightweight, pink-toned foundation evens out slightly blotchy skin. Rose blush on cheeks defines the area (Jane previously used an earthy cheek tint too dark for her natural coloring). Pink sheen shadow highlights eyelid. Blue shadow is applied to eyelid crease and surrounding eye. Eye-rimming blue pencil further opens eye area. Black mascara can work even for blondes—Jane felt it would be too harsh; she used to wear brown, but it was dull. Red lipliner, bright lipstick and raisin lip gloss transform lips. The lipliner makes the biggest difference by helping form seductive lips. Hair: cut and shaped, blonde-on-blonde streaks added.

Julie

To dramatically conceal the signs of approaching middle age: Cover-up conceals shadows and flaws. Julie relied on foundation alone for camouflage; past twenty-five, it's not enough. A soufflé-type foundation is best, because it doesn't settle into lines. Good cheekbones are emphasized via berry-colored blusher and brown contouring agent. Julie always colored her cheeks, but contouring (easy once you learn how) makes the difference. Very dark carbon-colored shadow above and under eyelids adds fire to the eye area. Earth-toned eye sheen highlights browbone. Black mascara—lots of it—completes the eyes. Brown lipliner helps keep lipstick from bleeding beyond lip borders, important when fine lines are starting to form above lip. Hair: natural henna adds life and body to softer hair style.

Nancy

To emphasize an all-American girl's wholesome glamour: Cover-up and peach foundation conceal youthful blemishes. Nancy thought foundation wasn't "natural," but we convinced her the right shade doesn't look obvious. Tawnied rose blush on cheeks brightens a pale face. Medium brown eyebrow pencil, new for Nancy, helps frame eyes. One-color eye shadow, pewter, is easy for a young girl to handle. Navy blue mascara finishes eyes. Rose lipstick and gloss shine lips, bring color to a small mouth. Hair: lightened via selected streaking.

Maria

To emphasize exquisite bone structure and sultry coloring: Tan foundation and transparent powder even
out skin tone. Maria never wore
foundation because she has good
skin, but good skin looks best when
it's all one color. Amber blusher
makes cheeks stand out. Soft brown
eye shadow doubles as cheek contouring agent. Nude tone shadow
lightens eyelids, taupe eye shadow
in and above crease contours eye and
looks better than Maria's usual very-
dark-brown-all-over lid. Lower lid is
lined in black, three coats of black
mascara make lashes look longer.
Hair: front and sides layered, pushed
away from cheekbones, back long.

Reggie

To make an outward appearance
mirror a vibrant personality: Beige
soufflé foundation adds a suggestion of color. Bright berry blusher,
applied sparingly, brings up a glow.
Reggie never bothered with eye
shadow because she felt her best
feature, bright blue eyes, could
stand alone. But a combination of
green and blue eye shadows, pink
eye sheen to highlight browbone,
blue line and black mascara are a
makeover in themselves. Auburn-
colored lip pencil, lipstick and gloss
are much more vibrant than pink,
Reggie's former favorite. Hair: very
blonde toner; hair set to give fuller,
thicker appearance.

Becky

To bring new life to a young career woman's looks: Blemishes and shadows are concealed with cover-up. Tinted makeup underbase—new to Becky—tones down ruddy complexion. Peach foundation, applied sparingly with complexion sponge, further evens skin tone. Tawny blusher colors cheeks. Taupe family eye shadows, dark brown eyeliner and black mascara make Becky's eyes special. Brown lip pencil and deep red lipstick make up lips. Hair: most important change for Becky. A sophisticated cut and set lifts whole face, eliminates sad, droopy look that often accompanies flat hair style.

Sandy and Elaine: to help two black women deal with very different skin tones—

Sandy

To clarify lighter skin tone, tan foundation is applied with sponge. Two shades of amber-toned blush are used on cheeks: Dark amber encircles a light amber center. Excellent eyebrows draw attention to large eyes, further enhanced with monochromatic earthy shadows, black eyeliner and mascara. Earth-toned lip pencil, lipstick and currant-colored shiny gloss bring subtle color to Sandy's mouth. Hair: cut to get rid of damaged ends and styled to frame face.

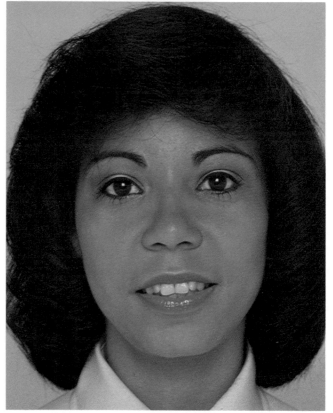

Elaine

To play up rich mahogany complexion, two shades of dark foundation
are blended and used sparingly to
even out skin tone. Berry blusher
highlights cheek area. Elaine felt
brighter eye shadows wouldn't complement black skin, but shades of
blue surrounding eyes provided
needed contrast. Navy eyeliner,
black mascara and false eyelashes
finish eyes. Red raisin gloss gives
lips a shiny, moist look they lacked
before.

Slim, Before

To transform an attractive woman into a real dazzler: Slim demonstrates some of the *exact* how-tos and techniques I'll be explaining throughout the makeup section of this book. You'll be adapting these steps for your own personal makeover.

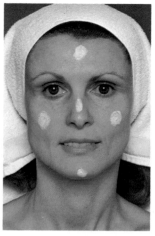

1

Color-correcting undermakeup tint base

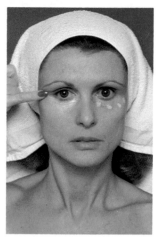

2

Concealing shadows and flaws

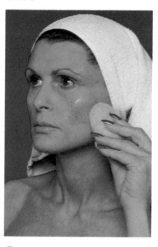

3

Applying foundation with cosmetic sponge

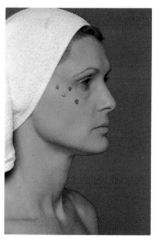

4

Applying cheek color in dot pattern to form "V"

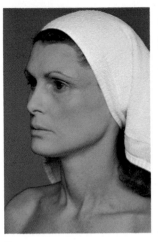

5

Blended cheek color

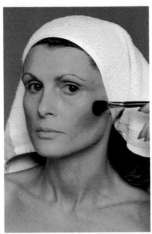

6

Cheek contouring

7

Lid eye shadow

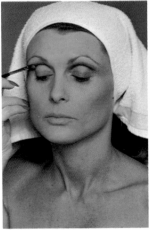

8

Darker "crease"
shadow

9

Browbone highlighting
eye shadow

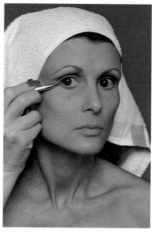

10

Eye-rimming blue pen-
cil

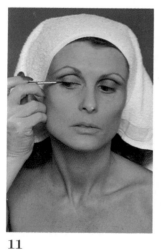

11

Eyeliner—straight line
method

12

Curling lashes

13

Mascara

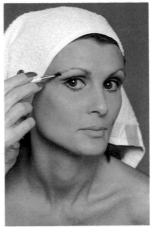

14

Brow shaping and coloring

15

Outlining lips

16

Filling in lip color

Slim, After

Soft, casual hair style perfect for woman of any age started Slim's makeover. She knew how to dramatize her cheekbones, but needed help giving her complexion a porcelain finish. Just how long did it take Slim to make herself over with makeup? Ten minutes. And you'll learn the speed-is-essential tricks on Days 15 to 19.

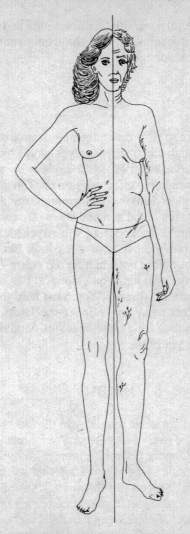

The Sag Alert: On the left, you can see how you'll look at forty if you take care of yourself; on the right you can see what happens if you don't.

only if you've got a smooth face and Lolita body. When the grays start coming, forget the flamboyant shades and you'll look younger.

EYES

Use eye cream to slow down the appearance of crow's feet. Get enough sleep so your eyes won't look puffy the next day. *Bad news basic:* Today's morning-afters will have a cumulative effect tomorrow. Too many late nights, too much drinking will prematurely age you. Wear dark glasses in the sun and stave off squint lines. Pink lenses are a look out of the psychedelic '60s, strictly for pre-teens. If your eyes look like you've spent the night before entertaining the entire 7th Fleet (when in reality it was lights out, alone, at 10 P.M.), read about eyelid plastic surgery. You must hold the newspaper three feet away to decipher the latest divorce statistics? It's time for an eye checkup. Straining your eyes wrinkles your face.

MOUTH

I've explained cosmetic dentistry in the last chapter— you needn't be twelve to correct your smile. As you age, you'll probably get a bit gummy. Did you know there's a cosmetic surgery operation that will help you show less gum? So you can throw back your head and laugh *without* looking as if you should be given a sugar cube or a bucket of oats! Keep it in mind and keep your lipstick light, subdued, so you won't draw attention to those little finely hatched lines developing above your lip. Consider correcting those upper lip lines with dermabrasion and chemical peels. Silicone *can* fill out the long, deep nose-to-mouth laugh lines. I'll tell you pros and cons shortly.

SKIN

If you spend 90-degree days playing "Beach Blanket Bingo," your face may soon look like a well-worn Italian handbag. Heredity plays a part, but plastic surgery can help restore some of the illusion of youth.

Bad new basic: You won't look twenty years younger after a face lift, but you will look better. Realize your face will keep aging after the surgery, so you may want to repeat the process. A face lift softens deep lines and furrows, and hanging skin—but it won't remove fine lines. (You'll need dermabrasion/chemabrasion for those.) The "lift" should be performed *before* you've completely crumbled for best effect.

THROAT

One well-known actress hasn't been seen without a turtleneck sweater or buttoned-up shirt since World War II. Rather than pretend you're a whiplash case, begin your throat cream therapy early—the richer the better. You can start at age nineteen. The throat is prone to turkey-wattle neck and other disasters; looks old before the face. Just cream, pray, and protect it from the elements.

BREASTS

The bigger they are, the faster (and farther) they fall. Gravity, baby-making, and heredity are the "big three" droop determiners. You know you're beyond hope (but not help) if you look at your breast profile in a mirror, and your nipple is on a level with the breast fold! Wear a bra (an underwire, especially if you're large), try the chest wall strengthening routine outlined in the exercise chapter. Remember this *bad news basic:* The breast itself is not a muscle, so even twirling them like "Suzy Stripper" won't help keep 'em high. If you can limit your husband's circle of acquaintances to your peers, he'll forget what an eighteen-year-old breast looks like. Avoid St. Tropez or Club Med vacations when you pass thirty-five and screen all baby-sitters carefully. Cosmetic breast surgery is a possibility.

MIDRIFF

I've yet to hear of the society that considers a pot belly a sex symbol (for women or men). You must exercise *now, faithfully and regularly* or you can kiss your waistline good-bye tomorrow. The stomach toners I describe in the exercise chapter would be a good way to start, especially if Mom and Grandma are rather thick around the middle. Your midriff is marred by stretch marks? *Bad news basic:* Cocoa butter, whether applied before, during, or after pregnancy, is useless. There is surgery . . . it won't remove 100 percent of your marks, but it may help if you don't mind trading stretch marks for scars.

THIGHS, HIPS, DERRIÈRE

If the rest of your body has fallen two inches since you were eighteen, these regions have probably dropped an

inch farther. They'll also get flabbier and lose tone—
even on thinnies—*unless you exercise*. Yes, it's a must
to keep you trim from the waist down . . . so keep that
jump rope handy, do your Body Bulge Attack exercises
like a good girl and (if heredity has been kind in the first
place) you can still have great legs in your forties and
onward. If the bulges are unbearable, and you're
considering body surgery, read about body sculpting
later on in this chapter.

FEET

Few people will see your exposed tootsies, but if
they're not working properly you'll hobble like an old
lady—pain is aging. Read all the feet treats and treatments outlined on Day 5, Part III.

THE BIG PICTURE

No one stays young forever, but you really can influ-
ence the way you'll look years from now by "good
living" today: The right foods and exercise, a program
of skin-saving facials, treatments that will keep your
hair looking alive, some attention to your posture. And,
most important: twice-yearly Pap smears, breast ex-
ams monthly, a yearly physical. No one wants to grow
old . . . but consider the alternative!

Now that you have a general idea what to expect,
learn what surgical procedures can/can't help correct
your flaws.

- *I'm considering having a face lift. How much younger will I look? What about scarring? How is it
  performed?*

A well-done face lift can take years off your appearance, make you look healthier and well-rested, but it won't turn you into a nymphet from the neck up. (You wouldn't really want that unless you plan to undress in the dark: the difference between your near-flawless face and forty-plus body could be too great a shock for your audience.)

The face lift helps get rid of sagging, droopy skin that seems to grow too big for your features as you age. The surgeon actually lifts your skin away from the support structures that lie beneath them. Then he trims the excess skin and repositions it back into place, making his incision and sutures where they won't be visible: in the hairline fold, behind the ear, or in the ear.

The operation is usually performed under a local anesthetic: It's safer, there's less bleeding, and the recovery period is shorter than if a general anesthetic is used. (Besides, when you're "put out" by a general anesthetic, your features are distorted, making the surgeon's job more difficult. You'll probably be in the hospital three or four days; the sutures will be removed in five to seven days and, if you don't mind being seen with some swelling or scabs, you can leave the house in about two weeks.

If you also have loose, hanging (turkey wattle) skin on your neck, this will be tightened during surgery. A double chin is usually corrected separately. The surgeon removes the fat pad lodged beneath the chin, leaving a z-shaped, hopefully hairline, incision in its place.

Another common procedure: nasal tip surgery. It seems as we age our noses start to droop, and many plastic surgeons now lift the tip while they're doing the rest of the face.

What a Face Lift Won't Do

While it will remove baggy, jowly skin, it won't eliminate those deep smile furrows or fine wrinkles that the
flesh is heir to. Dermabrasion or chemabrasion is
recommended for these remaining imperfections once
you've recuperated from your surgery. Nor will your
face lift keep you from aging: Gravity and constant use
of facial muscles continue to take their toll after the lift,
so you might feel the need to repeat the procedure in
five to eight years.

After Effects

You may feel some facial numbness following the
operation, but this should disappear. If your surgeon
isn't an artist as well as a craftsman, and he pulls the
skin too tight after he removes the excess, you may
wind up with a masklike effect. It's better to have skin a
little looser, to keep a few wrinkles, than to look like
certain aged movie stars who have had so many lifts
their faces are frozen in an expression of happy surprise.

After your lift, avoid the sun for two to three months.

● *Though I'm not ready for a face lift, I would like my
eyes to have a more youthful appearance. Now the
lids are droopy, and the undereye "bags" are becoming my most noticeable feature. Tell me about eye
jobs.*

Eyelid corrections can be performed to correct the
upper, or lower lid, or both. The operation (called a
blepharoplasty) can be performed as part of a face lift,
or alone.

If your upper lids give you that hooded, lizard-look

effect, the surgeon can make an incision in the fold of the upper lid, removing the excess skin and fat. If under-eye bags bother you (they can come from aging, heredity, a lack-of-sleep, lots-of-alcohol life style—good reasons to play the Spartan now), the skin and muscle below are lifted, and a portion of the herniated fat pad found beneath is removed.

Eye work is tricky: as Dr. Striker explains, the lids contain glands, muscles, tear ducts, nerves, packed into an area just one millimeter thick, so the surgeon must be skillful because you don't want the *protective* functions of the lid impaired.

Eye jobs have become very popular among both women and men. Stitches are usually removed within five days, the swelling should subside within ten days. Because the incisions are tiny, and can truly be made in the folds of the skin, they should not be detectable (notice I didn't promise invisibility).

After Effects

Remember I said the surgeon should have consummate skill? If he removes *too much* skin and fat, you could be left with that "basset hound" look: A droopy lower lid that seems to fall away from the eye. And, of course, you want to make sure you can close your upper lid, no matter how insomniac you are. (I hope you don't think I'm being too negative. I'm all for plastic surgery—but few books tell you the pitfalls, and it's better to know all the possibilities before you enter the operating room.)

There's another kind of youth-restoring eye surgery: the brow-lift. When we're seventeen, our brows rest comfortably above the bony ridge that's their home. As we age, the brows droop, sometimes below the ridge, giving a Neanderthal appearance. Some doctors compensate for this by making an incision just above the brow, and lifting it. The result: a visible, though inconspicuous, scar that you'll have to cover with brow makeup. Other surgeons might do a forehead lift, which will raise the brows and make the wrinkles of the forehead less conspicuous. Still other doctors *never* do brow lifts . . . they feel the effects aren't worth the effort (especially the scar that results from lifting the brow directly).

● *I'm afraid of having a total face lift, but I thought I'd try a mini-lift. How does this work, and what will it do for me?*

The idea behind a face lift is to pick up and tighten sagging, baggy skin and support muscles. A face lift can make a dramatic difference because it works against the effects of gravity that cause the jowls and sags of the lower third of the face. The so-called mini-lift involves a tuck by the ear that can help lift the upper third of the face, so if your brows are drooping, you've got some forehead lines, they may be lifted and smoothed. But you won't see much improvement because the lower third of your face remains untouched. For this reason, you should probably forget a mini-lift. Why submit to the scalpel knowing in advance you won't be totally happy with the results?

Note: There is one instance where a mini-lift does make sense. If you've already had a total face lift, a mini can correct the preliminary signs of aging that start to recur as the lift ages.

● *What's the procedure for having the bump on my nose removed . . . and can I be sure I'll get the nose that fits my face?*

Before you head for the doctor, consider that a bump can be beautiful because it gives you an individual look. Many top models have irregular features—the bumpy nose gives them an aristocratic European look. If you can't "carry" your bump stylishly and confidently, plastic surgery is a viable option.

I asked Dr. John Cinelli, director of plastic surgery of the New York Eye and Ear Infirmary, to describe the procedure. (This is the doctor who did my nose, and I hadn't seen him since. But I figure since I've been happy all these years, he would be a good man to ask.)

You're given a sedative before you enter the operating room and then injected with novocaine. Local anesthesia is always preferable because there is too much bleeding with a general (and the doctor can't see the not-so-fine details of your profile if they're covered with blood!), but you don't feel the pain.

The surgeon actually breaks your nose (some doctors use a saw; others use a hammer and chisels), then removes the bump. To fill in the wide gap that's left (and to give you something to rest your sunglasses on—you do need a bridge, you know), the bones of the wall of the nose are broken, moved closer together and reshaped. Excess bone is pulled out through the nostril, and the whole procedure is done internally, so you shouldn't see any visible scars. (Exception: if you're having your *nostrils* narrowed, this is done externally, and the scars might be visible. Black women especially prone to keloid scars might do better to avoid this procedure.)

You'll probably be in the hospital about three days, and you'll go home wearing bandages. You may be black and blue for a week, have traces of the procedure for another week, then you should look fine (though it will take several months before your new nose will assume its final shape). Your doctor may or may not ask you to wear a kind of splint or clamp on your nose to help the swelling go down faster during the recovery period.

Don't be surprised if your doctor says you need a chin correction, too. Sometimes a receding chin may be the cause of your less than harmonious profile: it makes your nose look larger than usual by contrast. The doctor inserts a silicone gel implant under your chin; the scar shouldn't be noticeable. In fact, if your doctor says you'll need a chin implant as well as a nose job and you refuse this complementary procedure, he may turn you down for surgery if he feels a nose-alone correction won't give the desired result.

After Effects

Will you get the nose that fits your face? That depends largely on the skill of your surgeon and how well you heal. If you're contemplating a nose job, look at friends who have had this surgery. Do their noses look individualized? Or do they look as if they were all cookie-cut from the same mold? Also, your doctor should be willing to show you before and after pictures of some of his patients. Naturally, he'll only show you his best work. But if you like what you see, you'll know you and the doctor are on the same wave length.

Choose your surgeon with care. Plastic surgery is a specialty in itself, and some doctors specialize *even further*. The man with the best reputation for face lifts may not be a nose-job superstar. You want a nose man, not a breast or eye job expert.

You aren't satisfied with the results? You can have a nose job two, even three times (waiting nine months in between). But as Dr. Daniel Weiner, associate professor of plastic surgery at Albert Einstein Medical College, explained, it's hard to redo a nose with terrific results because the doctor has less to work with the second time around. And, if your lack of total happiness is due to the unchangeable fact that you're a poor healer (something difficult to predict), re-surgery probably won't help at all.

● *My ears stick out from the side of my head like wings. What can be done about this?*

You're a candidate for otoplasty, cosmetic ear surgery, because you've got a thicker than usual wall of cartilage between your ear and head, so the ear protrudes. The doctor will either fold the cartilage back upon itself, or remove some cartilage and pin the ear back. In either case, the work is done behind the ear, so the scar will be visible to no one but the surgeon performing the work.

For most plastic surgery, doctors ask you to wait till you're fully grown to make any corrections. But, if your child has protruding ears he can have them corrected as young as five years old (he'll receive general anesthesia; adults have it done under a local). And he should. You know how cruel other children can be about a physical deformity. Why subject him (her) to classmates' torment? Childhood is difficult enough!

● *I'm considering breast augmentation surgery to increase what nature gave me. Will the results feel natural?*

First, let me tell you a little about the procedure. Most commonly, silicone gel implants are used. These are inserted beneath the breast wall (not in the breast tissue itself, so breast function, i.e., nursing, won't be impaired) via an incision made in the breast fold which will fade after several months and won't be *highly* visible if well-positioned, but it will still be there. An alternative: a "cut" made halfway around the nipple. The well-done nipple scar is even less visible, but the type of incision is a decision left to the surgeon.

You will be in the hospital for three to five days, and the operation will probably be performed under general anesthesia. Expect to feel uncomfortable afterward, and don't expect to do much moving around for two or three weeks. After this recovery period, you shouldn't feel any breast "heaviness" or discomfort.

While the silicone gel implant is still the most widely used (the silicone is encased in an envelope so it won't wander away from the insertion site—wandering was a drawback associated with the liquid silicone, now banned for breast operations), the newer inflatable saline implant (silicone envelope filled with a salt-water solution) is gaining adherents. The doctor inserts the saline implant via a tiny incision made halfway around the nipple. The incision can be small because the saline bag is inserted when deflated, *before* being filled. Then the doctor fills the bag through a valve until he gets the breast to the proper size. After the operation, further adjustments in size can be made with this procedure (by adding or subtracting small quantities of the saline solution) via another incision that once more exposes the valve to the surgeon.

After Effects

There are three questions women want answered: 1) Will it look natural? 2) Will it feel natural to the man in my life? 3) Will I still feel aroused when my breasts are touched?

LOOK. The surgically augmented breast won't look natural—if you define natural as a bit sagging, small, drooping with age, not quite sixteen-year-old firm. It *should* look better than natural.

FEEL. Will your man know? That depends on whom you ask. Some doctors say no one will be able to tell. Others feel the saline-implants pass the touch test better than the gel; gel-users say the reverse is true. One doctor confided that about one third of the breasts will seem firmer than natural—that seems like a reasonable figure. But, as Dr. Daniel Weiner explained, there's a new post-op office procedure that can soften firm breasts. That "hard" feeling is caused by a contraction of the tissue capsule covering the implant. Doctors can now "fracture" the capsule by hand-manipulating the breast. It takes less than five minutes and doesn't hurt. Dr. Weiner feels this technique is so successful it will make the overly-firm breast a side effect of the past.

AROUSAL. Will you wind up with a perfectly beautiful, perfectly insensitive breast? Again, there is some controversy surrounding this question. Some women do report decreased sensation; many other patients say their responsive mechanism isn't dimmed. Psychologically, a woman may feel *more* aroused after this procedure. If her smaller-than-average breasts made her feel inadequate, unfeminine, her newly acquired voluptuousness may turn her on along with her partner.

I should mention here that as many women opt for breast reduction as for breast enlargement. This is for functional as well as cosmetic reasons. Overly large breasts can give a woman backaches and fatigue (imagine all that extra weight they have to carry around!) as well as make wearing clinging clothes impossible. With the breast reduction, the nipple must be repositioned up higher on the breast after excess skin and fat have been excised. (You will have noticeable scars all around the nipple.) This incision around the nipple does not interrupt the ducts involved with nursing, although in some cases there may be a decrease in sensation after this operation. However, as Dr. Striker explains, erotic sensitivity has a great psychological component, and those who felt terribly self-conscious because of their large, pendulous breasts may feel so pleased with their normal profile they could have *more* sensation post-surgery than before.

You can also have drooping breasts lifted. Excess skin, tissue, and fat is cut away and the breast is resewn. This can be done with an implant if you also want enlargement; without, if you're just interested in perky, gravity-defying breasts.

The breast reduction is the most complex surgical procedure of the three; therefore, it is also the most expensive. The breast augmentation is usually the least expensive, the lift falls somewhere in the middle.

● *My pregnancy left me with stretch marks as well as twins. Can the marks be removed?*

You can't get rid of *all* your stretch marks surgically (or through any other method, for that matter), but some can be removed. If the stretch marks are accompanied by hanging skin the surgeon can make an incision near the pubic line, elevate the skin and cut away as much excess as possible. When the excess skin is trimmed away, so are the stretch marks imbedded therein. The rest of the skin is then *lowered* to meet the pubic line incision, so stretch marks that were once very obvious high on the abdomen will now be hidden from view (in a bathing suit) lower down on the body.

Because the scar is made near the pubic line, you *should* be able to wear a bikini. But, remember, you are trading your stretch marks for a long scar. And, stretch marks located near the center of your abdomen can be removed more easily than those from the sides. In short, your stretch marks can be improved, but not totally obliterated.

This method of elevating the skin, trimming the excess and pulling the remainder down to meet the incision is also used successfully for scar revision. Let's say you had an accident, or previous surgery, that left you with an abdominal region scar. By trimming the excess and pulling the scarred skin down, the surgeon can lower the scar into a less obvious position (down near the pubic bone rather than up around the waist). Scar revision can be done on any part of the body. Your surgeon may be able to trade an obvious scar for an inconspicuous hairline scar.

Did you know plastic surgery can even improve the shape of your belly button—giving you a graceful marquis-shaped "innie" rather than the bulging "outie" you may have developed with the years? Of course fashion models whose bellies (as well as their faces) are their fortune request this surgery more often than the rest of us.

● *The only pants that fit me are riding jodhpurs—my thighs have true saddlebag bulges, and I'm desperate to get rid of them. How does body surgery work?*

Body-sculpting surgery first came to prominence in this country via a *Vogue* article discussing the techniques of Rio's superstar surgeon Dr. Ivo Pitanguy, thigh, belly, and buttocks molder to the Jet Set. This type of surgery, unlike nose corrections or face lifts, is still surrounded by controversy. *The problem:* Are the results worth the scars that are an inevitable side effect of the procedures?

There is *no way* body molding, which is major surgery, will leave "invisible scars." An abdominal lipectomy (removal of gross excess skin and fat from the stomach region) is performed in the same manner that stretch mark removal is undertaken. As with any abdominal operation that involves major cutting, there will be discomfort following the procedure. Expect to stay in bed for two days. And, when you do get out of bed, you will have to walk around doubled over for an additional twelve days—the surgeon wants the scar to heal without break-open pressure being exerted on the wound. When you're in bed, you'll lie in a jacknife position (feet and head elevated by pillows) as long as practicable. For six weeks following surgery you must take it easy and avoid strain or exercise.

For bulging outer thighs or drooping buttocks, an incision is made in the buttock fold or the skin flap where the thigh meets the buttock. Excess skin and fat is trimmed away, and the "thinner" area is sewn together. Hopefully, the incision will be higher than the bottom of your bathing suit.

The scar will fade after several months, but it will still be visible. And they're not three-inch scars, but long incisions. As Dr. Weiner points out, the surgeon is working with tissue, bone, and fat—not sculpting with inert materials like clay, wood, stone—so perfection can't be guaranteed.

I think these body-sculpting procedures are highly overrated and should be considered last-ditch desperate measures only—the abdominal hanging apron surgery, buttock and thigh correction are major surgery, and that's serious business. You might be better off living with what you've got. One well-known cosmetic surgeon confessed that if he had his way he would never do below-the-waist body surgery again.

- *My lips look rubbery rather than sensuous. What can I do to make over my mouth?*

You can't choose a specific lip shape any more than you can select a certain style nose, but you can improve your mouth and bring it into harmony with the rest of your features. Full lips are associated with youth and are considered sexy, but truly bulbous lips are a cosmetic defect. Plastic surgeons can very effectively thin such lips, and because the incision is made within the mouth, the scar won't be visible.

If you have a gummy smile, an operative procedure devised in Paris may be for you: The surgeon makes an incision within the mucous membrane of the mouth, the upper lip muscles are detached from the jaw and the lip is allowed to drop down to a more pleasing (less gum showing) angle.

Your less-than-perfect mouth could really be an optical illusion caused by a receding chin, and silicone implants can correct this problem. (The silicone implant has many uses—it can even perk up a droopy penis! Yes, silicone is being used to correct impotence. But there *is* a tiny flaw, in case you're thinking of suggesting this option to a great and good friend: once implanted, the silicone causes a *permanent* erection. Though you may not consider this a drawback, the man might feel rather uncomfortable.)

If a Dick Tracy chin is your problem, aggressively protruding jaws can be corrected, too. If you decide to have this operation, be prepared to subsist on a liquid diet (your jaws/teeth are wired shut) for a month following the surgery.

● *My hands look like they should belong to the Ancient Mariner. Since I don't have a long gray beard or glittering eye, how do I make my hands look younger?*

Plastic surgery to get rid of excess skin on the hands is not recommended. Your hands' primary function is *function*. Any procedure (whether vein stripping or removal of wrinkled skin) that could possibly impair the mobility of your hands is not worth the cosmetic benefits.

Some doctors are experimenting with the injection of pure medical grade liquid silicone to plump up hands. Actually, only a handful of doctors in the whole United States are currently licensed by the FDA to experiment with liquid silicone, even though it's been used successfully in Europe for twenty years.

Liquid silicone is being employed to fill out facial wrinkles, too. But unless your doctor is highly skilled, you may not be pleased with the results. You don't want the silicone to pool up (causing a lumpy-looking forehead) or stray from the injection site. It seems to work best plumping up vertical grooves—between your eyebrows, the nose-to-mouth furrow. In these areas, many women are pleased with the results.

If you do opt for plastic surgery, consult a few doctors before making your final choice of surgeon. And, ask friends to recommend doctors they've heard give good results. If you personally don't know of any cosmetic surgeons, talk to those doctors on the teaching staffs of hospitals affiliated with well-known universities—they're usually most knowledgeable about all the latest techniques.

Three-Week
Makeover/Shapeover
Program

MAIN ACTIVITY. During each of the 21 days you'll be following this program, you will be asked to perform one activity geared to transform a specific face or body area. I've listed the time required to perform each of these rituals, so you can easily decide when to fit them into your individual schedule.

DAILY CHECK-OUT. In addition, there will be routines that must be made part of your daily calendar if you want to see results. These diet, exercise, and grooming reminders will be listed for you every day, so you won't forget their importance.

BEAUTY BONUS. Because I've gathered so many secrets from the experts, I've included extra beautifying activities you will want to try at your leisure in the days following your makeover.

Primal Scream Facial

TIME: 45 MINUTES

GET READY

Today I'm going to help rescue your skin by putting
your face into "group" therapy with my Primal Scream
Facial—a most successful salon deep-cleansing face
treatment for all skin types.

DAILY CHECK-OUT

If you're like me, you'd probably rather hang from your
manicured thumbs than estimate one more portion-size
serving or do one more deep-knee bend. That's why
I've given you fit-your-life-style diet and exercise re-
gimes that will produce results in three weeks.

Diet

Today, take the *Sacred Cow Vow*. You're not going to eat meat, you are going to follow the diet principles outlined in Chapter Four. *Weigh yourself*. You might as well learn this Bad News Basic up front!

Exercise

See what kind of shape you're in by taking the simple stamina-revealing tests listed in Chapter Three. Then, take your jump rope in hand and establish your own skip rope pattern and rhythm. Jump 25 times without stopping.

GET TO WORK. THE PRIMAL SCREAM FACIAL

1) First, remove makeup with Crisco vegetable shortening (it lubricates as it dissolves cosmetics), mineral oil, or your own cold cream.

2) Wash your skin with a gentle cooking cleanser: almond oil is effective and smells delicious. Or you might prefer sesame, avocado, peanut oil—whatever you have.

3) Steam open your pores. Put 2 tablespoons of camomile tea (or thyme, rosemary, whichever is your favorite) into a large pot of boiling water. (Herbs make inhaling the steam easier—and it smells nice.) Remove pot from stove, drape large towel over both your head and pot, making a "tent." Stay in this position for 10 minutes, making sure you don't put your face too close to the water. When you're finished, save the liquid for step 7. The steam will open your pores, getting your skin ready to . . .

4) *Spray* with your personalized pore-flushing formula:

DRY-TO-NORMAL SKINS: LEMON AND LIME FRESH-ENER. Combine ¾ ounce each of lemon and lime juice with 6 ounces water and ½ ounce of simple (not compound) tincture of benzoin, a preservative. If you want a nice minty color, add 5 drops green vegetable coloring. Shake, refrigerate in 8-ounce bottle.

OILY SKINS: HERBAL ASTRINGENT. Combine 1 ounce camomile, 3 tablespoons witch hazel, ½ teaspoon cider vinegar, 1 ounce peppermint herb, and ¼ ounce tincture of benzoin (optional—if you want to include a preservative). Boil the mixture in 8 ounces of water. Cool, add peppermint extract and a few drops of yellow coloring (both optional), and refrigerate.

TROUBLED SKINS: BLEMISH LOTION. Add ¼ teaspoon boric acid to the herbal astringent recipe.

How to spray? Simple. Just put your special formula in a plant spray or clean Windex bottle, hold 6 inches from face, and spray, spray, spray! This action flushes out pollution and makeup from pores.

5) Massage lightly, using your vegetable oil as a massage oil. Here's how: With fingertips, apply oil in circular motions all over the face. Apply to neck with upward and outward motions, starting at the base of the neck. Use small circular motions from the nostrils all the way up sides of nose, using both fingers simultaneously. Continue for a few minutes, till skin feels "relaxed."

6) Massage *honey and almond scrub* into skin with fingers and brush. This step is essential because it helps remove the "dead" surface skin layer that makes your complexion look muddy and lifeless. Here are two ways to make the scrub:

a) Use half of a small jar of cold cream as your base. Add to it one teaspoon honey. Whir slivered almonds in a blender till they're as fine as freshly ground pepper, mix with cold cream, and you have an inexpensive scrub-*cum*-cleansing grains.

b) If you're feeling ambitious, try this variation: Combine 4 ounces anhydrous lanolin, 2 egg yolks, 2 teaspoons honey, 2 teaspoons almond extract, 1 teaspoon lemon juice, ½ to 1 cup almond meal. Mix. If you like, add ½ tablespoon simple tincture of benzoin as a preservative. For further variety, substitute colloidal oatmeal (your drugstore has it), bran, or corn meal for the almonds.

To apply your finished scrub, massage into skin with fingertips, using technique you just learned.

For deeper cleansing, massage scrub into skin with a complexion brush for 5 minutes (in the salon we use an electric brush for this step). Leave the scrub in place for 5 to 10 minutes.

7) Cover with hot washcloth. With tongs, dip washcloth in your reheated steaming solution, drain cloth, place over scrub for 5 minutes. Remove all traces of scrub with tissue. Rinse washcloth and dip in steaming solution once more. Leave on face for a few minutes.

This brings us to the delicate question of blackhead removal. If you feel you can't leave it to chance, a dermatologist, or cosmetologist, extract with care. The steaming has softened your oil plugs. Now take a tissue, twine it around your index fingers, dip it in alcohol. If the nasties are ready to come out, a *gentle* squeeze (with your fingers about ¼ inch apart) should do it. Professional skin care people call it "lifting out"— that's how easily they should become dislodged. If you have to pry, your skin is becoming reddened, and you're leaving *nail marks* alongside the blackheads, forget it! You're doing more harm than good.

8) *Spray, spray, spray* with the special pore-flushing formula you used above.

9) Apply *draw-it-out* impurities masque, a strong face pack good for all skin types. Combine ½ cup brewers yeast (powder or flakes), 2 teaspoons witch hazel, a few drops of peppermint extract. Add enough water to form a paste, apply, let dry for 10 minutes. (If you already have a good strong masque, by all means use your own.)

10) Remove with cold water.

The Primal Scream Facial is one of the best treatments your skin will ever receive. Read the instructions twice, and you'll find it's really a super-easy, super-cleansing routine.

DAY
2

Nature and Nurture
Hair Treatments

TIME: 30 MINUTES

GET READY

Want to *really* get your head in shape? It may take more than one night to undamage your tangled psyche, but you can make a great leap forward by improving the quality of your hair. You look in the mirror and see drab, lifeless locks? You're not alone. Because so many women in our salons share this complaint, I have lots of information for you. Choose one of the treatments listed below—each is designed to get your hair on the road to health. Before you begin, try the strand test suggested in Chapter Two.

DAILY CHECK-OUT

Make sure you include diet and exercise in today's program.

Diet

Lean on the no-beef indulgence list in Chapter Four.

Exercise

Spend 5 minutes with your jump rope in the morning. In the evening, take a close look at your undressed body, see which areas you would like to improve. Turn to the Body Bulge Attack, Chapter Three, and ease into the specific trimming routine for your problem body spots.

GET TO WORK. NATURE AND NURTURE HAIR TREATMENTS

Something-for-Everyone Head-Mending Conditioner

Combine the following: ½ ounce condensed milk, 1 tablespoon citric acid crystals, 1 egg, 2 ounces water. Brush onto freshly washed, towel dried hair, leave for 30 minutes.

Variation: For more nourishment (which makes your hair look richer), add 1 tablespoon glycerine and 1 tablespoon wheat germ oil to the above.

Get-Happy Hair Rinse

People in mental institutions, people who are unhappy and depressed, always seem to have dull hair (your hair often reflects the state of your health). To get your *hair* out of the doldrums, follow your wash and conditioning routine with a rinse made from 1 tablespoon citric acid crystals and 4 ounces water. Leave on 30 seconds, rinse. The secret of this rinse is its acidic property.

Good Behavior Hair Rinse

If your hair has refused to shine since you passed your eighteenth birthday, try this one: Combine ½ cup apple cider vinegar and 2½ cups water. Leave on hair for 1 minute and rinse.

The odor bothers you? It will disappear when you rinse it out, but you can mask it by adding 5 drops of oil of cloves.

Caveat: Never pour straight vinegar on your head; it will strip the hair of essential oils.

Dandruff Rub-out

The following formula will help: Combine 5 tablespoons olive oil with a few drops of oil of rosemary. Comb through your clean hair. Cover your head with wax paper and a shower cap, or a Baggie. (The Baggie acts as a terrarium, helps keep moisture inside.) Leave on at least ½ hour; better still, sleep (alone preferably) with your head so encased. (Small warning: Don't use the 20-pound-turkey size Baggie. It may slip down over your nose, and when they find you in the morning they'll never believe it wasn't suicide!) Rinse with 2 ounces cider vinegar mixed with 2 ounces water. A teaspoon of your favorite cologne will help fade the smell.

Dry Hair Moisturizer

Towel blot hair. Combine 1 tablespoon citric acid crystals with 3 ounces of any protein conditioner. Leave on hair for 10 minutes. Massage 2 tablespoons mayonnaise into your hair, leave on an additional 3 minutes; rinse with cool water.

Permanent Rejuvenator

If your permanent is falling and with it your spirits, combine 1 tablespoon citric acid crystals, 4 ounces water, and 1 egg. Leave on hair 15 to 20 minutes and rinse . . . watch the bounce, curl, and resiliency return.

Odor Removers

To remove the odor of bleach, use your Get-Happy Hair Rinse. To remove all other processing odors, pour tomato juice through hair and rinse.

Off-with-the-Hair-Spray

Wash away clinging hair spray residue by combining 1 tablespoon baking soda and 6 ounces water. Work through hair and rinse.

The right conditioners and rinses can improve anyone's hair, and in this three-week makeover you'll be learning several additional helpful head treats.

3

Makeover Manicure (Including Nail Wrap Acrylic Application)

TIME: 1 HOUR, APPLICATION: 2 HOURS

GET READY

Fabulous, expressive hands begin with terrific nails. *Your* fingers look like they've done time in a Cuisinart food processor? Learn how to give yourself a professional manicure, and start building strong nails. The following nail wrap process costs $15 in a top New York salon ($5 for the manicure; $10 for a complete wrap job). For those of you who want long nails *now*, I've included instructions for applying acrylic nails, too—$35 *plus* if done professionally.

DAILY CHECK-OUT

Diet

Weigh yourself this morning, and on a regular every-other-day basis. Psychologically, it's easier to learn you've put on a pound or two than to schedule a *rare* weigh-in and suddenly find yourself over the limit for middleweights! Continue your *Sacred Cow Vow* of abstaining from beef, booze, and salt.

Exercise

Work out 5 minutes with your jump rope, gain greater proficiency with the exercises you've selected for your Body Bulge Attack. Complete all your exercises before you begin the manicure and nail-enhancing treatments scheduled for today.

GET TO WORK. THE MAKEOVER MANICURE

1) Wipe off all traces of old polish with cotton saturated in remover. Hold on nail about 15 seconds and polish will come off easier. Start at the base and work to the tip—this way, you won't push remover into the delicate cuticle.

2) Make sure hands are completely dry, then file with an emery board. The rules: *Don't* use a metal file; *never* file in the corners (you'll weaken the nail); file in one direction only—the shape you're aiming for is a squared oval.

3) Soak fingers in warm water and a mild, sudsy soap to soften the cuticle. (In some salons, we soak nails in heated hand lotion—try it.) Use nail brush to clean nails.

4) Dry your fingers and gently push back your cuticles using a small towel. Apply cuticle cream and continue to push back cuticles with an orangewood stick wrapped in cotton. The only cuticles you clip are the hanging, ragged edges. Leave firm skin alone.

5) Dip your cotton-wrapped orangewood stick in soapy water and gently clean under nails. You might want to dip the stick in hydrogen peroxide to further bleach the inside of the nail tip.

6) Always apply a protective base coat, so when you go *sans polish* your nails will look clear—not stained by old removed polish.

The Nail Wrap

Before I tell you how, let me tell you why. Wrapping protects your nails (along the edge and in the corners where they tend to break) by forming a paper cap over the nails. It helps prevent peeling, making your own nails stronger. If you're a biter, you won't like the taste . . . another plus.

In short, by protecting the tip, wrapping gives nails that never grow a chance. But you need some nail to wrap. If your nails barely extend beyond your fingertips, let them grow a bit first. One more point: Because the papers are so thin, the nails *do* breathe underneath, so the process isn't destructive to the nail. Here's how to do it:

1) You'll need coffee filter papers, or one of the nail mending kits now on the market. Cut a piece of filter paper in the size of a wedge that will fit over your nail. Soak it in liquid provided with kit and place over nail. The tip and corners should be covered for best results.

2) Let paper extend about ⅛ inch over the nail edge all around. Now, *tuck the end under,* smoothing into

THE NAIL WRAP

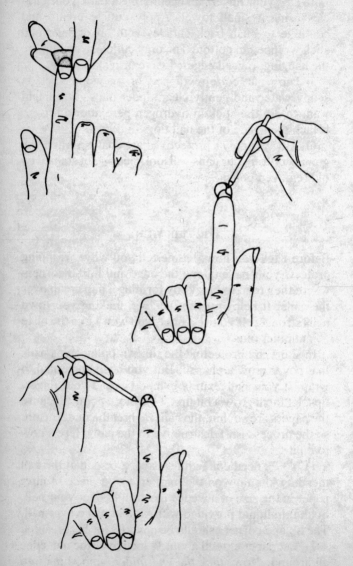

place with an orangewood stick. Dip stick in polish remover and work over nail to smooth out lumps. The paper should definitely extend *underneath* the nail edge; that's what helps strengthen nails.

3) Repeat this procedure for each nail, let dry, and apply coat of clear polish, making sure to polish over the nail edge.

4) Apply two coats of your favorite color, top with a sealer, and you've given yourself a salon-type treatment-plus-manicure.

Further Notes

If you don't want to nail wrap, give yourself a manicure once a week. Like a regular haircut, the scheduled manicure-nail trim seems to stimulate nail growth.

If you *do* nail wrap, a manicure *once* every 10 days—2 weeks is all that is necessary. Your polish will stay on longer. But, give yourself one new coat of nail enamel every night. Nail enamel protects and builds strong nails along with the paper.

Don't expect your first nail wrap to be perfection. It takes awhile to get the hang of it and achieve lump-free nails (you want to keep those papers smooth). But keep at it—it's a fabulous protective treatment.

Instant Gratification/Super Nails

Would you believe that in just two hours you can have nails long enough to satisfy the most demanding hand-fetishist (you know, the one who wants his back scratched before every meal). The secret: apply a little wizardry in the form of fool-everyone fakes. You can get kits to create them at cosmetic counters or drugstores.

I've been wearing acrylic nails for eight years now, and I asked my manicurist, Patty Milwaid, of The Nail Salon, in New York City, for a step-by-step description of how it's done. I'm giving you professional tips, but since materials vary with each manufacturer, follow package instructions, using the steps below as a guide.

1) *Prepping.* Proceed with a regular manicure, stopping before you apply a base coat. Examine your fingers—make sure your cuticles are healthy, there are no skin or nail injuries. Nails must be completely dry. Choose a "guide" (found in your at-home acrylic kit) that fits your finger and desired nail length and insert this mold around your nail, bending it so it will conform to your nail shape. The guide should fit snugly—you don't want the mixture to wind up on your skin.

2) *Roughing.* "Roughen" the nail by lightly stroking an emery board across it. Roughing helps the substance adhere better.

3) *Molding.* Mix the acrylic to the right texture (as indicated on package instructions), and brush over nail. This is where the artistry comes in: You now have to sculpt the material so it looks like the real thing. If you have a flat nail and would like a more arched look, you can add a thicker layer of acrylic (some call this nail building). You'll have to play around till you sculpt a nail that suits you. Work quickly to achieve the basic shape before your new nail dries.

4) *Breathing.* Cover the sides of the nail, but leave a space where the nail joins the cuticle. Acrylics don't allow your own nail to breathe, so you must leave the cuticle (or half-moon) area open to let in a little air. If you don't, the resulting "suffocation" may cause your own nail to grow improperly and your finger to blow up like a balloon.

SUPER NAILS

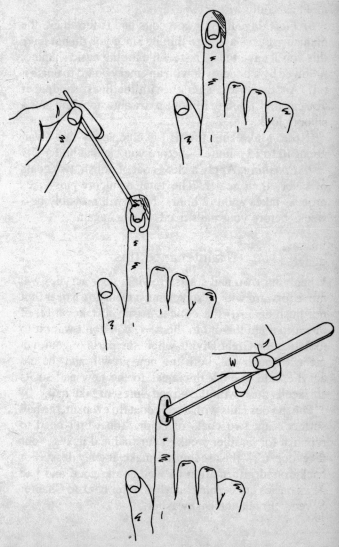

5) *Removing*. When the acrylic dries, remove the mold carefully with a tweezer.

6) *Finishing*. If your gorgeous nail is too thick, the manicurist uses a drill to thin it. Since you do not have this you'll have to use a steel file for the basic shaping, followed by a once-over with an emery board to finish it off. (Another trick: smooth with the finest sandpaper you can find.) Buff to remove extra abrasions and give a smooth look.

(Note: Make sure the nail is completely dry—wait about 10 to 15 minutes—before you file and buff.)

7) *Polishing*. Apply a clear coat of polish, two coats of color, then sealer. The total manicure-plus-fakes process takes about 2 hours, but it will probably be 3 weeks before your nails need "doing" again.

Maintenance Tips

When your own nail starts growing, your acrylics will move forward with it, so you must fill in down near (but not flush against) the cuticle. Again, it takes a bit of talent to meld the old to the new; you don't want it to look like the Great Divide where the parts of your nail meet. "Rough up" both the new growth and the old acrylic, add enough thickness to the new nail so its surface is flush with the already-present fake nail.

Polish your nails with a base coat (to even out the nail surface) and two coats of color. You won't need to repolish for another week. Your real nail flexes, your fake doesn't—this seems to make it chip less. For background information as well as the good and bad news basics concerning acrylics, refer back to Chapter Seven, "Freelance Dishwasher."

Climate Control Face Care

TIME: 10 TO 15 MINUTES

GET READY

Today you're going to learn skin-saving routines tailored to help your skin survive, beautifully, in any climate. Choose the facial geared to your own personal living environment. Reserve the others for when you travel and need to know how to treat your skin when you're in a different environment.

DAILY CHECK-OUT

Diet

Review the Abstinence and Indulgence food lists suggested by Dr. Levine (Part II, Chapter Four, "America's Second Most Popular Indoor Sport"). No cheating!

Exercise

Do your 5 minutes with the jump rope (how many times can you skip without stopping . . . or without becoming rope-tied?) in the morning. If the weather is nice, start your jogging routine (see Chapter Three) outdoors. Though indoors *is* just as effective, you may find it so rat-in-the-maze boring going round and round, you'll quit before you ever experience a jogging "high."

Grooming

If you gave yourself a regular manicure or nail wrap yesterday, add one coat of polish today. The enamel gives further protection against the "breaks" that keep nails from growing.

GET TO WORK. CLIMATE CONTROL FACE CARE

To paraphrase: You are where you live as well as what you eat, so the cosmetologists who staff my salons have different tricks to tone up skin in different parts of the country. I adopted these professional ideas for home use.

Big Apple Booster (Pollution Purifier)

If you live in New York or any large urban center, you've got to rid your skin of contaminating pollution (the sulfur dioxide in the air can eat away solid granite). Follow your usual cleansing routine, then use this slough-off to remove polluted surface skin and make way for the good skin below.

Combine ½ tablespoon epsom salts with the same

amount of table salt and drop the mix in a cup of hot water. Rub it into your face with the fingertips (avoiding the eye area) and you've performed a successful dermabrasion, an expensive dermatological skin-sloughing procedure.

Rinse and follow up with a mild astringent to "close" the pores.

The Sun-Scorcher

The perfect treat for those who live in a sizzling Sunbelt-type climate is the Penetrating Heat Pack. Place a small jar of opened Vaseline in the top of a double boiler; heat till warm and runny. Remove jar and massage contents liberally over face, cover with a piece of gauze, lie down and relax for 10 minutes. If your skin is dry as well as sun-struck, apply a warm heating pad (lowest setting) over the gauze to help insure rapid absorption (this step takes the place of our salons' electric heat masque). Try this treatment on any sun-exposed area of the body.

Windy-City Face Warmer

The biting cold known to Chicagoans and those in the Midwest in winter can be aging as well as drying. It also toughens the horny layer of the skin. To slough off this outer layer, work cleanser into your face with a gentle complexion brush moved in a circular motion. Follow the brush-boost with an herbal steam wrap: Steam over a pot as you did in the Primal Scream Facial, Day 1. Then, dip a washcloth into pot with tongs, wring out, and lie down with the heated square on your face for 10 minutes.

Sunset Strip

The road to hell *may* be paved with good intentions, but the freeway to Hollywood is *definitely* littered with complexion casualties. The villain: smog. To combat the soot and fog, you'll want a gritty cream to use as a sloughing preparation. Try this quick smog and dead cell lift-off: mix ½ tablespoon natural sea salt with 4 tablespoons Crisco or cold cream. And, don't leave home without a skin survival kit: A cleanser and freshener you can whisk over your face when the smog starts settling on your skin. If too much sun is aging your "California Girl" skin, try the Vaseline heat treat recommended for Sun Belters.

Rocky Mountain High

You don't have to live in Denver to be a ski fan—and to know what the dry winds of the slopes can do to your skin. Slather yourself in moisturizer, protect your face with makeup, and consider this après-ski masque: Combine 2 tablespoons mayonnaise, ¼ teaspoon alum (buy in drugstore), 2 tablespoons finely chopped (use your blender) almonds, and 1 drop peppermint extract. Store in the fridge ½ hour before using. Massage into face, and leave on for 10 to 15 minutes.

If your skin is thin and fragile, substitute 1 teaspoon lemon juice for the almonds. And if you're planning on spending your evenings sitting by the fire with the ski instructor, don't get too close to the blaze. Thin skin is prone to broken blood vessels (which means spidery red lines); heat exposure can cause the dilated vessels to pop.

Just Deserts

If you live in the sun-drying, desert-like climate that characterizes much of the West and Midwest in summer, you want to bring the moisture to your skin that the parched air won't provide. *A weekly head-over-kettle steaming is essential*. So is a refreshing gel masque: Take one package of lemon gelatin and substitute lemon juice for half the water required. Let it gel in the refrigerator until firm enough to coat face, then apply as a masque. After 10 minutes, remove with cool water. Your skin will feel refreshed, and there won't be any after-masque tightness.

Match up the climate in your home town with the environmental correctors listed above, then use the cleansing and conditioning routine that best fits your needs.

BEAUTY BONUS: THE TAILORED TREATMENTS

If you have a very specific skin or hair problem, you need to supplement your climate-control regimen with tailored treatments that will attack your particular problems. Try a tailored hair treat tonight, and save the facials for when your skin needs special help.

TAILORED HAIR TREATMENTS

Dry Scalp Moisture Treatment

Shampoo and towel blot hair. Mix 1 ounce glycerine with ¼ ounce apple cider vinegar and apply to scalp with Q-tips.

Leave on 10 minutes, rinse with citric acid rinse (Day 2). (This is a terrific soother for sunburned scalp and hair.)

Dry Hair Booster

Shampoo and towel blot hair. Combine 2 ounces wheat germ oil and 2 ounces vegetable oil. Heat till warm. Work through hair and cover head with a giant Baggie. The moisture will be sealed inside, where it will work wonders on hair.

Leave in place for 15 minutes. Rinse well, and follow with the citric acid rinse (see Day 2).

Egghead Damaged Hair Treat

Combine 1 tablespoon wheat germ oil and 1 tablespoon glycerine with a well-beaten egg. Warm the mix gently in the top of a double boiler, apply to hair and leave on 30 minutes.

Rinse with cool water and follow with the good-for-everyone citric acid rinse found in Day 2.

Body Building Shampoo (For Limp Hair)

Dissolve 1 packet gelatin in ½ cup boiling water. Add the amount of shampoo you would normally use for one soap, and let the concoction cool.

Shampoo in, remove, and rinse as usual.

Superior Natural Setting Lotion

Combine 1 packet dissolved gelatin (per package instructions) with ½ teaspoon lemon juice and 1 teaspoon light cologne.

Refer to these carefully tailored treatments whenever you've got skin or hair problems that need special attention.

TAILORED SKIN TREATMENTS

Oily Skin Cucumber Smash

Pulverize 2 cucumbers in blender. Mix with ½ teaspoon honey and 1 teaspoon witch hazel. Apply to face. Leave on 10 minutes. Rinse off. (Note: This facial provides excellent sunburn relief, too.)

Oily Skin Cuke Astringent

Put the cucumbers you used for the "Smash" in a cheesecloth. Strain. Take the remaining liquid and combine with enough water to equal 1 cup.

Let stand for 1 hour. Combine with 1 teaspoon witch hazel, and pour the whole into an 8 ounce bottle. Refrigerate before splashing on your face.

Cabbage Leaf Anti-Acne Skin Pack/Anti-Bacterial Masque

Soften cabbage leaves with vegetable oil or hot water. Let soak for an hour. Lay them flat on your face. Leave on at least ½ hour and follow with the Oily Skin Cuke Astringent (above).

If you have bad acne, soften the cabbage leaves in a boiled boric acid solution. (Cabbage has acidic qualities.)

Cabbage Cure Anti-Blemish Lotion

You'll need a vegetable juicer to prepare this one.

Put enough cabbage through your juicer to come out with 1½ ounces juice. Combine with ½ ounce simple tincture of benzoin and 6 ounces water.

Add a few drops of yellow vegetable coloring, and your favorite fragrant oil to counter the smell.

Dry Skin Cucumber Concoction

Follow steps 1–4 of the Primal Scream Facial (Day 1).

Skin a whole cucumber and slice into long strips. Press strips flat onto your face. Take gauze, dampen it in steaming solution, and wrap over cucumbers to keep them in place.

Leave on face for 10 minutes.

(Note: A slice of cucumber placed over each eye makes refreshing eye pad.)

Dry Skin Follow-up Freshener

Combine 1½ ounces cucumber liquid strained through cheesecloth with ½ ounce simple tincture of benzoin, 6 ounces water, and 5 drops green vegetable coloring.

Refrigerate. Use whenever skin needs a lift. (Important: A freshener has no alcohol, so it won't dry skin. Astringents do contain alcohol. Make sure you understand the difference.)

Amazing Pore Masker

If you're troubled by large pores, make this tonight.

Mix ½ cup quick rolled oats with 8 ounces buttermilk. Let sit for 10 hours in the refrigerator.

Strain through strainer or cheesecloth.

Keep strained mixture on face for 25 minutes; rinse with cool water and blot with ice cubes.

5

The Personalized Pedicure

TIME: 45 MINUTES

GET READY

I wonder if Paris realizes what it's done to our feet: platforms, knee-high skintight boots, *le western* cowboy boot. When I look inside my European-made shoes for the name of the designer, I always expect that illegible foreign script to read: Made by the Marquis de Sade!

Because I do so many personal appearances where I stand on my feet for 10 hours a day, I consider myself an authority on aching feet. You know that if your feet hurt it's reflected in your face . . . constantly grimacing in pain is *not* a recommended facial expression. Today, learn some terrific treatments that will help you revive tired feet and cure hurting feet.

DAILY CHECK-OUT

Diet

Weigh yourself this morning, make an interesting beef-less dinner tonight.

Exercise

No matter how tired you are, don't skip your skip rope. It should become a daily ritual—like brushing your teeth. (It doesn't take much longer.) Tonight, *double* your Body Bulge Attack . . . you've got to work up a sweat to work off the fat.

Grooming

Add another coat of nail polish to your manicure-wrap. Suggestion: Schedule your pedicure after your exercise routine. You'll feel doubly terrific.

GET TO WORK. THE PERSONALIZED (SALON-STYLE) PEDICURE

Before you even start your pedicure, take this true-false test to see if your feet are ready to be bared in public:

The Sandal-Foot Test

- You're sitting with your lover on the couch; you'd let him hold your hand, would never let him do the same to your foot.   T__ F__
- In all your sexual fantasies, you're always wearing tennis sneakers and sweat socks.   T__ F__
- You've given great thought to how Hopalong Cassidy got his name.   T__ F__

Cure your foot-inhibitions by making your feet as attractive as the rest of you.

1) Remove old polish from toenails.

2) Cut nails straight across. Cutting into corners encourages the development of ingrown toenails; so does trimming nails too short.

3) File nail edges till smooth (so they won't snag pantyhose.)

4) Soak feet in shallow basin filled with warm, soapy water for 3 minutes. Scrub toe region with soapy nailbrush. Remove feet and dry.

5) Apply *Foot Pumice Paste:* Mix 3 ounces epsom salts, 3 ounces table salt, and 3 ounces bicarbonate of soda with small amount of water to form a paste. Massage into feet and legs for 10 minutes. The paste sloughs off dead skin. (If you have varicose veins, don't give yourself *any* leg massage.) Rinse with lukewarm water, towel dry.

6) Treat your feet to the *Fragrant Foot Bath:* In a basin filled with warm water, pour 6 ounces epsom salts and 3 ounces bicarbonate of soda *or* 3 ounces boric acid. Add 6 ounces pine oil, cologne, or fragrant bath oil. Soak feet for 10 minutes, towel dry.

7) Push back cuticles with cotton-tipped orange-wood stick. Only ragged, hangnail-type cuticles should be removed.

8) Give your feet the *Magnificent Massage:*

a) Slather feet with emollient hand or body cream or Vaseline.

b) Sit in comfortable position (on bed or floor) that allows you to hold one foot in both hands.

c) Grab your foot, flex it toward, then away from you (6 times).

d) Squeeze each toe, holding for a count of three. Release and flex individual toes toward, then away from you. Rotate each toe in a circular motion.

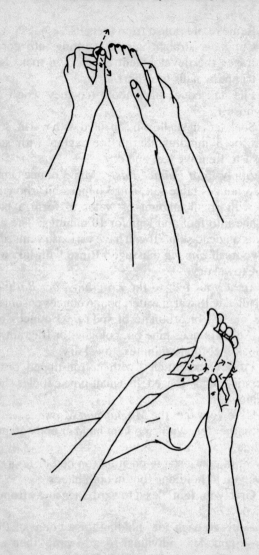

e) Work your fingers into position between each toe. Bend toes forward and back.

f) Hold your foot so it's facing you, with your thumbs on the sole of your foot. Thumb-massage the bottom of your foot in a circular motion.

g) Extend leg away from you. "Lasso" foot in your pedicuring towel. Use the towel to briskly massage the bottom of the foot: Grasp one end of towel in each hand, move it quickly back and forth till your foot feels warm.

h) Repeat entire procedure with other foot.

i) Stand up. "Shake out" each foot for a few seconds.

9) Remove cream with small towel you've heated over steaming kettle. Make sure you leave no trace of the cream on toenails.

10) Put a small piece of cotton between each toenail (or weave a folded tissue between the toes), enough to hold the toes apart so you can polish without smearing.

11) Apply base coat, two coats of color, one coat of sealer. You've completed your Personalized Pedicure.

12) Elevate your feet while your toenails dry.

BEAUTY BONUS: JUST FOR YOUR FEET

Check out this terrific collection of foot soothers, perfect for those fair ladies who sing, "I could have hobbled (rather than danced) all night."

Fetal Foot Wrap

For those days when you're ready to crawl feet first back into the womb: Heat enough olive oil (in a Pyrex dish) to cover your feet. Massage in oil thoroughly, up to and including ankles. Wrap hot wet towel (wring out till just damp) around each foot. Leave in place 10 minutes.

Herbal Waterfall

To revive tired feet, try this soothing brew: Mix a handful of your favorite herbs (camomile is terrific, so is rosemary) with a few drops of fragrant oils (i.e., sage, jasmine, mint, musk). Enclose in a cheesecloth and tie to the faucet in your bathtub, directly in the path of the water. Sit on side of tub, turn on the hot water, place your feet beneath for 5 minutes. Rinse with cool water.

Natural Foot Rinse

Drop 1½ cups cider vinegar and ½ cup lemon juice into foot basin filled with tepid water. Submerge your feet and relax.

For Yourself Foot Powder

Combine the following and dust over feet: ½ cup talcum, ½ cup bicarbonate of soda, 1 teaspoon witch hazel, 1 teaspoon cologne or fragrant oil. (This is a good odor absorber.)

All-Through-the-Night Foot Masque and Hard Skin Softener

Apply warm, runny Vaseline (heated in a double boiler) to your feet. Massage into skin. Cover feet with thin, inexpensive white cotton socks, and don't remove till morning.

The Sensuous Milk Farm

When F. Scott Fitzgerald wrote "the rich are different from you and me," he could have been describing their ability to spend $100 a day at de luxe health spas. No, you can't quite duplicate the luxe milk farm atmosphere in a studio apartment or in a house full of children . . . but you *can* incorporate some spa routines into your weekend existence.

For Days 6 and 7, I'm going to give you a whole variety of treats that duplicate expensive spa treatments. They're all based on the beautifying good health that's packed in cream, yogurt, eggs, honey and milk (everyone knows Cleopatra bathed in the stuff, probably with Marc Antony right beside her).

But remember, "food" recipes are as perishable as they are rich. Store them in the refrigerator and use as soon as possible to insure freshness. Whole milk helps under-forty dry skin, heavy cream or half-and-half (expensive, use only for facials, not baths) will fight over-forty dryness, skim milk aids oily skin. Protein-rich yogurt is good for all skins, helps thicken masques, and has anti-bacterial properties. The easiest and most economical way to make milk baths and masques is to use powdered milk. I've indicated when to use liquid or powder. Sour cream soothes dry skin.

6

Super Milk Farm Face Treat

TIME: 15 TO 30 MINUTES

GET READY

Take some time out of your busy weekend schedule to immerse your face and body in natural milk-based beautifiers; I've got two super treatments planned for you.

DAILY CHECK-OUT

Diet

Weekends bring all kinds of temptations . . . don't fall off the wagon! Dinner in a restaurant needn't add on the calories; stay away from heavy sauces, order your chicken or veal *au naturel,* eat fruit for dessert. Don't be afraid to tell the waiter you're on a diet; you'll find most good restaurants perfectly willing to adjust dishes to your taste (they'd rather you'd eat pickingly in *their* bistro than dine at home). As a rule of thumb, always leave something over on your plate. And, if the choice of a restaurant is left to you, *don't* suggest that American favorite, the steakhouse. When surrounded by all that beef, you may find it hard to stick to the Sacred Cow Vow.

Exercise

I'm assuming you've spent the last 5 days with your jump rope . . . it should be getting easier to prolong the skipping now. The weekend is also the best time to jog. Remember, no one's clocking you, and though you may feel self-conscious at first, no one's paying any attention to you, either. With some millions of joggers out there, you're *not* a unique phenomenon.

Grooming

I repeat: Don't forget your daily one-coat of nail enamel.

GET TO WORK. SUPER MILK FARM FACE TREAT

If you were spending $100 a day at a real milk farm, you'd expect more than a facial or two. For a considerably smaller investment (would you believe pennies?) the treatment you're about to perform contains a variety of proven complexion-boosting steps. I've reworked Day 1's Primal Scream Facial, incorporating milk-product formulas (rich in vitamin A, the skin-nourishing vitamin) for you to try and enjoy.

1) *Cleanse* with one of the formulas below. Use the appropriate one for your skin type.

NORMAL: Blend the contents of one vitamin A capsule into ½ cup yogurt.

DRY: Substitute ½ cup sour cream for the yogurt.

OILY: Mix buttermilk with enough table salt to make a grainy scrub (buttermilk is also a gentle skin lightener).

BLEMISHED SKIN: Add 3 tablespoons pulverized almonds (or almond meal) to ½ cup yogurt; massage into face. No matter which formula you choose, rinse with cool water.

2) *Steam* open pores (check the Primal Scream Facial, Day 1, for directions).

3) *Milk Rain Spray.* Fill your spray bottle with one of the following soothing liquids, one for each skin type.

NORMAL: ½ cup cold skim milk mixed with ½ cup cool camomile tea.

DRY: ½ cup cold milk and ½ cup rosewater mixture.

OILY: 2 tablespoons liquid skim milk, 2 tablespoons lemon juice, 2 tablespoons witch hazel, 1 cup camomile tea (brewed to triple its drinking strength). To prepare, mix lemon juice with the hot tea. Add skim milk, heat on very low flame in double boiler. Refrigerate when cool. Note: The color of camomile tea may not be esthetically pleasing, but camomile's been known as a skin soother, and all around beauty potion—it colors hair, and acts as a mild laxative and soporific—practically forever.

4) *Massage lightly* with heavy cream (follow the Primal Scream light massage steps, Day 1).

5) *Sloughing Scrub* (to remove dead surface cells and let young new skin shine through). The following is a handled mini-scrub "machine" that's easy to make:

Squeeze out the juice from half a small lemon, save for another use. Remove the pulp. Mix 2 tablespoons yogurt with the "dried" pulp and enough crushed almonds, cornmeal, or oatmeal to make the brew gritty. Return the thick, pasty scrub to the lemon rind, making sure the rind is packed full. Wrap the whole in wet cheesecloth. Secure with a rubber band. Now, work this mildly abrasive tool over your face for 5 minutes.

6) *Remove* traces of Scrub with hot, damp washcloth.

7) *Spray* again with the Milk Rain Spray suited to your skin type.

8) *Masque-it*. Finish your Super Milk Farm Face Treat with one of the many masques described below.

Milk 'n' Fruit Masques

In your blender combine enough powdered milk with any one of the following (remove skin first) to make a paste. The ingredients: ½ ripe banana, ½ strained avocado, ½ fresh peach, 1 whole apricot. If your skin is oily, use a fruit with stringent properties instead: try ½ cup fresh or thawed frozen strawberries. Apply to face, leave 10 minutes, rinse.

Vegetable Smash Milk Masques

For oily, broken-out skin, combine enough powdered milk to make a paste with strained tomato pulp in your blender—it contains vitamin C and potassium, both good healers.

Carrot pulp (rich in vitamin A) or cucumber (the vegetable that made Nefertiti such a smash) combined with powdered milk are also nourishing face treats.

Leave in place 10 minutes, rinse.

Don't Hold the Mayo

You don't have to be a short-order cook to use mayonnaise to soften rough skin. Just massage into your face, let sit for 15 minutes, tissue off, and rinse. Mayonnaise is considered a beauty treatment because the egg supplies protein, vinegar helps skin maintain its acid mantle, vegetable oil adds lubrication. (Same treatment works wonders for hair for the same reasons.)

Good Night Skin Clarifier

If your complexion is muddy and murky, follow your final facial massage with a mix of ½ cup yogurt and 1½ teaspoons lemon juice. Apply. Leave on overnight for a gentle bleaching effect that will help banish drabness.

GET TO WORK. SWEET DREAMS MILK BATHS

Here are two milk-based delights. If you're troubled by dry, flaky skin, choose the first. If you just want to u-n-w-i-n-d, consider the alternative.

Sloughing Milk Bath

If your skin is scaly, take 3 quarts of hot milk (made from milk powder and boiling water—it's cheaper), combine with 8 ounces of salt and perfume it with a dash of your own bath oil or a few drops of mint or pine oil. Dump the brew into a tub of warm water, soak for 15 minutes, then the dead skin cells will easily slough off with a loofah or a Body Buf Puf. (Note: a loofah is a strong natural sponge, great for sloughing off roughened skin and bringing up a glow on soft skin. Make it part of your bath paraphernalia. Body Buf Puf is another excellent slougher and it's available in most drugstores.)

Good-Enough-to-Drink Bath (For Already Soft Skins)

Make 3 quarts of the boiling water-powdered milk mix as above. Instead of salt, add 1 cup of honey and 1 cup of strong camomile tea. Mix again, pour into tub, relax.

When you're bathing, tepid-to-warm water is the best de-tenser. Hot water may cause your blood vessels and capillaries to expand and can cause you to jump out of the tub in a sweat before your muscles have a chance to de-kink.

The Egg-and-I Milk Farm Hair Treat

TIME: 10 MINUTES

GET READY

Today, dairy delights for your hair and a delicious bath oil for you to make and use more than once.

DAILY CHECK-OUT

Diet

Weigh in this morning and note your progress. If you're following the diet strictly, you will start dropping the pounds.

Exercise

Since it's the weekend, no excuses for not jogging . . . or at least jumping rope. You should also continue your Body Bulge Attack, as outlined earlier for spot reducing in Chapter Three. And, remember: jumping rope will trim those hips and thighs, if you'll give it time.

Grooming

Another coat of nail polish.

GET TO WORK. THE EGG-AND-I: NOURISHING MILK FARM HAIR TREAT

Separate 2 eggs. Beat whites slowly till almost stiff. Mix well with enough shampoo for 2 applications. Apply half the mix, leave on head for 5 minutes. Rinse, then put egg yolks on head, massage into hair for 5 minutes. Use the second half of your egg white-shampoo mix. Rinse well and allow hair to dry *au naturel* till "wetness" is 90 percent gone—hair should never be styled until it is practically dry. Use your blow dryer to style.

Crème de la Crème Bath Oil Soak

The following will make 3 cups of bath oil, enough for six soaks. You'll need: 3 whole eggs, ½ cup yogurt, ¼ cup plus 1 teaspoon witch hazel, 2 tablespoons melted butter, ¼ cup plus 1 teaspoon corn oil, 1¾ cups whole milk, 1 teaspoon cider vinegar, 1 cup peach or apricot juice (best made if you have a juicer; otherwise mash in blender), a few drops of peach or apricot oil.

Melt butter and mix with corn oil. Let stand 1 hour. Mix eggs and stir gently. Add all ingredients one at a time to electric blender—adding 1 cup of milk last. Beat at low speed. Turn off blender and add last ¾ cup milk unbeaten. Stir and enjoy. Keep refrigerated for freshness. Shake and add ½ cup of this rich mix to your tub each time you soak.

It does take some effort to make this, but it would be *much* more expensive to buy an oil of this quality.

BEAUTY BONUS: THE "SUPER SIX" MILK FARM FACE TREATS

Here is an additional collection of face treatments for a variety of skin problems.

Keep Up the Good Work Masque

If you've got normal skin, try this egg-and-honey masque: Beat 2 egg whites till stiff, add a few grains of alum, and apply directly to face. Leave on 10 to 20 minutes. Rinse, dry face, then cover with organic honey. Leave for 5 minutes, rinse off, dry and finish with your favorite freshener.

Drinkable Dry Skin Masque

Combine 1 tablespoon powdered milk with 1 stiff egg white. Slowly mix in the egg yolk and 1 teaspoon honey. Apply, leave on for 5 minutes.

Edible Dry Skin Cream

Combine the juice of one strained cucumber with an equal amount of heavy cream. Apply, leave for 15 minutes, rinse. If you're under 35 but dry, use milk instead of cream.

Yogurt Surprise

For oily skin, mix 3 teaspoons plain yogurt, 1 teaspoon Fuller's earth, 1 egg white, and 1 teaspoon honey. Leave on face 10 minutes, rinse.

Aging Skin Fighter

Good for wrinkling skin that is no longer plagued by break-outs: Combine 2 teaspoons plain yogurt, ½ teaspoon honey, and ½ teaspoon lemon juice. Prick open 3 capsules of vitamin E (the equivalent of 300 units) and fold into the mix. Leave on skin for 15 minutes. I prefer adding E to the face when it's mixed into another medium . . . less likely to cause a skin reaction.

8

The Skin Ironing Face Treatment

TIME: 30 MINUTES

GET READY

Begin week two with another great salon face treatment that I've adapted for your home use. Even if the ingredients don't startle you, the results will. (By the time you finish this program you'll know so many facial tricks, I just may have turned you into a competitor!)

DAILY CHECK-OUT

Diet

If you've followed the Sacred Cow Vow faithfully for seven days, you should be feeling better as well as looking thinner. Many beefeaters report a bloated, full feeling after a heavy steak dinner; fish and veal are satisfying, and you needn't take a nap after every meal!

Exercise

You should be jumping with less of a huff-and-puff. Retake the recovery from effort tests outlined in Chapter Three. Notice the improvement. The increased stamina you feel while jumping may be the motivation you need to get out there and jog . . . it helps to know you won't drop from exhaustion after jogging for just one block.

Grooming

Take two minutes out for your hands and feet. One coat of polish on your manicured/wrapped nails (by now you realize the daily nail enameling is as important as your vitamin pill!). Check for corns and calluses on your toes—it's easier to attend to them while they're still small.

GET TO WORK. THE SKIN IRONING FACE TREATMENT

You'll need 3 eggs, a facial pumice (3 M's Buf Puf Sponge), vegetable oil, cornmeal paste (if your skin is oily), complexion brush, a toy doll's iron (from toy store or the five and dime) or metal kitchen spatula, a small paint brush. I told you the ingredients would startle you, but what I've done is taken my salon treatment specifically designed to retexturize and renew spoiled city skin—and adapted it so you can try it *chez vous*.

We have introduced this treatment to our sophisticated European customers who love it because it's based on bits and pieces of principles they've seen practiced for years. The "skin ironing" you'll be performing is based on three beauty ideas from other times, other places, updated for today:

Ancient Egypt. Those clever Egyptians not only invented the art of mummifying and embalming, they were also interested in preserving the living. Witness the Wax Masque—a skin clarifier beloved by such as Cleopatra and Nefertiti.

Old Rumania. Bet you didn't know that Rumania, renowned as the home of Dracula, also saw the initiation of skin ironing, a wonder-working treatment performed over the wax (using paraffin only) to help soften incipient wrinkles and fine, dry skin lines.

Ultramodern Switzerland. In the pampered rejuvenation clinics of the rich/chic, the skin peel-off is a way of life. We do it with organic substances hard to duplicate at home. You'll do it with egg white.

Now that I've explained why, here's how:

1) *Cleanse* skin with mild, non-oily cleanser.

2) *Embryonic Peel-Off*. Crack open 3 eggs, remove the contents, and store for cooking. You're interested in the shells. Carefully peel off the membrane clinging tenaciously to the inside of the shells—try to remove it in large pieces. Smooth in place all over face, concentrating foremost on lined areas, large pores on inner cheeks, chin, nose. Leave in place till it dries, but can still be peeled off.

3) *Skin polishing/peel removal*. If your skin is oily, remove the egg membranes by gently polishing face with a Buf Puf. The rubbing action simulates a pumice effect—sloughs off dead cells. If your skin is dry, coat face with light layer of vegetable oil before using Buf Puf.

4) *Skin feeding*. If your skin is oily, apply a paste made of cornmeal and water. Massage with complexion brush and remove. If your skin is dry, apply vegetable

oil instead of paste, massage in with complexion brush, leave in place.

5) *Paraffin heat treatment* (Wax Masque). If skin is dry, make sure your vegetable oil base, step 4, is still in place. Melt paraffin in top of double boiler till it is of liquid consistency. Apply to face with paint brush. It should still be warm, but hold the brush away from face until you're sure paraffin isn't so hot it will burn your skin. Apply generously—warm paraffin forms a thin seal that precisely pinpoints lines, wrinkes, and blemishes by exaggerating their presence. It also helps melt sebaceous oils.

6) *Skin Ironing* (to be done over your paraffin wax masque). Heat your toy mini-iron (or metal spatula) by running the base of the iron across a pot of hot water (don't submerge the whole thing) until *just warm* to the touch, *not too hot*. Or rest iron on heating pad until warm. Press gently over whole face, concentrating on trouble spots—lines, wrinkles, bumps. Why iron over the masque? Heat is a great skin helper, but it would be too harsh if applied directly to skin. (The paraffin acts as a protective buffer between iron and skin.)

Work with the iron for 5 minutes, making sure it keeps warm to the touch, but not hot, and you'll be accomplishing the following: If your complexion is lined and dry, the iron helps penetrate the oil base deep into your skin. If you have problem skin or oily skin the heat will loosen the impurities and bring them toward the surface, where they'll stick to the wax masque.

7) *Pull off* wax in big pieces as soon as it solidifies—a few seconds after the ironing. You'll see imbedded within the skin debris, pollution, and stale makeup that normal cleansing just can't remove.

8) *Rinse* with cold water, and follow with freshener or astringent.

Highlight Your Hair— How to Henna

TIME: 1 HOUR

GET READY

To give a dramatic lift to your appearance, improve that most easily changeable part of your body—your hair. By adding highlights where none exist, or going a shade or two lighter or darker, you can project a more glamorous, together image.

Learn how to choose and use mistake-proof hair coloring by carefully re-reading Chapter Six, "Color Yourself Super"—it's a concise coloring primer, filled with tips that will enable you to select the right product for the effects you're seeking. Application instructions are included with every brand-name kit you can buy. Follow them carefully.

Which hair coloring process do I suggest? Either temporary rinses, semi-permanent colorings, or (if you're feeling adventurous) henna. I've explained about temps and semis and introduced you to henna in Chapter Six.

If you're one of the many women who want to heat up your hair color with henna, today's step by steps will show you how to successfully use this ancient, popular-again, natural coloring agent.

DAILY CHECK-OUT

Diet

Weigh yourself first thing this morning (you're doing this every other day, right?). Invite a meat-and-potatoes fan to dinner, serve neither. As a Sacred Cow believer, you've got to deprogram those friends who have been brainwashed into becoming part of the "meatloaf majority."

Exercise

If you're jumping rope with greater ease, start building up your skipping program. Tonight, go for 6 minutes instead of 5. A kitchen timer is essential—set it, then forget about checking your watch or clock; just stop when the bell rings.

GET TO WORK. HIGHLIGHT WITH HENNA

First, and most important, read all about henna in the mini-encyclopedia, Chapter Six. You can't use henna if your hair is more than 15 percent gray or if your hair has been bleached or permanented. If you're looking to become an ash blond—forget it! Henna doesn't penetrate the hair shaft, so it won't lighten (the brightening property comes from henna's ability to stain the hair with color).

Do consider henna if you want *additional body, high-shine color* that will fade gradually, leaving *no obvious root line*. If you're looking for a dramatic color change, use traditional coloring agents; henna's effects are difficult to control—if you're making a major color switch, you want to be able to predict as near as possible exactly the shade you'll wind up with.

Now that I've reviewed a few do's and don'ts, here's how to henna.

Color Selection

Today, henna means more than red. There are black, brown, and neutral hennas on the market. Just remember you're looking for *natural* (pure, organic, vegetable) henna (not the compound variety), preferably from Iran.

Connoisseurs claim that Iranian—or Persian—henna, like Iranian caviar, is superior. For your first try, choose the color closest to your natural shade—you don't want to do anything drastic; henna is difficult to remove.

The color you wind up with depends on the color of your own natural hair, plus the henna shade you choose:

Neutral henna gives body and shine, won't change natural hair color.

Red, black, and *brown* add the highlights and shades their names imply.

If nothing less than plum- or wine-colored hair will suit you, it's worth the $25 to $50 investment a professional will charge.

Hair Condition

As is true of any hair coloring, henna will take better on hair that is in good condition. It will be more unpredictable on porous or damaged hair; works best on a nice tight cuticle. So, make sure you've been washing your hair with acid-based shampoos and feeding it with protein conditioners before henna time. Don't henna if there are cuts or sores on your scalp.

APPLICATION

1) Buy natural henna. *Follow manufacturer's directions exactly*.

2) Get a friend to help. Though the henna makers don't say this is essential, you will be sectioning your hair—and four hands are better than two.

3) Protect your hairline skin with a coat of petroleum jelly—though Moroccans stain hands and feet with henna for special occasions, you're not interested in tattooing your forehead and temples.

4) Always mix the henna powder in a glass bowl—nothing metallic. Most manufacturers say to mix with hot water to make a paste. Mix till it forms creamy, not runny, consistency. If it gets too thick while you're working with it, add a little extra hot water.

5) Start by brushing paste onto scalp at rear of head, painting henna from root to ends. Continue parting and sectioning till whole head is covered.

6) Take a wide-tooth comb and work through hair to make sure you've got good coverage. Hair should be encased in a thick (not drippy) henna pack.

7) Wrap your henna-packed head in tin foil. Cover hairline with cotton and cover the whole with a plastic bag or shower cap.

8) Follow instructions for processing time and technique; some hennas require that you sit under a hair dryer, others don't. Processing takes at least 30 minutes; often, closer to an hour. Henna can't be rushed. If you leave it on for just a little time results won't be noticeable. The longer it stays on your head, the deeper the color becomes.

9) Rinse according to manufacturer's instructions. Here's where it really pays to have a friend available. Rinsing off your gloppy henna pack is an extremely messy job and you have to get rid of *all* traces of the henna.

Hints from the Pros

Henna is a cleanser and conditioner as well as a coloring agent. You don't have to wash your hair first; wash with an acid based shampoo afterward.

If you don't like the smell of henna, combine 1 ounce of lemon juice with 4 ounces cold water. Pour on hair, and don't bother rinsing out. The lemon juice is acidic and will help close the cuticle.

After you've used henna a few times successfully, you may want to customize your treatment.

If you're using neutral henna to give your hair a body and shine boost, mix in a whole egg—you'll get even more spectacular conditioning results.

To increase red highlights in dark brown hair, boil tea, remove the bag and let the liquid cool to the proper temperature. Use the tea instead of the plain hot water required.

For slight blonding, add lemon juice to a light brown henna.

Consider adding a dash of spice to the powder. Ginger is said to bring red highlights to brown henna; red pepper imparts a bright auburn glow. If you know anyone from Egypt, India, Iran, Morocco or Israel, ask them to ask their mothers for henna recipes. Women, men, and *horses* (their tails were dyed) have been using henna for some 2,000 years in these cultures, and know how to create special effects.

To deepen black henna still further, substitute strong coffee for the plain water required.

If you've got dark hair and are afraid the auburn highlights you seek may turn a metallic red, use less henna, more water.

Never use henna on hair that has been subjected to a metallic dye.

Henna Softening

You say you aren't satisfied? Removing henna is extremely difficult and not always possible. You may have to wait for it to wear out. In any case, you can't use the traditional chemical dye solvents. One manufacturer of natural henna says to slip into your rubber gloves once more, cover the hair with a generous supply of hot—not scalding—mineral oil and work the oil carefully through the hair. The oil slides under the henna, so henna theoretically slips off the hair shaft. Rinse; check whether you've removed enough. If not, oil again, rinse, and check again. When the shade is lightened to a color you can live with, rinse out and shampoo.

Another pro suggests coating dry hair with rubbing alcohol. Let it "marinate" for 5 minutes, then cover the alcohol with castor oil, coating hair completely. Cover your head with a Baggie, sit under the dryer for 20 minutes. Next, apply a concentrated shampoo to the castor oil (don't add water), work up a lather and let sit for 2 minutes. Rinse, rinse, rinse.

How About a "Hennicure"?

You know that hair and nails are both made largely of protein. And, since henna does such wonderful conditioning things to hair, it's natural that it can help strengthen and condition nails, too. To give yourself a hennicure (either mani- or pedi-) make up a small batch of *neutral* henna. Don't use a *colored* henna—you'll stain your nails. Coat bare finger- or toenails (including the cuticle) for 5 minutes. Rinse and continue with your favorite nail processes.

Removing Unwanted Hair

TIME: 15 MINUTES TO 1 HOUR

GET READY

Everyone is a little furry; how much excess hair you've got is a matter of degree. Today I'll give you the how tos of hair removal, as well as some soothing *après* treatments.

DAILY CHECK-OUT

Diet

If your urge to consume a side of beef is getting uncontrollable, consider liver for dinner—it's packed with good health. Just don't smother it with bacon!

Exercise

Keep on hopping, and do your trimming Body Bulge Attack.

Grooming

If your nail wraps feel like they're still in good shape under all that polish, take off nail enamel gently with a polish remover . . . you can do it without disturbing the wraps. Then simply re-manicure over them. If nail wraps look like they've had it, your polish remover makes them slip off easily. Remove wraps *and* polish, let your nails breathe for a day. You took the trouble to put on acrylics? They should still be in good shape.

GET TO WORK. GETTING OFF THE HAIR

Waxworks: What You Should Know

Waxing is a very important salon service. When done properly, there is minimum pain. I wax off the hair from my upper lip, eyebrows, arms, hands, and bikini line. Other possibilities include legs, stomach, under arms, and the nape of the neck. If you want to try it at home (much less expensive—leg waxing can cost $25 in a salon), you probably won't get as clean a result as the professional, but you will get rid of unsightly hair, and it will stay off your legs from 5 to 6 weeks; your face from 3 to 4 weeks. I think it's a worthwhile effort, especially in summer when your legs are on display.

Here's what you have to know:

TYPES. There are two kinds of wax available (at your

drugstore) for home use: hot and cold. No matter which type you use, wax is always smoothed on in the direction of hair growth and pulled off in the opposite direction.

Hot wax usually comes in cake form, looking like a bar of soap. Gently heat it till it reaches a runny consistency. It's most important to test the wax on a small area of your body to make sure it isn't *too hot*. Home disasters occur not from allergic reactions to the material itself, but from burns caused by swathing too-hot wax on the skin. When the wax starts to harden, you tug at it, pulling in the opposite direction to remove.

Cold wax comes imbedded in sheets of tape or paper. You open the sheet, smooth it wax-side-down onto the surface you want de-fuzzed, get a grip on the sheet and pull—again, in the opposite direction to hair growth.

I feel that cold wax is not as efficient as hot, especially if you're very hairy. But it is easier to use than hot wax.

No matter which kind you use, follow manufacturer's instructions *explicitly*. If you're doing it yourself, be *very* careful—this is not something for an inexpert teenager to try. It's a good idea to have it done once professionally so you'll see exactly how it's handled.

The first time you wax, test an inconspicuous area of your leg, just to see how you'll react. The most sensitive areas are the upper lip, under arms, and bikini area.

When waxing the hair above your lip, don't let any wax drip onto the lip itself. You might wind up tearing the delicate lip skin while removing the wax.

Wax only healthy skin. Avoid broken out, irritated, bruised, sunburned, chapped, or cut skin. Stay away from warts and moles (this is sound advice for any hair removal process).

If you wax your underarms (you're braver than I am!), don't use an antiperspirant for two days following the procedure. Use witch hazel instead.

Everyone's skin turns somewhat red after waxing; this reaction should fade in an hour. Women with sensitive skin may stay red overnight (these super-sensitives should avoid the use of deodorant soaps or any abrasives for several days).

You'll have best results if you allow leg and body hair to grow to ¼-inch; the wax needs enough hair to grip.

Waxing

1) Cleanse area to be waxed with witch hazel, applied with a clean cotton ball.

2) Dry skin thoroughly and dust lightly with talcum powder.

3) Make sure your face is devoid of creams or makeup.

4) Your skin must be gripped taut with your opposite hand as you remove the wax—give one good tug and pull it off in one quick stroke. This is the least painful, most effective method. A series of tiny little tugs prolongs the agony.

5) *Lip waxing.* Apply wax on one side of the mouth, in a diagonal line from below the nostril to the outer corner of the lip. Hold skin below the corner of the lip firm; remove wax quickly in an upward stroke. Now, do the other side of the lip. When you remove wax, quickly put your finger over waxed area and apply pressure; this helps prevent water blisters. Finger pressure should be applied over *any* just-waxed area.

6) *Chin hair.* Again, do one side first. Apply fresh wax to the opposite side. Grasp your skin under the neck to hold taut while you pull.

7) *Eyebrows*. Use just a little wax and a wooden orangestick or toothpick to apply the wax.

8) *Nape*. Short haircuts look better with the nape of the neck clean. First, scissor-trim scragglies till they're no more than ½-inch long. Divide the wax job into two parts: left side and right side. Cock your head to one side, holding your hair out of the way and pulling upward on the scalp with one hand while you pull off the wax with the other hand.

9) *Arms*. Proceed in the following order: fingers and back of the hand, side of the arm from elbow to thumb, front of arm. To get at the back of your arm, rest palm of hand on shoulder.

10) *Underarms*. Place one hand behind head, elbow pointing behind you. Apply wax in two steps: from the middle of underarm to the top; from the middle to the bottom. Always remove in the opposite direction of hair growth. Because this is such a sensitive area, don't rewax to take off what you miss. Tweeze the remaining hairs; it will hurt less.

11) *Legs*. Start with your calves; they're the least sensitive part of your legs. Bend your knees, so you have a smooth surface to work with. Your instep and toes need work? Do these last.

If you're doing your thighs, clear the outer thighs first, then the inner. Be sure to hold skin taut, especially if your thighs are less than firm. Manufacturers *say* you can rewax legs two or three times. But the process *does* sting, and once you've given one fast tug, you might not get up the courage to re-do it. Besides, waxing irritates the skin. Once is definitely enough.

Because I've been shaving since I was twelve, I can't wax my legs—my hair is too coarse and it hurts too much. But you should try it—if it doesn't bother you, you'll love the smoothness that results.

12) *Bikini line*. First, put on a pair of high-cut old bikini underpants to give yourself a guideline. Trim hairs in the bikini area till they're about ¼ inch long. Stuff a paper towel into your bikini pants (folding it back over the top of pants), to help keep the pants and your skin clean (and to keep the wax from touching pubic hair you don't want to remove).

I find the easiest way to do this is to sit on the bathroom floor, on an old towel. Do your outer thigh/bikini line region first. Now, bend your leg outward (as if you were on the gynecologist's table—if ever there was a "behind closed doors" routine, this is it!), and work in small sections . . . 1½ by 3 inches. Grasp your inner thigh *firmly*, pull swiftly.

13) *Stomach waxing*. The woman who has a hair line from the belly button to the pubic area can remove this by smoothing the wax into place in an upward motion, ending below the navel. Pull off in a down-sweep.

Some Bad News Basics

A day or so following waxing you may see some swelling, little pinpoints of redness (similar to the irritation a man gets when he shaves), and water blisters. Don't worry, these are common reactions.

If swelling is your problem, first apply finger pressure, then wrap some ice cubes in gauze and press gently over afflicted areas.

An effective *après*-wax blemish *preventer* is Zephiran Chloride Antiseptic 1:750 aqueous solution (available in drugstores). I use it right after waxing, morning and night, for two days—I find that this really prevents break-out. Just swab over skin with a cotton ball. Sea Breeze is another good follow-up antiseptic.

You may be troubled by ingrown hairs. Whether

caused by waxing or shaving, the best treatment is to use your loofah vigorously when you're in the shower. Loofah every other day and you may avoid ingrown hairs.

And don't get waxed the day before a bikini-wearing vacation. Give yourself a few days, to make sure all redness and slight blemishing completely disappear. After all, red thighs aren't much more attractive than the hirsute variety! Understand that bikini-line hair grows back faster than leg hair. If you're taking a month-long vacation, you may need to take your wax along for a week-four touch-up.

Bleaching

There are many commercial bleaching preparations for women who'd rather conceal than remove superfluous hair. Just consider the following:

1) Read package instructions carefully; measure formulas exactly.

2) If you're using a product for the first time, it's hard to judge how strong it will be. Leave it on a little less than the manufacturer's recommended bleaching time. Check to see how light your hair has become; you can always re-apply. If you leave it too long, you may wind up with a noticeably *platinum* mustache.

3) Don't make any plans for an hour or so following bleaching; your skin may turn red.

4) If you want to make your own batch of bleach, here is a well-known home formula: For every ounce of 20-volume peroxide (also called 6 percent hydrogen peroxide), add 20 drops of ammonia. Use either household ammonia or ammonia water (found in pharmacies). Make sure your peroxide is fresh. Patch test first.

Leave on homemade bleach for 30 minutes. If you're not satisfied with the result, wait a day, then re-bleach.

Shaving Points

Here is a quick review of the basics you probably know:

1) If you use a razor to shave your legs and underarms (don't shave your face—stubble on the leg is one thing; stubble above your lip is unsightly), make sure your hair is wet. Lather up with a good man's shaving cream rather than plain soap and water—the cream sets up your hair better.

2) Don't share razors with husband or lover. They always complain women clog up their razors and make the blade dull. Your very own razor should be part of your marriage contract.

3) Shave against the direction of hair growth.

4) If you're shaving your bikini line, and can't stand the stubble, the only recourse is to shave that area daily during the summer. Apply the *après*-waxing antiseptic lotions mentioned. Be generous with talcum powder to prevent chafing.

Chemical Depilatories

I personally don't like chemical depilatories. If you've been shaving for years, you may find your hair resistant to these preparations. And, if you leave the chemical on long enough to destroy the hair, you may cause irritation to the skin.

If you do want to try a chemical depilatory, follow instructions completely . . . and patch test first.

Plucking

The easiest way to deal with stray body hairs is to tweeze them. Many women tweeze the hairs surrounding the nipple. It may hurt in the moment of pulling, but it won't damage breast tissue. An alternative: clipping. Always use the best tweezers or scissors you can buy. And, remember, there's nothing to the myth that tweezing or cutting makes hair grow in thicker or faster. Don't pluck hair from a wart or mole; clip it.

BEAUTY BONUS: BODY FACIALS

Now that your body is beautifully hairless, consider these "facials" for every inch of you.

Dry Skin Body Facial

Heat almond oil in a Pyrex dish until warm; slather all over your body. Standing outside the shower, turn on the spray till the water is hot, closing the shower curtain or door till steam forms. Now, enter the shower and stand under the steam (not the hot water!) for 10 minutes. Feel the oil slip into your skin. Next, stand under the warm—not hot—water for 10 minutes . . . then wash as usual.

Blemished Skin Body Facial

Add enough water to almond or cornmeal to make a paste. Wet yourself under the shower and apply your meal paste all over your body, massaging in vigorously—first with your hands, then with a loofah, body brush or Body Buf-Puf. Skin will look pink and clear following your shower. (This treatment works well on broken-out backs.)

More back talk: If you're planning to wear a backless dress, and you've got one pimple that won't go away before the big night, use your dark brown or black eyebrow pencil to turn it into a beauty mark.

The Sensuous, Sensational Massage

TIME: 45 MINUTES

GET READY

You're halfway through the program, and I can't think of a better way to celebrate your progress than to teach you some sensational massage techniques. So far I've concentrated on beauty routines that will make over the physical you; massage can have both physical *and* psychological benefits. I've adapted one of the facial massages performed in my salons and included a scalp stimulator and body relaxing massage as well. All are both treat and treatment.

DAILY CHECK-OUT

Diet

Weigh in. Re-read the diet chapter, just to make sure you remember how to keep up the good work during the second half of your makeover.

Exercise

Jump rope with a friend age 10 or younger. A child skipping rope is the perfect example of real vitality.

Today's beauty is active, not passive. The "throwback" beauty (who spends her days sheltered under a parasol as if it were still 1915) just doesn't rate the attention of interesting, successful men. Even image-obsessed advertising shows women in motion. Ask the nearest man—a father, son, husband, lover—to mention his beauty ideal. No one is going to name Jean Harlow draped over a chaise longue.

Grooming

Acrylic nails need only one coat of polish a week. But start keeping an eye on their growth: in a few days you may have too much nail showing at the base—you might be due for a fill-in.

GET TO WORK. THE SENSUOUS, SENSATIONAL MASSAGE

Before I give you the how tos, I want to outline a very few when-not-tos. Don't give yourself (or a friend) a massage if:
- the area to be manipulated has any breakout (you don't want to spread anything) or varicose veins
- you have a heart condition or known blood clots
- you're pregnant.

The Set-up

Since you're trying to make your massages a sensual experience, you don't want to perform them in a men's locker-room type atmosphere. Soft lights and soft music help set the mood. And you needn't be a superannuated flower child to enjoy the aroma of incense.

The requirements are few. When you're performing a body massage you'll want some sort of oil to help your fingers glide easily across your skin. Baby oil, mineral oil, or any of your vegetable oils will do. Add a few drops of your favorite scent, heat the oil till just warm.

For the facial you'll need a massage cream (described in this section).

Cold, clammy hands are neither therapeutic nor relaxing—rub your palms briskly together for about 10 seconds to generate your own heat.

The Stimulating Scalp Massage

A tight scalp is a sign of tension, and means there's not enough blood flowing in the region. Since blood equals nourishment equals a healthy scalp and hair, a regular scalp massage is an important beauty treatment. Here's how:

1) Brush your hair to remove tangles.

2) Shake out hands and arms, rub palms together vigorously until warm.

3) Sit in a comfortable chair, drop your head to your chin, then rotate head slowly in a circle (over right shoulder, back, left shoulder back to chin) 4 times. Repeat, rotating head in the other direction. Make sure shoulders are loose; you're trying to de-tense.

4) Drop your head forward. Place palms (fingers separated) on scalp *underneath* your hair. Slide fingertips and palms upward toward the crown in a push-and-relax movement (short strokes). Never use your fingernails. Repeat this 3 times. Do you feel your scalp move? If not, you're not doing it properly.

5) Using the same short strokes, move your fingertips up your scalp in circular motions. Repeat over entire head 3 times.

6) Lift your head and perform these short, circular strokes at the hairline, working back toward the nape. Repeat this series 3 times.

7) Your head should feel tingly and warm; your scalp should now move easily beneath your fingers.

8) Place your palms at the base of the neck, fingertips touching. Using slow, deep, circular motions, massage up and down your neck till it feels warm. Using your fingertips, massage in small circles outward along your shoulders. The area is relaxed when you can easily grasp and lift skin between your fingers.

9) Rotate your head as indicated at the beginning of the massage. See how much easier it is?

10) Perform this de-kinking ritual whenever you're tense—and you don't have to worry how your hair will look *après*.

The Salon-Style Face Massage

Even if I weren't in the face care business, I would still have to say there's nothing more heavenly than a well-performed facial massage (except, perhaps, a body massage). No, you won't get the same total relaxation and skin benefits doing it yourself as you would if you were being treated by a cosmetologist, but you can learn how to do some basic, good-for-you facial massage routines at home.

Performing your own facial has an added benefit: you will learn a great deal about the contours of your face by touching it . . . and this will help you put on a professional makeup.

Again, set up a soft-focus mood for your treatment. Remove earrings and cover your hair. In order to reduce the "drag" of your hands across your sensitive facial tissues, you will want to substitute a massage cream for the massage oil you'll use for your body work. Use your favorite emollient cream, or make the following:

WARM MASSAGE GELÉE: Combine 2 ounces almond oil, 2 ounces coconut (or olive) oil, ½ to 1 teaspoon peppermint extract and 1 ounce Vaseline. Mix in double boiler over low flame till just warm.

For *lined* skin: substitute 1 ounce castor oil for 1 ounce coconut oil.

Now, here's how to perform a salon-style facial, based on just a few of the motions used by my staff.

1) Cleanse face according to your skin type.

2) Sitting in a comfortable position, apply generous amount of massage cream to palms of hands.

3) Using your right palm, fully extended, move upward and outward on left side of neck with rapid, smooth strokes. Repeat 5 times. Repeat procedure using left palm to massage right half of neck.

4) Apply more massage cream to hands. Start with fully extended palms on either side of mouth and lift upward and outward from mouth to cheekbone, using firm movements. Repeat 10 times.

5) Apply a small quantity of cream to fingertips. Using long extended strokes, sweep fingertips from center of forehead outward. Do approximately 8 times, alternating hands.

6) Now apply massage cream to outer sides of fingers. Make a fist and begin rapid movements with middle of fingers downward from the ears to the chin. Do 10 times.

7) Using the index and third fingers slightly sepa-

rated into a V, make 8 long firm strokes, from outer mouth to top of ear.

8) Repeat this procedure from outer nose to top of ear.

9) Make 5 circular motions (with both hands at the same time) all over face.

10) End your massage with a series of piano taps. Using both hands and every finger as you would to play the piano, tap the entire neck area, then the face. End the taps at the temple pressure point which you will tap a few times and then hold firm with the third and fourth finger for a moment.

11) Rest for 5 minutes with cream in place, tissue off, and follow your evening cleansing routine.

NOTE: This will take a while to perform on the first try; you may want to work with a mirror. Once you've gained proficiency, you'll find it an enjoyable, skin-helping experience.

The Sensuous Body Massage

I'd love to find a live-in masseur in my Christmas stocking . . . someone who would take the time to give me a relaxing or stimulating massage whenever I so demanded. A more reasonable expectation would be a considerate husband or lover who would rather give me a lengthy, once-over-gently than watch the Super Bowl or re-read last week's stock market quotations.

Since neither one of the above is always available, I've learned to give *myself* a proper massage. Here's what you have to know.

1) Start from the shoulders, working your way down to the feet, using a combination of strokes. Be generous with your massage oil.

2) Sit in a comfortable position, cross your arms,

and massage your shoulder and shoulderblades with kneading motions.

3) Still sitting, bend arms so you can comfortably reach hands, and massage oil into each palm. Massage each finger individually till it feels warm; massage back of hands.

4) Massage each arm firmly, working your way up from wrist to shoulder. Use small circular motions; don't massage the elbow. Finish by massaging up your entire arm with long, sweeping strokes.

5) Massage your chest and diaphragm region with gentle, circular motions. Go over abdomen with sweeping, large circular motions.

6) Lie down, rest your legs against the wall, and massage one leg at a time. Start above the ankle, knead up toward the knee. Resume your massage above the knee, working on thighs. Now, a couple of long strokes up your entire leg (as if you were putting on stockings).

7) Slowly stretch every area of your body . . . treat yourself to a nap.

12

The Revival Hour

TIME: 45 MINUTES

GET READY

Yesterday you learned a brace of soothing massages. But on those days when your eyes start closing involuntarily by lunchtime and your head dips precariously close to the *soup à l'oignon* (resting your head in onion soup is *not* a recommended facial procedure), revival, not relaxation, is the problem. Assuming you want a more pleasurable means of rousing yourself than a "Thanks, I needed that" slap on the face, I've included the following simple, fast routines. Pick yourself up long enough to try one or more of the following. (If the psychiatrist's "hour" lasts only 45 minutes, so can a cosmetic therapy session.)

DAILY CHECK-OUT

Diet

If your weight isn't dropping, review the Abstinence and Indulgence food lists, Chapter Four. Make sure you're not eating too much in the evening, before bedtime.

Exercise

Why not try jogging indoors—just so you know you can do it when a rainy day comes.

GET TO WORK. THE REVIVAL HOUR: WAKE UP YOUR FACE

Of the following skin-reviving routines, today try one of the four masques. Follow with the freshener and eye treats if needed.

Summertime Moisture Masque

Cut *very* thin slices of watermelon. Squeeze a lemon over them. Refrigerate till cold. Put on face and neck, leave on 15 minutes.

Tingling Grapefruit Rind Masque

Grind grapefruit rind till it is a fine consistency. Mix with an equal amount of skim milk powder. Add enough ice water to make a paste. Leave on 10 minutes; watch your pores tighten.

Oily Skin Reviving Masque

Combine 2 teaspoons brewers yeast, 1 teaspoon ice water, and 1 tablespoon witch hazel.

Make into paste. Leave on face 10 minutes.

The Fruit Punch Facial

Here, another oily skin refresher: combine ½ cup lemon yogurt, 1 teaspoon lemon juice, 1 teaspoon lime juice, and 1 teaspoon grapefruit juice.

Mix, leave on face 10 minutes. Rinse with cold club soda.

NOTE: Club soda is a good all-around *non-alcoholic* pick-me-up skin freshener. If your skin is super-oily, add 1 tablespoon witch hazel to the club soda for astringent power.

The Frozen Freshener

Combine 1 teaspoon camomile tea and 1 teaspoon crushed rosemary.

Pour 1 cup boiling water over, and let steep 1 hour. Refrigerate when cool. Use as needed to bring life to "blah" skin.

Eye Cubes

Make ice cubes but replace half the water with camomile tea. Rub around tired eyes before applying makeup.

Refrigerator Eye Wrinkle Oil

Combine 1 carrot, blended into pulp, 1 teaspoon castor oil.

Refrigerate 1 hour. Apply by first dotting plain castor oil under eyes. Apply mix over it. Leave in place 30 minutes while you relax.

THE REVIVAL HOUR: WAKE UP YOUR HAIR

The Refrigerated Setting Lotion

Here, the simplest way to resuscitate hair:
- Shampoo.
- Towel dry.
- Make lemon- or lime-flavored gelatin according to package directions.
- When slightly gelled, comb through hair.
- Style as usual.

THE REVIVAL HOUR: WAKE UP YOUR BODY

Choose one of the following quick body pick-ups:

Do-It-Yourself Friction Lotion

Combine ½ cup lime juice, ½ cup lemon juice, and 1 cup warm club soda.

Mix, apply in shower with clean sponge, work over skin vigorously, and feel body come alive.

Body Bath (For Oily Skins)

If you never take showers, adapt the Friction Lotion above for the tub:

Combine ½ cup lemon juice, ½ cup lime juice, and 5 drops lemon extract.

Mix and drop into tepid tub.

The "Sea Cures" Spa

The life- and health-giving benefits associated with the sea have been known to man since he first began looking for ways to restore his body. (True, *ancient* beauties didn't have to cope with tension and air pollution, but it took more than a strong cup of coffee to recover from those Roman orgies.)

The Island of Cos was famous to the ancients not only as the birthplace of Hippocrates, it also boasted the first European sea-spa in history. Modern jet-setters who take the cure in select Austrian and German baths are following in the bare footsteps of wealthy Romans who retreated to these spas some 2,000 years ago.

Spas devoted to bringing forth the health gifts from the sea now exist in virtually every country on the Continent. Yes, it *would* be nice to experience first hand the rejuvenatory, therapeutic, or beauty benefits of, say, the saline Swiss spa, Bain-les-Bains, or the mudbaths of Ischia, Italy. But since the overwhelming majority of women can't, I introduced a deep-cleansing sea-spa treatment into my salon facial program. Because it has proved so successful, I've adapted it (along with other sea-mud cures) for you to try this weekend.

Your special ingredients will be sea salts, kelp powder . . . and mud.

13

The Deep-Cleansing Sea-Spa Skin Treatment

TIME: 45 MINUTES

GET READY

Today you're going to experience a unique face treatment that combines the best elements from the sea—and you don't even need a passport or wallet full of traveler's checks to indulge.

DAILY CHECK-OUT

Diet

It's a jungle out there . . . a junk food jungle! There have been songs written about snack foods; Madison Avenue even gives awards for the cleverest junk food jingles . . . but the only award the consumer gets for indulging is the booby prize. Natural, wholesome food is what you need as well as what you should want. Do you know why there are *two* cupcakes in a package? One for each hip! So recondition your thinking, decondition your body to junk foods. (P.S. Weigh in this morning.)

Exercise

Use your jump rope. Keep in mind your *long-range* goal: *5 minutes a day, 5 days a week, 500 skips nonstop*.

Grooming

Check your manicure; polish your nails.

GET TO WORK. THE DEEP-CLEANSING SEA-SPA SKIN TREATMENT

Following is my salon treatment, adapted for the dedicated do-it-yourselfer.

1) *Deep Sea-Kelp Cleansing*

If you have been a resident at any of the famed international "thalassotherapy" ("sea cure") clinics, you would have been introduced to sea kelp, believed to have healing properties. Buy sea-kelp powder at the health food store. Here's how to make and use your cleanser, step one of this comprehensive facial.

Combine 1 teaspoon sea-kelp powder and 2 table-spoons cold cream, Crisco, or creamy cleanser. Work kelp cleanser into your skin with a natural (not synthetic) sea sponge. Make sure the sponge is soft and wrung out but still wet so it doesn't feel harsh against your face. Massage for 5 minutes. Remove with water.

Spray, spray, spray with mineral water. Famous models drink mineral water to flush out the system— but they also know it's as good for you externally as internally. And what would a sea-spa treatment be without a special water?

2) *Sea Salt Slough-off*

To separate and remove skin cells which are already dead, without harm to living tissue, make your sea-salt cream.

Start with 1 teaspoon natural sea salt (available from health food stores). Salts from the Dead Sea are the best (richest in iodine, magnesium, and bromide) if you can find them. Add to this 2 tablespoons cold cream, Crisco, or creamy cleanser. Massage mixture vigorously into skin with fingers for 5 minutes. NOTE: If you can't find sea salt, mix ½ teaspoon of epsom salts with ½ teaspoon table salt.

Leave on face, cover with thin coat of see-through gauze.

3) *Steam*

Bring a large pot of water to a boil. Add pine or bayberry fragrance to give a fresh sea-side scent. Remove from stove.

With face covered with gauze, bend over pot, making tent with towel. Steam for 5 minutes. The steam will open the pores, allowing the skin-benefiting minerals in the salt to penetrate.

Spray with mineral water.

4) *Sun-warmed Massage*

Give yourself a 5-minute relaxing facial by using the Warm Massage Gelée you made on Day 11. Or just warm coconut oil and stroke gently over face with fingers.

5) *Heat Treatment*

In the salon, we use infra-red rays, a heatless-heat treatment. At home, sit under the sun lamp for 2 minutes. (Your skin should be clean and dry.) No sun lamp? Skip this step and go on to your . . .

6) *Mud Pack Masque*

Combine 1 teaspoon honey, ½ cup yogurt, 1 tablespoon Fuller's earth (from drug or health food store), 2 drops extract of mint, and 1 pinch bicarbonate of soda.

If your skin is dry, precede the mud pack with a light protective layer of cream. If skin is oily, apply mud masque directly.

Cover masque tightly with large, dampened strips of cotton. Lie down for 10 minutes.

7) *Finnish Facial Finish*

Scandinavians always finish their sauna and other heat treatments with a dip in bracing cold water. Wake up your face by removing your masque with cold, refrigerated mineral water. Alternating hot and cold temperatures stimulates the circulation.

You've just given your skin an excellent rejuvenating treatment. It should glow with new-found health, cleanliness, and clarity.

BEAUTY BONUS. SEA SALT BODY TREAT

For your consideration, a way to clarify and beautify your body skin with sea salts.

Sea Salt Bath

Mix 1 cup of sea salts with enough warm water to form a paste. Massage vigorously over wet skin with a loofah, being especially diligent over body blemishes. This may actually hurt if you have open blemishes (you know what they say about rubbing salt into wounds!), but it's a great curative treatment. Keeping the salt in place, jump into a warm tub, relax, and bathe as usual.

If you don't want to massage, just dump 1 cup of sea salts into your bath water. Stir the salts around so they don't dive immediately to the bottom of the tub. Bathe as usual—sea salts make the bath invigorating, help rev-up your tired body.

14

Sea-Spa Hair Treatment

TIME: 10 MINUTES

GET READY

Today, you'll let kelp go to your head to do its rejuve-nating work on your hair. You'll let mud go to your body, with a treatment that would make Cleopatra envious.

DAILY CHECK-OUT

Diet

Test your willpower . . . go to an Italian restaurant. Before the waiter has a chance to lure you down the fattening path with such temptations as lasagne, ziti, or spaghetti with meatballs, say "basta pasta." Forsake the tomato/meat-sauced Sicilian delights for the cuisine of the north. Elegant Venetian and Milanese women dine on veal simply prepared. It's the only way to "diet" when the rest of your group insists you must join them and *"mangia" a l'italiano*.

Need I remind you to skip the garlic bread? I've been told the real reason many Italian men have mistresses is that their wives eat garlic bread at every meal! Garlic bread and romance (not to mention dieting) definitely don't mix.

Exercise

If you miss the nice high an occasional drink provides (you're abstaining for three weeks, remember?) you really should get into jogging. Devotees of the sport claim one of the side effects is a light-headed feeling better than that produced by drugs or drinks. Worth looking into, no?

Grooming

If you put on acrylic nails during Day 3 of this program, it might now be time to fill in near the cuticle. Your regular manicure and nail wrap just needs another coat of polish. Have you noticed? All the polishing and wrapping is actually making your nails *stronger*.

GET TO WORK. SEA-SPA HAIR TREATMENT

Choose one of these for fast hair rejuvenation.

Kelp-Plus Hair Treatment (For All Hair Types)

Combine ½ cup yogurt, 1 beaten egg yolk, ½ teaspoon kelp powder, and 1 teaspoon grated lemon rind.

Rub into dry scalp, leave 10 minutes. Comb through and shampoo. Do your final washout with regular water and the final rinse with mineral water.

Mayo-Kelp Hair Conditioner (For Damaged Hair)

Combine 1 tablespoon mayonnaise and ½ teaspoon kelp powder.

Leave on 10 minutes, comb through hair and wash with your pH-tested shampoo.

GET TO WORK. MINERAL MUD BODY TREATMENT

The lure of the spas lies not in the blue skies above, but in the mud below. Just as the mud pack has been used on the face for thousands of years, mud baths have been used on the body. Here's how you can adapt the mud body rub concept for at-home use.

The ingredients are easy to find: You'll need sterilized plant (potting) soil, powdered milk, mineral water, and a soft, inexpensive shaving brush.

Combine mineral water and powdered milk to form a paste the consistency of creamy cake frosting.

Add your sterilized soil a little at a time. To keep the creamy/pasty consistency, add a little mineral water as needed.

When you have enough mud to cover your body, apply generously with your soft shaving brush. Keep in place 15 minutes (answer the door so encased *only* to beyond-the-grave horror aficionados). Shower as usual.

BEAUTY BONUS. TWO FOR YOUR FACE

Two masques that continue our fascination with mud and salt—to perform when you don't have the time for the deep-penetrating facial outlined for you yesterday.

Dry Skin Nutritious Face Pack

Combine 4 teaspoons mayonnaise, 1 teaspoon Fuller's earth, and ½ teaspoon kelp powder.

Make into a paste. Leave on 10 minutes.

If skin is *super* dry or very lined, do the following first: Take clean, thick artist's brush or blush brush. Separate one egg and brush yolk on the face, heavier where lined, lightly over the rest of face.

Apply the paste over this egg yolk base; keep on face for 10 minutes.

Oily Skin Face Masque

Combine 2 tablespoons alcohol, 2 teaspoons Fuller's earth, and 1 teaspoon peppermint extract.

Leave on face for 10 minutes.

You've completed the first two weeks of your makeover/shapeover and you're about to begin your makeover *makeup*. Just how much difference can a knowledge of cosmetics make in your appearance? The color photographs (see insert) show how women like yourself learned to make the most of what they've got. And there's a pictorial guide that shows the steps needed to complete the transformation.

Now, before you start to work, let me explain how Week Three's makeup lesson will work.

Day 15. Necessary tools and procedures will be outlined. The rest of the week will zero in on specific makeup areas and problems, giving you the tips I use to create a better look on the women who come to me personally in Saks Fifth Avenue, Neiman-Marcus, Bloomingdale's, Lord & Taylor, and other top department store face treatment salons. The learning breakdown will be as follows.

Day 16. The how-tos of contouring/coloring/cheek color to improve what you've got.

Day 17. Eye makeup tricks that can help any woman dramatize her eyes; a step-by-step eye shapeover and enhancer.

Day 18. The makeover mouth: how to transform your too thin, too thick, too blah lips into a sensual mouth.

Day 19. The Arpel ten-minute makeup method.

Organizing
for a Perfect Makeup

GET READY

If you've followed my face and hair treatment program, been diligent with your diet and exercise regimens and manicure-pedicure suggestions, you should already see (and feel) a big difference in the way you look.

Week Three will cap the improvements you've made so far by teaching you, simply and clearly, how to apply makeup like an expert. I'm going to teach you the tricks I've used to successfully transform the thousands of women I make over in my salons each year. I *do* believe that the right application of makeup can dramatically improve any woman's appearance. Just look at the color photos in this book . . . then get ready to work the same magic on yourself.

DAILY CHECK-OUT

Diet

Weigh in this morning. You will be devoting this week to what goes *on* your face—but that's no excuse for growing lax about what goes *in* your mouth!

Exercise

A super face and flabby body makes your final unveiling disappointing. You're working with your jump rope, of course. But make sure you don't neglect your Body Bulge Attack during Week Three. Review Chapter Three.

Grooming

Let's start Week Three with a quick nail review: If you give yourself a manicure or nail wrap, give your nails one coat of polish a night. If you work with acrylics, you'll need just one coat a week. No, I'm not a nail *fetishist,* but well-groomed nails are so easy to maintain, once you get the habit.

GET TO WORK. THE TRICKS OF THE TRADE

A master chef doesn't attempt to create the perfect omelette without the proper whisk and pan; a consummate artist uses only the best paints and brushes. You, the clever makeup expert, must also use the proper tools and products. Consider the following list (you probably have most of them already).

The Products

As the makeover progresses, I'll explain these essentials in detail. This list provides a glimpse of what you'll be learning to use this week.

- makeup removers and skin cleansers
- astringent, freshener, blemish lotion (as indicated by skin type)
- treatment creams and oils
- moisturizer
- underbase (to correct skin tone)
- cover-up
- foundation
- contour agents
- blushers
- lip color(s)
- eye shadows
- eye liners (pencil or liquid)
- mascara
- face powder (optional)

The Tools

A good set of brushes is essential. You will need:

- A large, long-handled soft brush for applying blusher and loose face powder
- A child's toothbrush to brush up brows (there are also professional brow mini-toothbrushes that can be flipped over and used to comb your eyelashes)
- A brow brush, angled and firm, almost stiff (used to apply brow color)
- An eyeliner brush, tapered to a thin, thin point
- Two brushes for applying shadow—an all-purpose, flat-top brush to sweep over your whole eyelid; a "crease" brush, angled like your brow brush, but

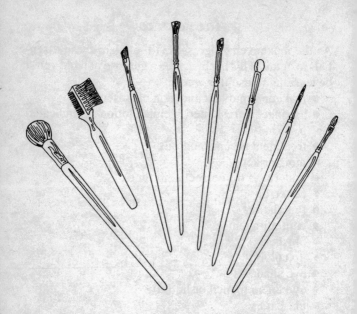

softer (note: a sponge-tip applicator is also excellent for applying shadow)
- A tapered lip brush, narrower at the top than at the base (not too soft—you don't want it to flop around as you're using it)

Besides brushes, you will need:
- Q-tips (handy for removing cream from jars as well as applying various products)
- makeup sponges
- cotton balls
- lip outline pencils, eye shadow and face blush pencils are always clearly defined in the store, though sometimes you can use them interchangeably

- headband or hair clips (to keep hair away from face)
- eyelash curler (optional)

Confronting the Cosmetic Saleswoman

A cooperative and knowledgeable cosmetic saleswoman can be your greatest ally. In order to make sure you can guide her in helping you get the look you want, consider the following:

Look for someone you can associate with. If the woman has teased red hair, purple eye shadow, a six-meal-a-day body, she probably won't understand what you have in mind. When you do find one who meets your general physical requirements (you're not searching for your idol, just someone neat, well-groomed, perhaps glamorous, whose makeup you admire), ask this *key* question: "Do you have time to answer specific questions about your products and how they work?" If she starts out by telling you everything in the world is wrong with you, forget her. The good salesperson starts by emphasizing your good points, she isn't cruel.

Remember that your life style as well as your age and general coloring has a lot to do with the makeup that's right for you—what works for the receptionist at a high-powered movie studio isn't necessarily correct for the woman who juggles her time between children, a part-time job, and PTA meetings—even if these two women have a similar appearance. Your goal is to look like yourself, only better.

Think over what you want to say before you approach the counter. Learn to articulate your needs—whether you're after the natural look, sultry eyes, or a cleanser geared to your skin type. You're more likely to get specific answers if you ask specific questions.

Be flexible about fashion colors. You should try new shades so you won't date your look, but that doesn't mean you have to abandon the spectrum you're most comfortable with. If red lipstick is popular and you've always worn pink, ask the saleswoman to show you a muted, subtle red. Did you know the biggest selling colors in the United States and Europe are still pink for the lips and blue for the eyes? But instead of wearing a light-blue eye shadow, see how you'd look with a smoky blue-gray.

Make "try before you buy" your new cosmetics shopping credo. Cosmetics are more concentrated in the bottle or tube, and will look different on your face. *Be assertive:* insist on trying your intended purchase where you'd normally wear it. Dabbing foundation on your wrist or lipstick on the back of your hand won't give you a true clue to the way it will look on your face when you get it home. And make sure you're shown how to apply the products as well. (Surely we're liberated enough to demand these minimal rights when we buy expensive cosmetics.)

If the salesperson doesn't have what you want, but wants to show you something else she thinks you might like, look and listen. Improved products are always coming out, and it doesn't cost anything to take advantage of the well-trained saleswoman's expertise. If a new product looks interesting, and you can try before you buy, why not experiment?

Now, the pencil story. In the cosmetics industry we talk about "drag"—how difficult it is to pull a product across your skin. If, when you try an eyeliner or shadow pencil, you have to pull on your delicate eyelids in order for the pencil to do its job, forget it. Any pencil to be used on your eyelids must be extremely soft. If you're looking for a pencil to line your *inner* eye, ask the woman if what you intend to buy is specifically formulated for this area; if she doesn't know, forget it.

Lip pencils are usually made with a thin, hard point—their purpose is to keep color from bleeding beyond your lips onto your skin and seeping into fine lines (if you have any) above your lips. Even though you think your brown lip lining pencil would make a terrific eyeshadow, this product probably can't do double duty: lip pencils aren't always soft enough to glide along your more delicate eyelid.

There are fatter pencils used as blushers. But I would recommend these only for young women or those with oily skin—the oil will help the pencil glide along your cheek without pulling.

Keep the above in mind when you're quizzing the saleswoman about pencils.

Does your saleswoman know the difference between a freshener and an astringent? A freshener usually contains no alcohol, and it's the only toner to be used by women with normal to dry skin. Astringents are made to blot up oil, and they do contain alcohol. Just to be doubly sure you know what you're getting, read the label. The chemicals do sound like "newspeak," but all you have to know is: Alcohol is listed as SD Alcohol (which means special denatured) or isopropyl alcohol. An astringent usually contains anywhere from 8 to 15 percent alcohol.

All major lines also contain blemish lotions, but don't buy a teenage product unless you fit that age category. It will dry your skin too much if it promises results between Monday and Saturday's junior prom! If you do need a blemish lotion, explain you want something gentle and apply only on troubled areas; don't smear it all over your face. Helpful, gentle blemish lotion ingredients include: isopropyl alcohol (to strip excess oil); a detergent (TEA Lauryl Sulfate) for cleansing; Polysorbate 20 (helps remove dirt); propylene glycol (a humectant to keep the skin supple); and urea (a natural, organic compound to help protect skin from chemicals).

When it comes to buying lipstick, understand the vocabulary, consider the look you want, and you won't have a failure to communicate. Remember, you can't use a high-fashion, deep plum lipstick color on an otherwise blank face—you have to work with the whole muted plum palette for eyes and cheeks to "get away" with such a dramatic mouth. But you can get a high fashion *mood* by asking for a plum or wine in a more transparent stain. These stains come in either a stick or pot; they're more sheer than the opaque sticks, easier to wear if you don't like the feel of a thick, rich lipstick on your mouth. If your current lipstick is creamy and seems to smear too easily, mention this problem, too. (You have to tell the woman your likes and dislikes; if there were any clairvoyant saleswomen around, I'd hire them in a minute. Most rely on input from you.)

What about lip gloss? A soft gloss provides the most transparent stain of all—really just a shine. If you're buying gloss in the summer, look for the slightly stiffer formulas (open the pot and examine) so they won't melt in the heat. Don't keep any creamy formulas in the sun.

I'll explain the different types of eye shadows in detail on Day 17, but for now, understand that oil-based is creamier, greasier, and may have a tendency to smear, while you have to make sure a water-based shadow doesn't dry out. To keep the water-base moist, buy it in the newer wand-type applicator. Experiments with our own products have proved that a water-based eye shadow packed in a pot has a tendency to dry out: the seal isn't tight enough so the water evaporates.

(Cosmetic technology is always being perfected—that's why you should at least browse through the cosmetic counters now and then. You might find a product you love in new improved packaging, which leads to longer shelf life—which means the product will last longer when you get it home.)

When you're ready to buy mascara, ask the saleswoman whether or not the one she's showing you contains fibers. These are good if you want your lashes to appear thicker, bad if your eyes have a tendency to tear or you wear contact lenses. Certain applicators are made for the woman who wants each hair to stand out individually; these same mascaras are thinner in consistency. (Note: You can get this same separated look with any mascara by combing lashes with the narrow teeth of a small comb.) I personally like the look of thick, rich lashes—there are mascaras that give the thick look, of course. But you've got to tell the saleswoman what you're after.

A word about mascara color. Write-in cosmetics companies often say blondes should wear brown; blue-eyed women should choose blue mascara. But if you want an intense look, wear black. Even if you're fair and wear little other makeup, black mascara won't make you look hard; it will give you oomph. I do think colored mascaras can be very pretty, but only if they're very dark. A royal blue or bright green can make you look like a Sesame Street character. You need dark wine, navy blue, or deep olive—the best test is to see how your colored mascara looks in the sunlight.

Waterproof mascara will do as promised if you walk through a spring rain or sniffle through a one-Kleenex movie. But if you're taking up scuba diving, this mascara won't withstand the waterfall. You have to have reasonable expectations.

Take It All Off

I want to say a few words about makeup removal, and several words about skin cleansing. You learned how to judge your skin type in Chapter One, "The Good, The Bad, and The Ugly." Now learn the daily care routine suited for you.

MAKEUP REMOVAL. No matter what type of skin you've got, it's better to remove makeup with a makeup melt (a solvent especially designed to clear your skin of cosmetic remnants) before cleansing.

Normal-to-oily skins should use a cold-cream type (comes in a jar) melt/remover. Put it on, leave in place one minute (so it has a chance to melt the makeup), remove with a wet washcloth rather than a skimpy tissue.

Cleansing oils should be used by only *normal-to-dry* or aging skins. The oil has less pull, so it's better if your skin is fragile and sensitive.

This step takes an extra minute, but if you really don't want to use a separate makeup remover, use a gentle non-detergent foam cleanser as your general solvent-plus-cleanser; a detergent soap doesn't do a good cosmetics-removing job while a makeup melt used alone doesn't do a deep-cleansing job.

CLEANSING. *Normal-to-oily skins.* Start the morning with a gentle nature-based scrub (like the sea-kelp scrub you made for Weekend Two) or a honey and apricot/almond type soap (made by many companies) if you have young, oily skin.

If your skin is leaving its oily phase and really tending toward normal, use a non-detergent foam cleanser three mornings a week, your mild abrasive four times.

The next step is an astringent, to help control oil flow and bacteria. If your're beaking out, you'll also need a blemish lotion. Dip a Q-tip in lotion, dot the lotion on the blemish *only,* and throw Q-tip away.

If your skin is young and unlined, you don't need a treatment cream during the day, but it is a wonderful precaution. If you're over twenty-five, it's a necessity.

Wash your face at night with a gentle non-detergent foam cleanser. It acts as a soap replacement, washes off with water, and is especially good for those who don't feel clean without that soap-scrub feeling.

If you've got *normal-to-dry skin,* and you wash before bed with a gentle non-detergent foam, all you have to do in the morning is rinse your face with thirty splashes of cold water.

Follow your morning splashes with a nature-based non-alcoholic freshener (mine is lemon and lime—there are many to choose from). Your day care should also include a non-greasy collagen protein under-makeup treatment cream to help your skin stay supple.

Treatments for Everyone

Unless the skin is truly oily, and you're young enough not to need any cream, wear a non-greasy night cream to bed. The new technology combines all the youth and suppleness-saving properties of protein-rich night creams *without* that greasy kid stuff feeling, so you don't have to sleep looking like you should be wearing skid chains! There are a wide variety of non-greasy daytime treatment creams available, too—experiment till you find one you like.

Have you ever stopped at the circus booth where the man guesses your age? All he does is ask you to say "cheese." When you smile, he tells your age (with alarming accuracy) by the number of eye crinkles you've got. And, since they rarely ever give away those gigantic pandas, it's true that you can guess someone's age by checking the skin surrounding their eyes, which "goes" first. That's why everybody needs an *eye oil;* there are no oil glands in this area, so the skin surrounding your eye needs special moisturizing protection. Put it on your upper lid, too.

Your *neck and throat* take a different kind of cream. You want to firm up these oil-glandless areas, so the manufacturer puts in tightening agents (massage this cream into your bust, too).

Why can't one cream do it all? Don't blame the cosmetics manufacturers. Instead, study your body. Our skin just isn't the same consistency from scalp to soles of the feet—you can tell that by looking and feeling. If you see a "miracle cream" that promises to do it all, keep looking.

Many women wrongly feel their moisturizer provides all the skin nourishing treatment they'll need. This is a myth. Your moisturizer *is* terribly important, but while it provides some lubrication, it primarily acts as a *shield,* like a glass mask protecting your skin from pollution and the elements. Your moisturizer can be worn with or without make-up. If you wear a treatment cream, give it a moment to sink in, and apply your moisturizer over it during the day. At bedtime, your treatment cream alone will suffice.

THE BASIC MAKEUP

Today's lesson will concentrate on the first steps in your makeup: Moisturizer, underbase, cover-up, and foundation. As the how tos proceed, remember I am not trying to make you create one particular look. It's up to you to add and subtract those steps that make the most sense for your life style and your skill level.

MOISTURIZER. Everyone over the age of eighteen needs some moisturizer. If your skin is dry, apply generously all over face. If you have oily or combination skin, apply moisturizer where needed, including the throat. Choose a light moisturizer (liquid, cream, or oil—as long as your chosen formula doesn't sit on your face giving a greasy look) for under makeup. After applying, give it a minute or two to settle before continuing with your makeup. (Note: Some under-make-up moisturizers are tinted and serve to help balance skin color while providing light lubrication and protection.)

UNDERBASE. An underbase blended all over your skin helps correct skin tone defects by stripping out color flaws (ruddy or yellow undertones, for example). The lightweight underbases act as a primer, helping your makeup stay on, giving your skin a smooth porcelain finish. When you use the right underbase, you don't need as much foundation. (*Note:* Because it corrects skin tone (color), an underbase is often called a toner.)

COVER-UP. Next, lighten under-eye shadows with one of the special creams for this purpose. Apply sparingly. My cream is modeled after "TV blue." In the early days of television, men wore blue shirts because blue casts shadows *away* from the face. Blue cover-up still works best. (Don't wear white—it makes you look like a raccoon.) Of course, you can only wear blue if you'll be putting other makeup over it—otherwise you'll look mighty strange!

If you're just planning on wearing moisturizer and a bit of blush, but you still want to camouflage those dark circles, choose a covering product one or two shades lighter than your own skin color. Blend well. Your cover-up should be creamy, and must contain enough oil so it glides on easily and doesn't collect in the little lines under the eyes—so don't put on a thick layer. If you're using a stick, make sure it's super-emollient, so you won't have to use too much force to drag it across your delicate under-eye skin. These under-eye lighteners can also be worn on the top lid to lighten the area without applying shadow.

FOUNDATION (or makeup base) improves skin tone and texture. The kind you'll need depends on your skin type. If you have *oily* skin, choose a water-based liquid. If you're *dry,* you'll want an oil-based formula. (Ask the saleswomen what kind of formula she's giving you.) If you're plagued by broken capillaries or just plain breakouts, you may want a heavier base for extra coverage. But if your skin is very broken out, here's the Catch 22: Save the super-covering for special occasions. Try one of the "liquid" powders made from glycerine and powder. They contain no oil or water, yet offer good coverage without being greasy. They're excellent for all skin types.

There are many kinds of foundation on the market. The basic rule is: the better your skin, the sheerer the foundation. By all means *experiment.* A whipped soufflé foundation (light, fluffy, subtle) may appeal to you. Or you may find a cream in a compact convenient. Just be realistic—you can't use a super-sheer, totally natural foundation if you have flaws you want minimized.

The *color* of your chosen foundation is as important as the formula (after all, skin tone correction is the major purpose of foundation).

COLOR ANALYSIS:	YOU NEED THIS FOUNDATION:
To brighten a sallow, yellow complexion	Warm, rosy
To tone down ruddy colors	Beige or peach
To color up dark olives	Play it up with a bronze tone
To enhance delicate, pale shades	Enhance it with ivory; warm it with the palest peach.

Always complement your natural look. If you're pale, go for a porcelain-finish effect. You just weren't meant to be a rosy-cheeked milkmaid type, so play to crowds who love Camille.

If your foundation looks unnatural on your skin, it's either the wrong color, or the right shade, wrongly applied. Base must be blended in completely; there should be no obvious line of demarcation between face and throat. If you're heavy-handed with application, apply to a dampened cosmetic sponge, then wipe sponge over face. The sponge will blot the excess for you; too much foundation, and you'll look like you're wearing a mask.

Forget about your neck; you don't want cosmetic residue on your clothes.

Secrets from the salons. We tell our customers to wear *less* foundation as they get older. No matter how excellent the formulation, base has a tendency to collect in tiny wrinkles and crevices as the day wears on.

When applying foundation or any face *makeup* (as opposed to cleansing or treatment products), always smooth on with *downward* strokes. We all have some practically invisible downy hair on our face; the down strokes help them lie flat. Your makeup also looks more finished, polished, when it's stroked on from top to bottom rather than against the grain . . . and it won't sink into the pores and fade as fast when it's applied this way.

Your basic makeup also will consist of the following steps which I'll be explaining in detail in the days to come:

CONTOURING can help you chisel out high cheekbones and features even if you've got a pudding face. It's an art worth learning, and it's based on simple principles. You emphasize good points with light colors, minimize the less-than-perfect with dark shadings. You can learn to contour with powder blushers, tawny-colored creams, eye shadows, and pencils. On Day 16 I'll give you the step by step of contouring, cheek coloring and highlighting. For your basic makeup, just remember everyone—whether you have the high cheekbones of Pocahontas or a Humpty-Dumpty face lacking in definition—needs cheek color to look alive.

EYES. If Dorothy Parker were here today, I'm sure she would say, "Men seldom make passes at girls without lashes." You will devote the most attention to your eye makeup, because well-defined eyes most quickly change you from a plain Jane to a spectacular creature. The tools: eyelid foundation, an assortment of muted shadows (powders are the longest-lasting because they contain little or no oil. If you have dry skin, you may prefer the glide creams provide. Sticks—make sure they're soft—offer the most control), eyeliner liquid or pencil, baby powder, mascara, tweezers, brow color, eyelash curler (optional). The detailed how tos for using these products to make any eye shape look open, more expressive, are listed on Day 17.

MOUTH. Essential gear: Lip brush, lip liner pencil, gloss, stabilizer (a gold stick to keep your lip color from picking up a blue cast), lipsticks. I'm going to teach you how to correct your mouth shape on Day 18. Why do some lipsticks fade faster than others? Glosses use less wax and more oil; an oil base melts faster, has less staying power. So if you're interested in longevity, use a wax-heavy lipstick formulation instead of one labeled lip gloss. If you're an older woman, never use gloss alone. The slippery gloss may bleed over into the fine lines above your upper lip. Use only on lower lip or not at all. The prettiest way to apply lipstick is to outline the mouth first. Everything about lips will be told on Day 18.

SETTING. You take the trouble to set your hair to make sure it stays a certain way; you'll want to set your makeup, too.

If you want a matte finish but oil has a tendency to break through your makeup, finish with a light dusting of moisturizing powder (many companies make this new kind of powder with moisturizing agents built in). If your skin is partly oily, dust only in T-zone where oil collects. I'm not a big powder fan. I end my makeup by putting a dab of moisturizer on a sponge and gently patting it over my face. This softens the look and minimizes the tendency of makeup to collect in fine lines.

If you want a glowing look, a light misting of mineral water sprayed gently over your face will do it. Buy a plant mister, a quart of mineral water, and you're set.

16

Contour and Face Color

GET READY

If you were permitted to get a close-up look at top models preparing for a photography session it would (surprisingly) be a terrific *ego booster*. Because many of these $100-an-hour girls look positively blah when they enter the studio. But they know one secret: A *natural* beauty is a rarity, so these models have learned to create a more beautiful self by the application of makeup to contour and color the face.

They spend hours practicing this art till they can punch up their appearance in a few minutes. Today you're going to learn the secrets of minimizing flaws and playing up good points that top makeup artists teach the models—secrets we teach the women who visit our salons. Don't expect perfect results the very first time. Refer back to this session and practice till you get this particularly tricky lesson right.

DAILY CHECK-OUT

Diet

The French have a word for it: *cuisine minceur,* slimming food. It's the newest rage in Paris, and freely translated means—lay off the sauce. Clever French chefs are preparing elegant, rich-tasting foods that are low in calories by forsaking the traditional butter-flour fattening sauce bases. If the notoriously resistant-to-change Gallic cooking consciousness can be raised to the point where *minceur* is being accepted because it's so much healthier, you can turn around your less-entrenched cooking and dining ideas. When you're in a French restaurant, ask the waiter for *cuisine minceur* suggestions . . . your meal will be more interesting when you stop relying on *"le fromage-burger," n'est-ce pas?*

Exercise

When jogging in a pollution-rich atmosphere, always wear moisturizer and foundation for double protection.

You're in a relatively soot, smog, and sulfur-dioxide free neighborhood? Remember, a thin film of moisturizer never hurt anyone (except the acne prone).

Grooming

Touch up your manicure with one coat of polish.

Makeup buildup: Apply moisturizer, tinted underbase, cover-up, foundation.

GET TO WORK. CONTOURING AND CHEEK COLOR

The essential gear for cheek color is the following:

1) Powder or soft, fat pencil if you have normal-to-oily skin; cream or liquid if you have normal-to-dry skin. Exception: If you cover your oily skin with a matte foundation you might feel you look very dry. If so, try a cream cheek tint *sparingly* for a moister look.

2) Contour color: brown eyeshadow (powder, cream, liquid—depending on skin type), second blusher/foundation darker than your primary coloring blush/foundation or just-for-contouring cream or powder. Use light coffee-colored browns—*dark* browns in an unskilled hand make the face look dirty. Creams are easier to blend than powders, but powders give a more chiseled, high cheekbone look. Powder fans, remember, a pearlized powder glides on easier. Highlight with white or pale shades.

3) Applicators: Sable brush for dry powder; sponges for liquid or cream. Important: When you use a brush to apply makeup anywhere, always blow on the brush and shake it first, so you don't deposit too much color at a stroke.

The essential philosophy is simple: light colors bring emphasis to an area; dark, matte colors introduce an illusion of shadow that makes an area recede. So we minimize flaws with darker shades, highlight good points with brighter tones.

At what point you color your cheeks and contour, like almost everything else in makeup application, depends on your skin type. If you're oily, and intend using powder formulas *everywhere* from cheek color to contouring agents, you contour *after* you cover foundation with a light dusting of moisturizing face powder. If you're using creams and liquids, contour before applying (if at all) final face powders. In either case, your tinted underbase, cover-up, and foundation come first.

Rules for Cheek Contouring and Coloring

1) *Make sure your hair is tied back,* you're sitting in front of a well-lit mirror, you have everything you need.

2) *Suck in your cheekbones* (make a fish face). Feel the hollow beneath. Pat a dab of your coffee brown contouring agent in the holllow. Blend outward, following the under-line of your cheekbones.

3) Bring your face back to normal; now break into a grin. See and feel the fleshy "apple" part of your cheek. Apply your chosen blusher here, following cheekbone out to in front of your ear. Blend in with darker contour line you applied beneath the cheek, and you've got more defined cheekbones. Whether you apply cheek color alone, or make your cheek color part of a contouring effort, remember the following:

   a) You want cheek highlights in the center of the cheeks, not underneath (that's for shading only).

   b) Don't bring cheek color up near the eyes—it will emphasize crow's feet and detract from your iris. Instead, sweep the color out—not up—toward the side of your face.

   c) Color too close to the nose draws emphasis to the nose itself. Look straight in the mirror, dab color on your cheek's fleshy center, no closer to your nose than an imaginary vertical line drawn from the pupil of your eye would indicate.

4) Play around with the use of color and contouring in the cheek region. When your cheeks look more pronounced (you've made more obvious cheekbones) you're on the right track. Be careful with color: Cheek color, unlike foundation, is supposed to show—to give you a healthy glow. But bright red clown circles staring back from your mirror are not your goal. Your cheek color should *not* be a definite red or orange. You want a muted pink or bronze blusher with brown undertones. But a true brown powder is only for contouring and would be too flat as your main cheek tint. A *softened* red is another possibility, and pearl often softens the look of any color.

Here are more flaw-minimizing tricks:

Beaked nose. Keep cheek color away from nose, as described above. Use a shade darker foundation or your contour agent down the center of the nose, blend well.

Too-broad nose. Draw your contouring agent in a thin line down either side of nose. Blend with foundation.

Too-short nose. Cover center of nose with highlighter or lighter-than-usual foundation to make the smaller nose more prominent.

Receding, weak chin. Highlight with lighter foundation or cheek color.

Double chin. Minimize with touch of contour color down the center, blend outward.

Dick Tracy jaws. Add a dark shadow from below ear all across jawline. For narrow jaws, use a highlighter in this area.

BEAKED NOSE

TOO-BROAD NOSE

TOO-SHORT NOSE

RECEDING, WEAK CHIN

DOUBLE CHIN

DICK TRACY CHIN

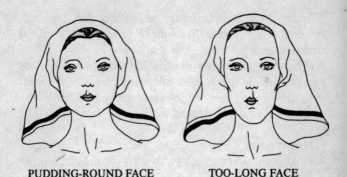

PUDDING-ROUND FACE   TOO-LONG FACE

Pudding-round face. Draw two side-by-side vertical stripes from below cheekbone out to jawbone; blend well.

Too-long face. Draw attention up to your eyes, add a bit of blush to the temples. Use cheek color to further emphasize upper half of face.

Putting It Together

Your first few attempts at this procedure may reveal a series of beige, brown, tawny stripes all over your face, resembling warpaint. Don't be discouraged. This is how the models start, and they don't give up. The secret of successful cheek coloring and contouring lies in *blending* and being *subtle*.

If you're blending powders, use a dry brush, 1 to 1½ inches wide. (A good source of makeup brushes is an art supply store. All manner of fine paint brushes are available in every width, and the long handles give better control. The little stubby brushes given out with the products are not good for beginners.)

Today you're practicing, so expect the contour-coloring procedure to take time. Eventually this critical step will take no more than 2 minutes.

When you're finished contouring, check to make sure you have given the *illusion* of creating a better-defined, more interesting face without leaving behind the *reality* of the lines and angles that work together to form it.

NIGHTWORK:
- At night you can get away with greater contouring contrasts.
- Experiment with a pearlized look. Pearlized (or frosted) products contain metallic salts and mica that reflect light, make your face glimmer. (Bad news basic: if your skin is allergy-prone, skip the glitter—pearlized makeups cause more allergic reactions than regular.)
- Put your blusher on temples and chin as well as cheeks.

MAKEUP LANGUAGE: The older woman who paints bright doll-like circles on her cheeks is revealing she's trying to capture the last blush of youth. It's better to use a more subtle color, smoothly applied.

17

Eye Makeovers

GET READY

Once you've got your flaws concealed, your good points emphasized, and your cheeks in place, you're ready to dramatize your eyes. You may go light on the blush and gloss over your lips, but if you don't know the tricks for creating look-at-me eyes, you're at a disadvantage . . . a disadvantage that I'm going to correct today.

DAILY CHECK-OUT

Diet

Weigh in. If you really feel as if you're missing something by skipping booze and beef, take heart—you're nearing the end of your three-week makeover. The maintenance diet is less stringent on its abstinence requirements.

Exercise

As you skip rope today, think back to Day 1, and how out of breath you were. Notice the improvement.

Grooming

Polish your nails.

Makeup build-up: Put on moisturizer, underbase, cover-up, foundation, contour, and cheek color.

GET TO WORK. THE EYES HAVE IT

Build a Better Brow

When your eyebrows work with your eye and face shape, they aren't really noticed—they just seem to fit. But a disastrously *wrong* brow—too thin, thick, short, arched—not only draws attention away from the eye, it gives your whole face a bizarre appearance. Here is all you need to know to shape up your brows.

The essential gear is:

- alcohol
- cotton
- stiff eyebrow brush (or child's toothbrush)
- tweezers
- powdered eyebrow makeup and brush

Steps for Everyone

1) Find your browbone: Close your eyes, rub fingers over brow, and locate bony prominence. Open your eyes and keep rubbing. If you have many hairs that fall below this ridge, you need to do some weeding out underneath.

2) Follow your natural brow shape. Yes, you want to get rid of strays and improve your brow's appearance, but an artificially high arch (you know those women who always look startled!), a pencil-thin line, and other contrived shapes are no longer considered chic.

3) Your eyebrow should be almost the same width all the way across, tapering slightly at the outer edge. Don't keep it thick to the arch, skinny from mid-brow to edge.

4) If your eyes are close set, look more wide-eyed by tweezing a few extra hairs from the center. Don't overdo.

5) A natural-look brow follows these contours:

a) The *outer* corner follows a diagonal line from your nostril to the outer corner of your eyelid.

b) For a subtle arch, place the lift on a line above the outer corner of your iris.

c) If your face is long, forsake the arch for a straight brow—this straighter line cuts the length of the face.

d) To elongate a moon face, make the arch a little more pronounced.

e) Thick and bushy brows leave you less lid to emphasize with eye makeup—an important reason for tweezing into shape.

The Mechanics of Shaping

1) Wipe alcohol-dampened cotton over brows.

2) With your small stiff (tooth) brush, sweep brows upward, brush back into place. (This clears debris—old makeup, dry, flaky skin—from brows. Should be done regularly.)

3) Remove strays between brows. Wherever you tweeze, pluck in the direction of hair growth. Pull with a

quick motion, grasping one hair at a time, so you won't overtweeze.

4) To clean out underbrow area, brush hairs up toward forehead, so you can see where the low-down strays begin. Tweeze a row at a time, working from inner to outer corner of brow.

5) Your arch should be a gentle lift, not a point.

6) After you do a little plucking, brush brow hairs back to regular position, so you can see how they're shaping up.

7) Never tweeze above the brow—do your shaping from below.

8) Don't overtweeze. Brows that are continually shaped into a pencil-thin line never seem to return to their original fullness—a drawback when styles change.

9) Bushy brows that are unmanageable behave better when tweezed. After tweezing underneath, brush brows straight up, tweeze out every fourth hair and you'll be letting daylight into the forest. Hold thick or unruly brows in place with a dab of Vaseline or lip gloss.

10) You just can't seem to find the right shape? Have it done once professionally (an inexpensive salon service), then keep the new contour by plucking strays daily so you don't lose the line.

Brow Color

Shape is only part of the story. Study the color of your brows, relating it to skin tone and hair color.

Soft color is the look you want. If your hair is dark, brows should be a shade or two lighter. If your hair is pale blond, you don't want your brows to match (matching hair and brow colors exactly is passé anyway)—draw brows one shade darker than your color so they won't fade into invisibility. Here's how to draw on natural color:

Brush powdered brow color on dry with angled brush. Use short, feathery strokes following the direction of hair growth for a natural look, brush brows lightly back into place. Brush-on brow color is best when you want to fill in; if you want to draw on a better shape, use a brow pencil to create short diagonal hair-like lines. Then take a little toothbrush and brush through to soften.

If your prefer to bleach your brows, have it done *professionally*. Green or orange brows are a common result of at-home bleaching.

After you complete your entire makeup, brush brows lightly to remove any freshly deposited cosmetics.

The Eye to Have

Once your eyebrows are set, you're ready to dramatize the eye area itself. A well-shaped and colored eye can be yours, even if you've got tiny eyes. The secret is the proper eye makeup(s), properly applied.

What you'll need depends on the effects you want to create and the flaws you want to conceal. Consider the following essentials; you'll add to this list as you identify the tools and colors needed to give you the individualized look you'd like:

- under-shadow eyelid base
- gray, taupe, brown shadows: basic shadows, can be worn by any eye color
- eyeliner tool—either pencil or liquid
- baby powder to dust on lashes
- mascara
- eyelash curler (optional)

Eye-Dentify

Makeup artists see your upper eyelid as a surface divided into three parts: *the lid proper,* which extends from the base of your lashes up to the point where your eye socket indents (close eyes and feel—remove contacts first!); *the contour line* (or lid crease), the indentation itself; *the browbone,* the bony ridge above the crease, extending right up to the eyebrow.

These three areas are the "canvas" you'll cover to make the most of your eyes.

Determine your eye shape and lid problems. Take a close look at your eyes. Are they really round? Do they droop at the corners? Does the upper lid hang down so far you're afraid it's going to block out your vision one day? Be merciless in your assessment, but don't do your eye study first thing in the morning: Many people wake up puffy and bleary-eyed. Give your eyes a chance to settle before your eye exam.

Hint: If you're really not sure what shape eyes you've got, have someone take a close-up Polaroid of your eye area, and go over the photo with tracing paper. Then you can easily match your true eye shape to the illustrations.

If you're not used to wearing eye makeup, too little is better than too much. Learn how to perfect what you're using before you pour it on.

If your eyelids are dry or wrinkled (or if they are so oily that shadow slides off quickly), "prime" your canvas by applying a moisturizing eyeshadow undercoat designed to protect lids and help shadows stay in place longer. Use when applying a cream shadow.

Remember the contouring rules: dark colors minimize, bright colors bring an area forward.

It's your *eye* you want to draw attention to, *not* your lid. So if you're going for green shadow because you've got green eyes, don't use a bright grass green; it will overpower your own iris color. So will a bright blue if you've got green eyes. Muted, smoky tones are best. Don't think you have to match your shadow to your eyes. Experiment with color, keeping the following suggestions in mind:

All eyes: gray, taupe, and brown are good basic shades to work with, no matter what your eye color.

Brown eyes: any deep, smoky colors—including plum, olive green, charcoal—will flatter you.

Blue: soft, heathery tones; muted amethysts and topaz, smoky turquoise and soft green. (Avoid bright blue.)

Green eyes: add navy to the palette listed for blue eyes, try gold pearlized colors. (Avoid bright green.)

Hazel: warm apricots and toasts, olive greens and grays, gold pearlized colors.

As you learn more about your eye shape, and eye makeup in general, you'll add different colors that work well with your skin as well as your eyes.

If you have dry or crepey eyelid skin, moist creamy powders will stay in place better, won't make lid look wrinkled. Powdered shadows last longest because they're oil free. Eye shadow sticks or pencils are good if you're in a hurry, but they must be soft enough to glide across your lid without pulling on your delicate skin. Experiment with different formulas till you hit on the method you like best. Here's a surprise: Some women with oily lids tell me they prefer cream. When it collects in the creases a fingertip can easily smudge the line away—it's harder to rub powder off the crease.

The browbone section of the lid is not oily, and can be highlighted with a creamy sheen—candlelight or soft pink tints—to open up the eye area. A pearlized shine is nice, but if your eyes sometimes bother you when you wear eye makeup, avoid anything with pearl: it causes the most (though still small in number) allergic reactions.

If you'd like your powdered shadow to look deeper, wet a small shadow brush, dip in color, and apply. Water makes it darker.

Even if you have poor dexterity and less than 20-20 vision, you can apply eyeliner the new softer way it's being worn today via the smudge technique. Using liquid or pencil, dot liner on close to the lashes. Connect the dots with a Q-tip or sponge-tipped applicator for a soft, smudgy line that's both natural and effective.

To make the whites of your eyes look whiter, line *inside* the lower lid with cobalt blue pencil specifically formulated for the inner lid.

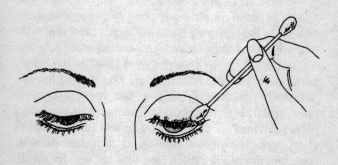

An eyelash curler—used before you put on mascara—can make an incredible difference in your lashes. The rubber insert is the safety valve, protects your lashes from breaking off. Many women don't feel comfortable using a curler, you don't know till you try.

Mascara is for everyone, all the time, whenever you show your face:

Make your eyelashes appear more voluminous by dusting the topside of your upper lashes with baby powder. Put a dab on your finger, dust on lashes. Now, apply mascara.

Don't just hold wand stationary and wipe across lash. Roll the wand along the topside of your upper lashes. The rolling motion helps deposit all the mascara onto the lashes and prevents clumping.

Roll wand along underside of lashes from roots to tip.

Let dry, repeat two or three times. If lashes look like they're sticking together, hold wand vertically and use the point to de-clump, or comb through with the small teeth of a regular comb.

To mascara lower lashes, hold the wand vertically and use the tip to lightly flick mascara onto each lash individually. If you're prone to under-eye mascara smudging, wind a piece of tissue tightly, hold in place under bottom lashes while applying mascara. Or apply mascara up from underneath your bottom lashes.

Best way to apply mascara: If lashes touch top lid when you look straight ahead, look down into hand mirror. Even better (though not always practical), lie down with your head resting on back of couch, hold mirror up at an angle so lashes are pointing straight ahead, not up.

Reminder: In the instructions to follow, whenever I say mascara, I want you to powder your lashes first.

False lashes are not for everyone, but there is still a place for them: if your own lashes are skimpy (even *with* mascara) or if you can improve the shape of your eye with a few strategically placed lashes.

After you learn the shadow-contour rules, I'll give you my no-fail lash instructions; they're a lesson in themselves.

Correcting Nature's Mistakes

After making eyes for (not at) thousands of women, I've learned that there are eight basic eye flaws that can be dramatically improved with makeup. Compare your eye shape with those below, and learn the corrective steps.

PROBLEM: Small eyes
SOLUTION: Use a pale lid color up to crease; contour crease with a dark, smoky color, smudge to soften—this is your most important color area.

BEFORE   AFTER

Repeat pale lid color on browbone just under eyebrow; apply from center of eye to outer edge of brow.

Line eyes with coordinated, smoky liner, using the "smudge" method explained above; line upper lid completely, lower lid from just below pupil out to the edge. Caution: If you have small eyes, don't line inside the lower rim; this makes the eye look smaller.

PROBLEM: Deep-set sunken eyes
SOLUTION: To bring them into view remember that dark colors make an area recede, light colors bring it forward. Lid color should be pale and frosted nearest lashes, both above and under eye. Instead of applying

BEFORE   AFTER

darker smoky color right in crease, apply it just above indentation and blend up and out.

Skip eyeliner, apply lots of mascara, and consider false lashes to make sunken eyes more prominent.

PROBLEM: Protruding, bulging eyes

BEFORE   AFTER

SOLUTION: Start with a murky, smoky lid shadow. Your contour color should be an even darker version of the shadow. If browbone also protrudes, leave bare or cover with your smoky lid shadow.

Never use frosted shadows or white highlight. Surround eye with smoky, dotted-on liner. Be especially generous with mascara.

PROBLEM: Round eyes
SOLUTION: Saucer-shaped "leapin' lizard!" eyes should be elongated.

BEFORE　　　　　　　　　AFTER

Apply just one color of shadow over entire lid, starting above inner iris and working diagonally up and out onto the browbone. Where shadow meets lashes, extend it lightly beyond eye. Smudge your shadow under your lower lashes along the outer half of your eye. The upper and lower shadows should meet in a sideways-V just beyond the outer corner of your eye.

Line entire upper lid with a smoke color using the dot-and-smudge method; extend liner out just beyond outer edge of eye.

Don't mascara lashes closest to your nose; add extra mascara (and individual false lashes) to frame the outer corner of your eye.

PROBLEM: Close-set eyes
SOLUTION: Tweeze a few extra hairs from between brows to create illusion of space, and put light, highlighter shadow on corner portion of lid above tear ducts.

BEFORE　　　　　　　　　AFTER

Contour eye vertically: Your primary lid shadow (a muted tone) should extend from your upper lashes up toward your browbone, covering the rest of your eye. Blend the two colors (lid color plus highlighter) well so there's no obvious demarcation.

Extend smoky shadow slightly beyond outer edge of eye, both above and below.

Start eyeliner a third of the way from the inner corner of upper lid.

Place heavier mascara on outer two-thirds of above and below lashes. Individual lashes, upper and lower, along outer corner of eye will also pull eyes apart.

Put a Lid on It

The last three corrections are for those whose eye shape is fine, but whose eyelid leaves something to be desired.

PROBLEM: Narrow lid
SOLUTION: You don't have much space to work with, so use one medium-tone eye shadow, extend almost (but not quite) to browbone.

BEFORE   AFTER

Use this same shadow to outline around outer third of lower eyelid.

Line inner rim of entire lower lid with pencil (blue makes the whites of your eyes look whiter) to draw attention away from narrow upper lid.

PROBLEM: Overhanging upper lid

SOLUTION: If you look half asleep even when wide awake and your eyes appear to be mere slits, plastic surgery might be necessary some day. Here's how to compensate with makeup:

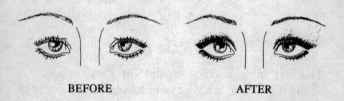

BEFORE   AFTER

Shadow with light color on lid proper, flush against lashes. Use dark color in crease right up to browbone to make the overhang appear to recede.

Smudge light shadow under lower lid, covering outer half of eye.

Use mascara.

PROBLEM: Falling outer corner

SOLUTION: When the outer lid starts succumbing to terminal droop, give a lift to your eye, if not your spirits, by: Stopping your lid, contour, and highlight shadows just before they reach outer corner.

Give entire upper-lid lashes one coat of mascara; apply additional coats above iris to draw attention to center of eye rather than corner.

BEFORE   AFTER

Lash of the Red Hot Lovers

That's how *Vogue* described my applied one-at-a-time lashes, and though fewer women wear false eyelashes today, add-on lashes are still an important accessory if you want to open up your eyes, correct eye shape flaws, and dramatize what you've got. Choose a natural-look human-hair lash—feathery and realistically long rather than inch-and-a-half spiky clumps. (In case you're interested, many models whose eyes jump out from the pages of magazines often rely on individual or soft strip lashes for special effects. . . . why not you?)

There are two types of lashes, strip and individualized. Here are the how tos for both.

Putting on the Strip

The best way to buy is to have lashes custom-cut to fit your eye (many department store beauty salons and large drugstores employing a cosmetician provide this service when you purchase lashes).

Don't look straight ahead into mirror. Instead, put a hand mirror down on the table, and apply the lashes looking down.

Apply the adhesive (surgical glue) with a toothpick, blow on the glue, and count to 20. Don't try to put the whole lash on at once—that's where many women make a mistake. Instead, put the middle in place, then press the ends in place a second or two later. To position, use your fingers or an orangewood stick for the middle section, a long fingernail, toothpick, or the end of a tiny makeup brush for the outer sections.

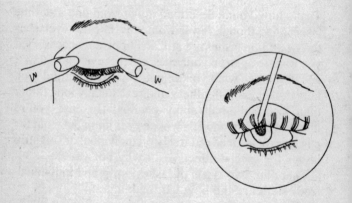

Don't curl, powder, or put mascara on false lashes. First mascara your own lashes, let dry and pinch your own together with the fakes so they blend.

Note: This process takes practice; try it when you're relaxed, and give yourself a few sessions before giving up!

To remove: Get a good grip on the strip (not just the edge) and peel off lightly, then peel adhesive off the strip. Human hair lashes (the only kind to use—synthetics make you look like a kewpie doll) don't need washing.

Putting on Individual Lashes

Sold in department and drugstores, these come in kits with adhesive and remover. They're grouped in clusters of short and long hairs, so you can add lashes wherever you need them. If you're using these, apply before rest of eye makeup.

1) Clean lashes of all cosmetics, dust, and oil (with cool water and washcloth). Your lashes must be perfectly dry and clean, or fakes will fall off.

2) Using a tweezer, dip the tiny cluster into the adhesive so that half of the lash is covered with the surgical glue.

3) Place lash adhesive against your own lash (cover three-quarters of your own lash). Professionals often apply lashes underneath your own, but this is so tricky that if you're doing it yourself, apply on top of your own lashes.

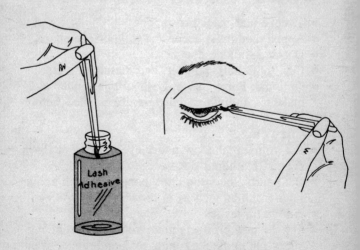

4) If you're doing your whole eye, work from the center of your lashes to the outer corner, then return to center of lid and continue toward nose, stopping ⅛ of an inch from the inner corner.

5) Apply these lashes directly to your own lashes, *not* to eyelid.

6) For bottom lashes, reverse this process.

7) Don't use cream or oil around the eye after application.

8) To clean lashes, use Q-tip and cool water.

9) To remove top lashes, dampen cotton pad with lukewarm water and apply to eye area for 3 minutes. Remove cotton pad and hold under eye area. Dip a Q-tip into remover and stroke eyelash. Keep your eye closed. Lashes will ease right off; do not pull. For bottom lashes, reverse this process.

Review of Steps to Create Fabulous Eyes

- Tweeze and color brows.
- Apply shadow(s) according to your eye shape.
- Dot-and-smudge eyeliner.
- Curl (optional), powder, and mascara lashes.
- Optional: False lashes. Lash *strip* is applied after makeup. Individual *clusters* are applied before makeup.

NIGHTWORK:

- Put your eyeshadow under eye, narrow at inner corner, feathered out widely at outer corner.
- Put pearly sheen on cheekbone very high above your blush as well as in browbone area.
- Add extra lashes.
- Try the new products made with heavy shimmer/ super glitter flecked with gold or bronze. Wear

over shadow or alone—use to glitter up cheeks, too.

MAKEUP LANGUAGE:

- Bright eye shadows usually signal a flamboyant personality.
- The woman who wears no eye makeup may be afraid to compete . . . and lose. She's often the first to lower her gaze in eyeball-to-eyeball confrontations.
- The older woman who puts on eye makeup well indicates that she hasn't given up, is determined to age gracefully and glamorously.
- The woman who sticks to her light blue shadow and pink cheeks often has the sunny Doris Day-type personality that goes with this pastel palette. More stubborn than her smiling face indicates, she sticks with the look that expresses how she feels, no matter what fashion dictates.

BEAUTY BONUS. MEN ALWAYS MAKE PASSES . . .

at women who wear attractive eyeglasses. The vogue for *sunglasses* as year-round fashion accessory really began in the 1960s, when Jackie Onassis started appearing everywhere in those big, bug-eyed shades. Today, *regular* eyeglasses can greatly enhance a woman's appearance, if she chooses the right frame style. Before I leave the eye makeover section, a few words to help girls who wear glasses:

New York optician Alfred Poll suggests the following:

1) Make sure the lenses are large enough to allow eyeshadow/makeup to show through (wear your everyday eye makeup when you're selecting a frame).

2) To minimize a long nose, choose frames with a bridge that sits low on the nose.

3) If you have a too-round face, oval frames longer than they are wide will help. Don't choose round frames; a frame that's angled and has corners is more flattering.

4) Round frames, or angled frames wider than they are long, will shorten your face.

5) If you have a "sad" face, don't wear frames so large they droop down onto your cheeks.

6) Minimize under-eye bags by wearing round frames thick of width (skinny wire-frames won't camouflage).

7) Frame colors follow the lead of fashion; choose a color that looks well on you rather than opting for the color of the moment.

8) If you wear contact lenses and are considering going tinted, understand you can't make your dark brown eyes light blue by inserting a colored lens. You can make light eyes look deeper in tone (by going from a watery blue to a deep-sea blue, for example).

18

The Makeover Mouth

GET READY

While it takes a certain amount of expertise and flair (practice, and you'll get both) to create the perfect eye, all you need to improve your lips is a steady hand, the right tools and knowledge of a few simple rules. Make a little effort, and today you'll learn the easy way to make over your own mouth.

DAILY CHECK-OUT

Diet

If you feel *déclassé* sipping your "Shirley Temple" while those around you are enjoying more spirited drinks, you'll be surprised to learn that a few internationally notorious drinkers (famous barroom brawling actors) have taken the no-booze vow, and are sticking to it. Their secret? Elegant, delicious, good-for-you

Perrier, one of the world's legendary mineral waters. Drink yours with a twist of lime or lemon (or both—why not?).

Exercise

What's the perfect gift for the woman who has everything—in the way of bulges—and nothing—in the way of energy? A jump rope. Buy one for a friend, and include a pep talk and a demonstration.

Grooming

Makeup build-up: Apply moisturizer, underbase, cover-up/camouflage, foundation; contour and color cheeks, do eyes.

Something for Everyone

Before I discuss the how tos for correcting individual lip shapes, I want to give you a bit of information every woman should know.

If your lip color starts to fade before you walk out the door in the morning, make sure you're wearing the traditional lip*stick,* which contains more wax (and therefore more staying power) than the slippery glosses.

Never let your lips go naked. Because they contain no oil glands, lips have a tendency to get parched and cracked even in the best of weather. If you don't want to wander around the house with lipstick on, wear gloss or Vaseline. To make your own gloss, mix a few drops of food coloring with Vaseline for subtle color, or cut the top off a favorite old lipstick with a razor blade, crush the color and blend with Vaseline.

While your lips should have color, the color must coordinate with your own natural skin shade and cheek coloring. If you're very fair, and wear just a hint of pink cheek color, bright red lips will stand out from your white skin like an open wound! It's always better to err on the side of subtlety.

Find a lip color formulation you're comfortable with so you don't feel the need to blot, which strips off color. A moist-looking mouth is more appealing than flat color. Just remember that greasy lips are unattractive, so don't layer on the lipstick.

GET TO WORK. THE MECHANICS OF MAKING UP LIPS

Your essential gear consists of:
- lip lining pencil
- lip brush
- lip stabilizer
- lipsticks
- lip gloss

Here are the steps you'll use, no matter what your lip shape.

1) Outline. Use a lip pencil a shade darker than your chosen lip color, and outline your lips. The outline will help keep creamy lipstick in place, prevent it from bleeding over the edges of your mouth, because a pencil is of a heavier consistency, neither waxy nor oily nor runny. Even a beginner can use a lip pencil.

2) If your lipstick has a tendency to turn blue, apply a stabilizer first—it's a special gold stick designed to keep color true.

3) Fill in, using a lip brush for prettiest results. The surface of the stick is really too wide to let you cleanly

paint the relatively small lip area. Slide the brush over the tube in one direction only; don't smash the brush into the lipstick. (Use brush to apply stabilizer, too.)

4) Blend color into pencil line with the brush so there is no demarcation. Your penciled-in lip outline shouldn't show unless you want a high-fashion two-toned mouth look.

5) If you want to lighten the shade of your lipstick, put gloss on first, lipstick last.

6) For added shine, dot lip gloss over lipstick in the center of your mouth only. A complete overlay of gloss is too greasy.

The mechanics of working with the right lip tools are easily learned. Your next lesson: Using the tools to make over your mouth.

Correcting Nature's Faults

Make yourself a better mouth by "cheating" on the basic outline and learning how the makeup artists in our salons camouflage with color. You can improve your lip shape, but you can't turn narrow lips into a full, voluptuous mouth. Small corrections work; attempts at large corrections are too obvious in the lip region.

If your mouth does need some correcting, extend your foundation to cover outer edges of lips before beginning.

PROBLEM: Thin, narrow lips

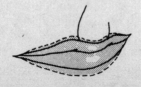

SOLUTION: Thin lips sometimes make a woman look grim. To open up this kind of mouth, remember that dark colors recede, so the deep mahoganies are not for you. Rust or toast shades are about as dark as you can get.

Outline lips in the same color pencil, making your line just beyond the outer edges of your own lips. Stop your line just short of the corners; this will place more emphasis on the center of your lips, making them appear fuller.

Blend line and color especially carefully so the old contour of your lip doesn't show through.

Dab gloss over the center of your mouth to highlight this fullest area.

PROBLEM: Lips too full

SOLUTION: If you've got too much of a good thing, first line lower lip just inside the natural lip, extending the line a tiny fraction beyond the lip's own contour at the sides. By elongating the mouth slightly, it will appear less full.

Repeat this same procedure with the upper lip, making sure your corner edges meet.

If it's compatible with your skin tone and cheek color, choose deep, dark shades of lipstick. Don't wear lipstick plus gloss; it will overemphasize your Brigitte Bardot pout.

PROBLEM: Uneven lips

SOLUTION: A mismatched full lower lip and narrow upper lip is a common problem. To bring your lips into balance, line your lower lip just inside its natural contour; line upper lip as it is.

Correct with color, using a deeper shade on the lower lip, a lighter color in the *same* shade family on the upper lip.

The two shades should be close enough in color so the viewer doesn't notice an obvious difference between upper and lower lip; you're trying to create an impression of harmony.

PROBLEM: Down-in-the-mouth lips

SOLUTION: If your mouth seems to droop in the corners, lift the lower corners by extending the outline of your lower lip slightly upward. Outline the center of your upper lip to focus attention away from the corners of your mouth.

Use a color one shade darker on the lower lip.
Dot gloss in the center of your upper lip only.

MAKEUP LANGUAGE:

- Some say the woman who wears no mouth color is afraid of sex (remember, the mouth is an erogenous zone).
- If you only wear a moist gloss, you're subtle, but a tease.
- Smeared lipstick indicates a careless attitude—it goes with rundown heels and a torn hem.
- The woman who removes her lipstick before making love is too fastidious and controlled.
- The woman who wears her lipstick to an even point is fastidious and frugal.
- Does your lipstick wear down to a shape resembling a phallic symbol? You're erotic and uninhibited.
- A lipstick worn to a flat plane indicates a possibly aggressive personality.

The Ten-Minute
Everyday Makeup

GET READY

Just how long should it take to put on a complete makeup that can transform your face? Ten minutes, when you follow my outline.

DAILY CHECK-OUT

Diet

Yogurt, one of nature's healthiest foods, should be part of your diet. But don't confuse the term "99% fat free" with calorie-free. Fat-free yogurts do indeed have calories—an 8 ounce container of vanilla adds 200 calories to your total; fruited yogurts contain 260 calories. If you're making a meal out of it, fine. But if you down an 8 ounce container as a daily between-meal snack, you're treating yourself too richly.

Exercise

If the idea of jogging appeals to you, but you always find excuses to put off getting into the reality, form a jogging club with friends. Not only will your own conscience be telling you to slip into your sweatsuit, you'll also have your friends urging you onto the track.

Grooming

After you jog, soak your feet in one of the refreshing footbaths listed on Day 5. Polish your fingernails.

GET TO WORK. THE TEN-MINUTE MAKEUP

Time-Saving Tips

Invest in a clear, Lucite-type makeup holder with several compartments, so you'll have easy access to all your gear, including your hair tie-back tools. Sewing notions departments in the major stores usually sell this type of (inexpensive) organizer.

To simplify your life, buy duplicates of those items you'll need for away-from-home touch-ups. Your carry-along makeup case and your stay-at-home organizer should be two separate entities.

Apply makeup in the north light, if possible. This is the "true" light artists paint by, and large cosmetics firms always have their color-matching facilities facing north. If you can't face north, make sure the light you do have is adequate.

The Ten-Minute Makeup: Time Check

You've already cleansed and toned (with freshener or astringent) your face, and put on a treatment cream if your skin type demands it. Now, take this makeup proficiency test: Can you complete these steps in 10 minutes? (Check the pictorial how-to guide in the full color makeover section.)

MOISTURIZER. Apply all over face. If you have oily skin, buy a non-greasy moisturizer. (If acne-prone, avoid blemished area.) Apply to throat no matter what skin type you have. Important: let moisturizer settle so it won't interfere with the smooth application of the rest of your makeup. If you've been too heavy-handed, blot up excess with a small cosmetic sponge.

UNDERBASE. Wash underbase all over your skin to correct color flaws. Check your profile to make sure there is no demarcation line between face and neck. And, of course, you're applying all makeup with downward strokes, right?

COVER-UP. Lighten those late-night under-eye dark circles with your cream cover-up. Apply sparingly, let set and "smile." Has the cover-up gathered in your "crinkles"? If so, remove excess.

FOUNDATION. Dot your chosen formula on forehead, cheeks, nose, eyelids and chin (you'll need a couple of dots in each area to insure adequate coverage), blend with downward strokes. Don't rub hard; you want base to coat the skin, not penetrate into your pores. Check for demarcation lines.

CHEEK COLOR. Smile. Apply cheek color to "apples" of your cheeks. Make sure it's not too close to your nose or eyes (especially if you have crow's feet).

CONTOURING. Remembering that dark shades and matte finishes minimize, while light shades emphasize, draw and blend in your contouring lines according to facial structure. Blend extremely well; you don't want any angular lines showing on your face.

EYE MAKEUP. Check the shape of your brows; tweeze any stray hairs. If your brows need color-correcting, follow explicit directions from Day 17.

Apply a moisturizing eye shadow undercoat, follow with your chosen shadow(s).

Next, apply eyeliner using the dot-and-smudge technique. To make your eye whites look brighter, line inside the lower lid with a cobalt blue pencil. (Skip this step if you have tiny eyes or you're uncomfortable with the dark look inside the eye.)

Curl your eyelashes (optional), daub baby powder on top lashes, apply mascara. Let mascara dry between coats; use as much mascara as you need to give lashes the thickness you want.

If you're applying false lashes (optional), don't time yourself at the beginning. You need practice before you can get them on in the couple of minutes it takes me.

LIP MAKEUP. Outline the mouth with pencil, then prepare lips with a lip stabilizer, so lipstick won't change color. Fill in (you'll get a better look if you use a lipstick brush). If you want extra shine, dot gloss in center of mouth. Don't blot lips.

SETTING. Depending on the look you're trying to achieve, you may want to dust your face with a moisturizing powder; spritz it with mineral water for a moist look; dampen a sponge with moisturizer and pat on lightly for a dewy look. Setting steps are optional.

It takes me 10 minutes to do a complete makeup. How long did it take you? Look at the clock, and consider the following:

10 minutes, my makeup looks terrific

Congratulations, and go to the head of the class! Just keep one thing in mind: your face should look terrific, not your makeup.

10 minutes, but I look like a painted lady

You're still not comfortable using the assembled tools and products. Lightening your makeup after each step with a just-slightly-damp cosmetic sponge will help compensate for your heavy hand until you become more skilled. Remember, it's better to take 20 minutes at the beginning than to rush and not be pleased with the results.

8 minutes, and I look terrific

Consider becoming a cosmetician.

18 minutes, and I haven't begun my mouth

You need plenty of practice (that's all it really takes). You also might want to consult a department store makeup artist for further advice, and don't be embarrassed to return to the woman who sold you the cosmetics and ask for a further "try *after* you buy" lesson.

I can barely draw a straight line with a ruler; all these brushes and pencils confuse me

When I first started in business, I realized that some women just can't wield a brush or pencil, so I devised the Arpel Fingerpaint Method. If you use makeup with a cream or liquid consistency, you can put your face on with your fingers (even Picasso probably learned to fingerpaint before he learned to draw). The key (though inelegant) word is *smear:* Dot everything on (one layer at a time), and smear into place using fingertips. Everything can be blended in this way, and by fingerpainting, by touching your face, you become more familiar with facial flaws and contours. Once you gain the confidence successful fingerpainting brings, you'll be ready to work up to brushes. Save pencils for last.

NIGHTWORK:

Your nighttime makeup is just an intensified version of what you wear by day. You may be adding more glitter and sheen, but if you do you'll be subtracting matte finish products to make room. The point: Night makeup can be accomplished in 10 minutes, too.

MAKEUP LANGUAGE:

To sum it up, when I look in the mirror and see that my makeup is on correctly, and I feel attractive, I speak and act with more confidence. I'm sure cosmetics can do the same for you.

Body and Soul Spa

You've already exerted so much energy (enjoyably, I hope) during the past 19 days that I want to wind up with two major activities—one for each day—geared to help you unwind while shaping up your body.

20

The European Cellulite Treatment Wrap

GET READY

In European health spas women who want to lose a few pounds fast opt for this specialized treatment that takes off water weight. One word of warning: It's not for those with circulatory problems, so check with your doctor first.

DAILY CHECK-OUT

Diet

These last two days separate the women from the girls. Stick to your Sacred Cow Vow for two more days, and you won't make it a lost weekend.

Exercise

Jump for joy . . . you've established a quick exercise program that will stay with you a lifetime.

Grooming

Polish fingers and toes.

GET TO WORK. THE EUROPEAN CELLULITE TREATMENT WRAP

1) Gently massage your body with the massage cream you used on Day 11. Shower off.

2) Next, the key step: The Herbal Towel Wrap. Take a large bath towel and dampen with an herbal brew (mix of your favorite herbs—camomile, thyme, rosemary—steeped in boiling water and strained). Liquid should be hot but not unbearable. Encase yourself in the towel.

3) Wrap yourself in a plastic drop cloth (buy in any hardware store) placed on your bed.

4) Have someone throw heavy blankets over your body and a cold washcloth over your forehead.

5) While your body is thus encased, and you're (we hope) sweating away the cellulite, let your mind rest.

6) Stay in position for 10 minutes. Set a timer so you won't overdo, and when you wake up, both your body and soul will feel lightweight and refreshed.

7) Don't follow up with any strenuous activity; come to gradually.

Total Relaxation Routine

TIME: 15 MINUTES

GET READY

When every muscle of your body has reached the breaking point, there's a 15-minute minimum exertion exercise that will help unkink your body and soul. If you've ever attended a yoga class, this is the routine yogis use to make sure their disciples leave the exercise room with a feeling of tranquility. (Of course it works— have you ever seen a tense guru?!)

DAILY CHECK-OUT

Diet

Weigh yourself. Compare with your weight at the beginning of your makeover/shapeover. I hope self-congratulations are in order.

GET TO WORK. TOTAL RELAXATION ROUTINE

Find a quiet corner where you can be alone, wear comfortable minimal clothing (a leotard is fine), turn off the lights, lie down on a softly carpeted floor. You should be lying on your back, arms a few inches from your sides, palms facing up. Feet should be about twelve inches apart and relaxed. (Yogis call this the corpse pose.) Eyes must remain closed at all times.

Breathe deeply, in and out. Concentrate on your breathing, feel and hear the rhythm. Think of nothing else.

Once you feel calm and comfortable in this position, you are going to contract and relax every muscle of your body, working from toes to top of head. Start by curling your toes under tightly, lift off the floor, hold for 15 seconds, and let drop heavily back to the floor.

Tighten your feet and calf muscles, lift off the floor and hold for slow count of 15, let drop heavily back to floor. Direct your consciousness toward the feeling in your calves as you tense and relax this area.

Continue with your thighs, hips, stomach, and chest. Take your time. Contract each set of muscles, lift off the floor, hold, let drop back to the floor.

Tense fists and arms, raise from the floor, hold and count to 15, lower.

Knit your brows, grimace and hold your facial muscles tight. Let them relax.

Do a complete body stretch by crossing your ankles, clasping your hands and placing arms on the floor behind your head. Stretch your whole body while in this elongated position.

Return to the starting "corpse" position. Breathe in and out deeply and rhythmically, feel your whole body relax completely. Concentrate on a relaxed image—let your mind's eye see yourself floating on a raft in a calm ocean. Remain "at sea" for 5 minutes.

When you stand up, you'll notice your kinks have disappeared, your muscles are no longer tight and tense, your mind feels as tranquil as your body.

NOW WHAT?

The past three weeks have been both a learning and doing experience geared to help you become a more attractive person. You've shared some of the routines I've worked out for the thousands of women who visit our salons, and I hope you've also shared their success.

From now on when you look in the mirror I trust you will be able to do more than recite this line (I don't remember who said it—but it seems the right way to end a beauty book):

> *Wrinkle, wrinkle go away . . .*
> *Go and visit Doris Day!*

Index